Confidentiality & Record Keeping in Counselling and Psychotherapy

Legal Resources for Counsellors and Psychotherapists

Legal Resources for Counsellors and Psychotherapists is a series of highly practical books, themed around broad topics which reflect the most 'frequently asked questions' put to the BACP's professional advice line.

Books in the series:

Therapists in Court: Providing Evidence and Supporting Witnesses

Tim Bond and Amanpreet Sandhu

Confidentiality and Record Keeping in Counselling and Psychotheraphy, 2nd edition

Tim Bond and Barbara Mitchels

Essential Law for Counsellors and Psychotherapists

Barbara Mitchels and Tim Bond

Legal Issues Across Counselling and Psychotherapy Settings

Barbara Mitchels and Tim Bond

2nd Edition

Confidentiality & Record Keeping in Counselling and Psychotherapy

bacp

British Association for
Counselling & Psychotherapy

Tim Bond and Barbara Mitchels

Los Angeles | London | New Delhi
Singapore | Washington DC

Los Angeles | London | New Delhi
Singapore | Washington DC

SAGE Publications Ltd
1 Oliver's Yard
55 City Road
London EC1Y 1SP

SAGE Publications Inc.
2455 Teller Road
Thousand Oaks, California 91320

SAGE Publications India Pvt Ltd
B 1/I 1 Mohan Cooperative Industrial Area
Mathura Road
New Delhi 110 044

SAGE Publications Asia-Pacific Pte Ltd
3 Church Street
#10-04 Samsung Hub
Singapore 049483

Editor: Susannah Trefgarne
Assistant editor: Laura Walmsley
Production editor: Tom Bedford
Copyeditor: Solveig Gardner Servian
Proofreader: Derek Markham
Indexer: Silvia Benvenuto
Marketing manager: Camille Richmond
Cover design: Lisa Harper-Wells
Typeset by: C&M Digitals (P) Ltd, Chennai, India
Printed and bound by CPI Group (UK) Ltd,
Croydon, CR0 4YY

Library of Congress Control Number: 2014936871

British Library Cataloguing in Publication data

A catalogue record for this book is available from
the British Library

ISBN 978–1–4462–7451–4
ISBN 978–1–4462–7452–1 (pbk)

At SAGE we take sustainability seriously. Most of our products are printed in the UK using FSC papers and boards.
When we print overseas we ensure sustainable papers are used as measured by the Egmont grading system.
We undertake an annual audit to monitor our sustainability.

Contents

List of Figures, Tables and Boxes

Figures

Tables

Boxes

About the Authors

Dr Barbara Mitchels, LL.B., PhD., FBACP (Snr Accred), BACP Registered, combines the professions of law and therapy. A retired solicitor, Barbara is Director of the Watershed Counselling Service in Devon, and also runs Therapy Law, providing a specialist consultancy and mediation service for therapists and others in the helping professions, and CPD workshops (see www.therapylaw.co.uk). Her publications include books and papers on law, therapy issues, trauma, child protection and peacemaking.

Tim Bond is an Emeritus Professor of the University of Bristol and Visiting Professor to the University of Malta. His extensive research and publications about professional ethics include *Standards and Ethics for Counselling in Action* (2009, Sage). He is currently a consultant to the British Association for Counselling and Psychotherapy on professional ethics and standards and a member of the Ethics Committee for the British Psychological Society.

Acknowledgements

We are indebted to all the hundreds of therapists from many different backgrounds and settings who have shared their experience of their dilemmas concerning confidentiality and record keeping and how the law has helped or hindered them. There is no way of naming them individually but we hope that they can recognise some of their concerns in how we have developed this book.

Trying to find the answers to some of the questions that have been posed to us has been challenging. In relation to the first edition of this book, we are particularly grateful to Amanpreet Sandhu who conducted the early legal research in her post as Legal Resources Manager at BACP before leaving for a new post in London, and to Roisin Higgins for her helpful comments and addition of the Scottish law in the manuscript.

We would also like to express our especial gratitude to all those experienced practitioners who willingly shared their experience at a crucial time in developing the first edition of this book. We particularly thank Cindy Bedor for enhancing this new edition of the book with her contribution of Chapter 10 with her ideas and examples from practice on the development of organisational policies and procedures.

Above all we are grateful to the current and former staff of BACP, especially to Kathleen Daymond, Denise Chaytor and Wendy Brewer who worked with BACP's Information Services and drew on their experience of answering members' queries to inform us about the issues that we needed to address. We have also been helped by the expertise of Grainne Griffin, who has now left BACP for private practice, and John O'Dowd, Head of BACP's Professional Conduct Department.

Finally, we want to express our appreciation to BACP, who sponsored and supported the writing of the first edition of this book, and subsequently encouraged us to write this new edition. The ultimate responsibility for this new second edition rests with us as the authors.

Note on jurisdiction: This book covers the law in England. The law in Northern Ireland, Scotland and Wales is covered only where specifically mentioned.

Introduction

Confidentiality and Record Keeping in Counselling and Psychotherapy, published in summer 2008, as part of the BACP's Legal Resource series, has proved popular. In response to the significant developments in law and practice over the last five years, we have been encouraged to produce a new 2nd edition, reflecting changes in the law relevant to counselling and psychotherapy and taking into consideration new and exciting developments in practice: for example, the growing popularity of modalities such as coaching and mentoring, online therapy and counselling psychology.

We are aware that many trainees and practitioners have a portfolio of work, and that they may be working across a range of modalities and practice settings. The aim of this book is to help practitioners and trainees understand the legal issues, values and ethics of confidentiality and record keeping, and to apply this understanding across a variety of settings. We also explore how the law, organisational policy, and the ethical frameworks in which we practice will apply to particular aspects of our work, seen from the perspective of a variety of practice contexts.

The book is intended not only for counsellors and psychotherapists; we aim to include other developing forms of therapy, including coaching. We intend the book to be useful for trainees, trainers, managers, supervisors, other practitioners and clients to assist them to recognise when there are significant issues at stake that require specific ethical or legal advice or to understand the advice that has been given to them. We have included practical resources and visual aids in the form of checklists, diagrams, tables, and flowcharts where appropriate. We also include a comprehensive index of resources and organisations, which practitioners tell us are helpful in obtaining additional information and guidance.

In our own respective therapy practices, workshops and in Barbara's consultancy and mediation service for therapists, we hear at first hand practitioners' dilemmas and concerns. In writing this new edition, we have taken into account comments from peer reviews, professionals, trainees, publishers, the BACP as well as our own ideas for updating. Confidentiality involves an approach which includes ethics, good practice guidance and law. Since writing the last edition, the BACP has produced the *Ethical Framework* 2010, revised in 2013, and this book takes into account the current *Ethical Framework*, providing a user-friendly guide, bringing ethics, good practice and the law alive with practical examples and applications which are drawn from practice and relevant to practitioners.

What is new?

The 2nd edition of the book includes, in addition to the topics covered in the 1st edition, an exploration of confidentiality and record keeping issues in relation to:

- Online therapy, telephone counselling, web-based (cloud) information storage texts, emails and other electronic communication.
- The role of supervision.
- Insurance.
- Recent changes in child protection law and procedure.
- Confidentiality and the Director of Public Prosecution's guidance on assisted suicide.
- Privacy and confidentiality in working with vulnerable adult and child witnesses in the context of court proceedings and compliance with current Crown Prosecution Service guidance.
- Changes in therapy practice arising from new law and voluntary registration, ethical developments and practice guidance updates.

There may be new law making reporting child protection concerns compulsory, but the draft law and protocols are not yet resolved. Readers should watch out for any new legislation/guidance on this issue. We find in our workshops that practitioners consider specific scenarios and case studies most helpful to their practice. In this new edition, we include a new Part V with questions, dilemmas and short scenarios to form the basis for personal reflection, supervision or group activities, which we hope will be helpful to bring the concepts alive for trainees and practitioners.

This book reflects the law in England and where indicated, includes the law in Scotland, Northern Ireland and Wales. The content of this book is general in nature and cannot constitute legal advice on any specific cases, because the context of every dilemma is different. We would advise any practitioner concerned about a specific case to seek legal advice, which may be available as part of the cover offered through their professional insurer.

We use the terms 'he' and 'she' intending them to be inclusive and interchangeable and the singular to include the plural in this book, unless the terms are specific to a particular context. Similarly, when we use the terms 'counselling', 'psychotherapy', 'therapist' and 'client' we intend to include professionals practising all forms of psychological therapy and coaching and their clients, unless specifically stated otherwise.

Our two earlier books in the BACP's Legal Resource series, *Essential Law for Counsellors and Psychotherapists* (2010) and *Legal Issues Across Counselling and Psychotherapy Settings: A Guide to Practice* (2011), reflect the law in other jurisdictions. This book reflects the law in England and, where indicated, includes references and further reading for the relevant law in Scotland, Northern Ireland and Wales.

We value practitioners' comments and feedback, and we thank everyone who has contributed their thoughts, ideas and scenarios for us to include in this new edition. We look forward to hearing your thoughts about this new 2nd edition!

Tim and Barbara

Part I

Confidentiality and the Law

1 Recording Confidences

I am a reasonably good therapist with many years' experience. My clients are well satisfied with what I offer ... but I do feel nervous about whether what I do concerning confidentiality is legally correct.

I provide counselling in two places. My employer's policy on confidentiality is so different from what I do in my private practice that I cannot see how they can both be right.

I know what I am doing when I am counselling or coaching ... I feel confident about when I need to get extra support. When the law is mentioned I feel exactly the opposite. The law seems so big and I feel so small in comparison that I feel uncertain, anxious and watch myself becoming defensive.

To make things simple, I have decided to treat everything my clients tell me as absolutely confidential. It's worked so far but I know that one day it may get me into trouble. I have had a few awkward moments and think that I ought to get clearer about what the law requires.

I don't keep any records – am I wrong?

I usually keep client records. One client says she won't work with me if I keep records – can I agree to this or should I refuse to work with her?

When we ask therapists how they approach confidentiality and record keeping in their practice, these are some of the typical comments we receive. We understand therapists' concern about making and keeping boundaries in confidentiality and records and it seems to us that few issues raise greater anxiety for counsellors and psychotherapists than the appropriate management of their clients' confidences, particularly where a client's trust is at risk.

Well-managed good practice concerning confidentiality and record keeping can strengthen the therapeutic relationship as trust is deepened and clients feel increasingly secure and respected. This is critically important in counselling and psychotherapy, where clients need to feel able to discuss sensitive thoughts and issues without worrying that their confidences might be communicated to others in ways that could harm the client by damaging their reputation or upsetting others. Therapy is usually possible only where there is a high degree of respect for clients' confidences and privacy.

On the other hand, badly managed confidentiality and record keeping can have the completely opposite effect, destroying ways of working together and leaving the client feeling betrayed, hurt and misunderstood and the therapist's reputation or integrity undermined. It is therefore not surprising that confidentiality is one of the issues most frequently raised by therapists. This indicates both its importance to everyday practice and the level of difficulty involved in managing it well.

On an issue of such importance to therapists and their clients, it is both reasonable and professionally responsible to turn first to the law for guidance. For many therapists, this is where the problems begin. Those who hope for clear and unequivocal guidance leading to certainty will be disappointed in most legal systems based on English and Scottish law or other legal systems closely related. Instead of precise rules that can be automatically applied, the law operates as a framework in which professionals, including therapists, are required to exercise a degree of judgement in how they apply the law to the specific circumstances of their work. It is also an area of law where therapists may receive contradictory advice from different sources. Our aim in writing this book is to provide information for therapists so that they can base their judgement on a reasonable degree of knowledge about the essential points of law involved, spot the 'hidden traps', and develop an understanding of some of the complexities and points of tension in the existing law.

Confidentiality and record keeping have been combined in a single book because the two issues are often experienced as increasingly linked and existing in tension with each other. One therapist memorably likened recording her clients' confidence to 'walking a tightrope ... wearing a blindfold'. She worked in a service for young people and their parents which had seen a steadily increasing number of requests for copies of clients' records from lawyers for use as evidence in court cases and growing pressures on therapists to co-operate more closely with other professionals. As she reflected on these pressures in her work, she observed:

> I feel that I am walking a tightrope. So long as I stay on the rope I am OK but keeping my balance can be difficult. If I wobble too much towards either side I will fall off. If I lean too far in one direction, by keeping the briefest possible records to protect my client's confidences, I reduce my competence to help my client because my records become too skimpy to help me deliver the therapy. If I lean too far towards on the other side by keeping over-detailed records, I may compromise my client's privacy when I am required to reveal those records. It feels like a balancing act. Sometimes I feel that I am walking the tightrope wearing a blindfold because I cannot always identify what is legally expected of me.

In this book, we hope to be able to remove the 'blindfold' by adequately explaining the relevant law. We set out the legal frameworks that apply to confidentiality and record keeping in order to help therapists develop and review their practice in ways that are compatible with the law. Because the law needs to be flexible and so cannot always provide absolute certainty, and because client and therapist circumstances vary widely, we may not be able to eliminate the difficulty of balancing competing legal responsibilities and conflicting legal opinions. We intend that well-informed therapists will be able to use the law to support their work and to resist unjustified intrusions into their clients' confidentiality and privacy. Knowledge of the law is no substitute for being a competent therapist. However, competent therapists who are knowledgeable about the law are best placed to establish some of the essential conditions from which to deliver the highest quality therapy.

1.1 Using this book

Throughout the book we include extracts and quotations at the start of chapters from comments made to us by therapists, clients and service managers. These illustrate a wide range of views on confidentiality and record keeping, and they have influenced the way we present the legal information and analysis which we have designed to be easily applied by therapists. We have deliberately avoided the traditional style of legal textbooks written for lawyers, but will include references to them where they provide useful sources of further information. We are particularly interested in understanding how the law works in the context of therapy practice. It is seldom more complex than when therapists are working in large organisations with multiple responsibilities to their service users and the community as a whole.

We have developed the structure of the second edition of this book for busy therapists. Some may read the book from cover to cover, but we imagine that most will pick topics of particular relevance to whatever issue is causing concern or is of interest. To meet most needs, we have attempted to ensure that each chapter is complete in itself, even if this sometimes means some repetition between chapters or including cross-references to other sources in the book. The best way of navigating around the book will be to use the Contents page or Index. There are inevitably technical terms in any area of law. We have attempted to keep these to a minimum and have provided a glossary to briefly explain the important ones.

We have included in this new edition a range of short practice scenarios for reflection and discussion, and checklists to help practitioners think through issues and dilemmas and for discussion in supervision. We hope that these may prove useful to understand and implement the law, ethics and guidance in the context of practice.

1.2 The importance of obtaining legal advice

Breaches of confidence and poor record keeping may incur legal liabilities or penalties. There is no substitute for obtaining good up-to-date legal advice on any issues that are of importance to you or your service. The law is constantly developing and legal opinion frequently depends on the precise circumstances of a particular case. Many professional bodies and insurance services provide access to legal advice or can guide you on where to find the best available legal resources.

This book should not be used as substitute for obtaining advice from a lawyer who is qualified and experienced in the relevant field. The book is intended to help readers understand the broader legal issues concerning confidentiality and record keeping. It may also help managers, practitioners and clients to recognise when there are significant issues at stake that require specific legal advice or to understand the advice that has been given to them.

1.3 Defining key terms

There are many technical terms used in the law concerning professional confidentiality and record keeping. We have provided explanations of these terms in the Glossary at the end of the book, but three terms are so fundamental to understanding this topic that they merit consideration here. These key terms are 'confidentiality', 'privacy' and 'records'. Each of these terms takes on technical meanings in law that differ from their use in everyday life or their routine practice by counsellors and psychotherapists. In this section, we consider their legal meaning and applications.

1.3.1 Confidentiality

To confide in someone is to put your trust in that person. The word's origin lies in Latin, with *con* acting as an intensifier of *fidere*, meaning to trust or put one's faith in, and is probably best translated as 'to strongly trust someone'. Confidentiality presupposes trust between two people in a community of at least three people. For example, confidentiality occurs when two people decide to restrict the communication of information, keeping it between themselves in order to prevent it being communicated to a third person or to more people. In a professional relationship, 'confidentiality' means protecting information that could only be disclosed at some cost to another's privacy in order to protect that privacy from being compromised any further. In her extended consideration of *The Law of Professional – Client Confidentiality* (2003), Rosemary Pattenden observed that recent developments in the law have removed the need for a relationship of trust as a prior condition to create legally binding confidentiality. All that is necessary is that the professional was aware, or a reasonable person in her position would have been aware, that the information is private to the subject of that information (Pattenden, 2003: 13).

1.3.2 Privacy

The *Shorter Oxford Dictionary* defines 'privacy' as the 'state or condition of being withdrawn from the society of others or from public attention; freedom from disturbance or intrusion; seclusion' (Trumble and Stevenson, 2002). The ordinary meaning of the word closely matches its legal use. In contrast to confidentiality (which requires at least three people), privacy only requires that one person be able to keep information to him or herself. It can exist in a world without trust and may take on its greatest significance in circumstances of mistrust. It is a more fundamental condition than confidentiality, in that privacy does not require confidentiality but confidentiality requires privacy. For such a core concept in the relationship between people and the relationship between the public and private spheres of life, it is surprisingly hard to be more precise than the dictionary definition in either everyday life or in law. The right to privacy has gained significance with the growth of cities and urbanisation, where it is possible to live anonymously and with sufficient independence from others. Discussion of the legal origins of privacy goes back a hundred years in the USA in the case of *Boyd v US* [1885] (see Pattenden, 2003: 7). 'Breach of confidence' has long been a concept in English law, but notions of privacy became particularly significant when the Human Rights Act 1998 bound the courts to apply the law in compliance with the Human Rights Act 1998 and the European Convention on Human Rights (ECHR), which includes Article 8, the right to privacy. Accordingly, the courts are currently endeavouring to apply the common law provisions of the law of confidence in a way which protects the Article 8 right to privacy: see, for example, the speech of Lord Nicholls in *Campbell v Mirror Group Newspapers* [2004], and the decision in *Douglas v Hello!* [2007].

1.3.3 Records

When therapists refer to 'records' they are typically thinking of any notes they keep about their work with their clients, but as we will see below, legally, client records may include more than notes.

There are many possible options for record keeping, and their respective advantages and disadvantages are considered in the chapters that follow. Here are just a few examples of the record keeping systems that we have seen in practice:

- *Single file system*: All records concerning a single client are kept together in one file, i.e. name, contact details, correspondence, session notes and finances.
- *Two file systems*: The client's name and contact information, with details of any financial transactions may be kept together in one file; correspondence and session notes may be kept separately.
- Another two file system is to keep the client's name with details of any financial transactions together in one file; and contact information, correspondence and session notes may be kept in a separate file.
- An alternative approach to keeping two files is to store client names and contact details with correspondence and notes of sessions in one file, and to keep financial information in a different file for accounting and taxation purposes.
- *Multiple file systems*: Client names and contact details in one place; finances kept in another for accounting and taxation purposes; correspondence and notes of sessions kept separately to maximise client privacy. Additional files may be used for other records such as audio recordings, items created by the therapist or client during the session, or notes to be presented in supervision.

The legal meaning of the term 'records' encompasses all these different approaches to records but stretches further than what is usually thought of as the formal client record. The legal meaning of records may include a diary in which appointments have been made; any surviving jottings on scrap paper made before writing the case notes; the client's drawing or writing made in a therapy session; records of assessment and psychological measurements, reviews and reports, emails about the work with the client; and notes prepared for discussion in supervision, research or training. A record is any form of document, whether paper-based or electronic, and therefore could include audio or video recordings, recorded telephone messages, handwritten or computerised charts and photographs. Verbal or text messages on a mobile phone if still existing, or notes of the content of texts or verbal messages may also form part of a client record.

In relation to written records, the courts require the best evidence possible, and so the greatest legal weight is given to records which are made closest in time to the event to which they relate. The extent to which the law will be interested in records beyond those contained in a therapist's file about a specific client will depend on the circumstances.

Should lawyers request a copy of the client records, the file of case notes will usually be adequate for providing evidence to the courts about therapy where the legal issues concern matters between the client and a third party, for example where the client is suing someone following an accident, or where an employer is blamed for an industrial injury. If a client is suing the therapist, the quest for notes may be more wide-ranging and could reasonably include any separately recorded process notes that reveal the therapist's subjective responses as well as any supervision notes. A criminal inquiry might wish to explore all possible documentary sources both for their content as well as for any potential forensic evidence, such as fingerprints and DNA, that might be gathered from those documents or indeed any other sources. Further information about disclosure of records can be found in volume one of the BACP's Legal Resource Series, *Therapists in Court: Providing Evidence and Supporting Witnesses* (Bond and Sandhu, 2005).

If records are requested by a lawyer or a court, the imprecise and inclusive way that lawyers refer to records means that therapists are well advised to clarify with lawyers what is being referred to and whether the records requested are confined to the client's case file.

Information is the currency of everyday life. In *Commissioner of Police v Ombudsman* [1998] it was defined as 'that which informs, instructs, tells or makes aware'. However, it is the nature of the information that is shared in counselling and psychotherapy that makes the practices of record keeping, confidentiality and privacy so critical and interlocked. The information that clients disclose in therapy is typically both intimate and personal to the client. For this reason we start with the client's perspective in the next chapter.

2 Confidentiality as a legal entitlement – the Clients' Perspective

I want to be able to take confidentiality for granted. I want to be able to talk freely. I don't want to be distracted by worries about confidentiality.

I don't think that I gave confidentiality a thought when I saw my counsellor. I had so much to talk about and had waited several weeks to get started. I was pouring it all out almost before I sat down.

I am a very private person and don't find talking about personal issues easy. I need to know that there is confidentiality about whatever I say.

What I wanted to talk about is so personal that I really don't want anyone else to know about it unless I tell them. It could affect both my family and my work so I need to be in control.

You know I haven't given confidentiality much thought. My counsellor is clearly careful to be ethical and respectful of me. I trust her to do what she thinks is right for me or to discuss it with me if she is uncertain or sees a problem arising.

When I first saw my counsellor I was so desperate that I was talking to anyone who would listen: friends, neighbours and even strangers in bus queues. I didn't care who knew. I just needed help.

When I was looking for a therapist I wanted the three Cs – someone who is caring, confidential and competent. I couldn't imagine a good experience of therapy without all three being present. I needed all three personal qualities to be present, as a serious deficiency in any one of these would undermine the others and give me a false sense of security.

2.1 Clients' needs and expectations

The comments above present a variety of views about the significance of confidentiality to clients. They reveal that there are no standard needs in relation to confidentiality. 'A very private person' may want absolute confidentiality to feel safe. A very troubled person may be willing to disregard confidentiality in the urgency of seeking help which has become an overwhelming priority. For all, confidentiality is not the primary purpose of therapy but a necessary condition that makes therapy possible. Without an expectation of confidentiality, most of these clients would either have felt constrained in what they could say to their therapist or that it would be too risky to engage in therapy until the need for therapy overwhelms sensible self-protection.

For the client there is potentially a lot at stake. Personal information in the wrong hands can be very damaging to personal relationships, employment and public reputation in the wider community. Clients are taking a risk in talking to a therapist and it is only the expectation of confidentiality that makes this risk acceptable. Many clients may want to discuss sensitive personal information about themselves and they may also give information about other people involved in the events they want to discuss. Furthermore, the process of therapy may expose other information that had not previously been put into words, typically troubling feelings and the impact of difficult experiences. In order to be able to deepen their sense of themselves and to discover the personal resourcefulness to enhance their lives, clients need to be able to trust the therapist to respect and protect their confidences.

It is understandable that clients who are concerned about confidentiality desire simplicity, straightforwardness and predictability backed by high levels of certainty over such a sensitive issue. The diversity of backgrounds of clients also favours a basis for confidentiality that is simple enough to be easily communicated and readily understood by people with different abilities and experiencing various levels of distress so that clients are not distracted from their primary purpose in coming to therapy: that is, to receive help. When we discuss confidentiality with clients, words need to mean what they seem to mean and not be subject to lots of exceptions and interpretations or to be contradicted by actual practice. Clients need to know that what is offered at the outset will reliably predict what will follow. With enough certainty about what is being offered, confidentiality takes its proper place by providing clients with sufficient safety and protection from the risk of having difficulties and sensitivities exposed to others. A straightforward and robust approach to confidentiality, with a clear agreement with the client about the limits of confidentiality, leaves the client much better placed to talk frankly, with only their own personal constraints and internal censors to limit what can be said.

Some clients may hope for absolute confidentiality and total control over what is disclosed in therapy.

2.2 A fantasy of the legal consequences of creating total and absolute protection of clients' confidences

The purpose of this brief excursion into legal fantasy is to explore what the law might look like if it were to meet a client's needs for simplicity, straightforwardness and certainty about almost total protection of their confidences. We offer this example of an imaginary 'Therapeutic Secrets Act', written entirely with the purpose of totally protecting clients' confidences, in order to highlight the types of issue that have led to the current complexity of the law that is challenging for both clients and therapists alike. A law that sought only to protect clients' confidences, without considering public responsibilities and the public interest might contain the following provisions:

- An obligation of strict confidentiality would be placed on all recipients of personally sensitive information disclosed during therapy, with no exceptions.
- Disclosure of therapeutic confidences would only be permitted with the client's explicit consent in circumstances that ensure that the consent has been conscientiously sought and given.
- Wrongful disclosure of therapeutic confidences would be a serious punishable offence regardless of the intentions of the person making the disclosure, and the client would be automatically entitled to compensation for damages for the disclosure.
- Legal privilege would be granted for therapeutic confidences in order to protect them from disclosure to any court, public authority or law officers.

This imaginary legal framework would provide a high degree of certainty and security over the protection of confidences that is superficially attractive. It would provide excellent legal protection of clients' confidences but could compromise the provision of good therapy intended to serve the client's wellbeing in other ways:

- How can clients' confidences be protected without preventing therapists from receiving training and professional support and supervision intended to promote the quality of service on offer to their clients?
- What are the limits of managing confidentiality solely on the basis of client consent?
- How should therapists respond to people who are incapable of expressing what they want due to their immaturity, intoxication, disability, illness or extreme distress?
- How should therapists work with people whose autonomy is disrupted by their vulnerability created by any of these circumstances?
- When is it appropriate for therapists to breach confidentiality against the wishes of their clients in order to prevent clients inflicting serious harm to themselves such as self-mutilation or suicide? At what point ought a therapist to intervene to protect a client who is unwilling or unable to protect themselves from abuse by others, such as child or elder abuse?
- When is it appropriate to override clients' confidentiality in order to investigate or prevent suspected misconduct or the exploitation of clients by therapists?

A single-minded and absolute protection of client confidentiality could require an extraordinary degree of self-sacrifice by therapists where their professional and personal wellbeing could be sacrificed to preserving client confidentiality. For example:

- When is it appropriate for therapists to breach a client's confidences in order to protect themselves from being harassed or endangered by a client?

Such instances are fortunately rare but have been seriously harmful to the therapists concerned, who have been stalked, assaulted and on very rare occasions, therapists have been murdered. Services to other clients may also have been disrupted or diminished in quality.

Similarly, the protection of client confidentiality may be gained at the cost of preventing harm to others:

- When is it appropriate to breach confidentiality in order to prevent a client inflicting serious harm on another person? At what point is the client's right to confidentiality overridden by the rights of others?
- When is it appropriate to breach client confidentiality to prevent serious harm to another person? For example, when a client discloses abuse, to prevent another member of the client's family or friendship group suffering similar abuse?

There is also the question of the balance between the good that can be achieved by providing therapy on a confidential basis and the overall wellbeing of society as a whole:

- Where does the balance lie between avoiding deterring people from seeking therapy because of fear of breaches of confidentiality, and the benefits to society in enabling the prevention of serious harm or the investigation and detection of serious crime even when this requires therapists to breach confidences?
- At what point do the principles of justice and fairness between citizens require that any court cases are decided on the basis of all the relevant information being made available to the court, even if this means intruding on what would otherwise be confidential to the persons concerned? In some situations such cases may be observed by members of the public or reported by the press, which extends the intrusion on what has originally been disclosed in confidence. Should information disclosed in therapeutic confidence be given legal privilege to protect it from being required to be disclosed in court cases?

This list of issues indicates the potential for complexity when confidentiality is considered in the wider context of competing interests in society. It is not surprising therefore that our fantasy of a 'Therapeutic Secrets Act' is just that – a fantasy. It is unlikely ever to become a legal reality. In so far as law is a form of public morality, there are competing moral interests that impact in different ways on the provision of confidentiality. The protection of a client's confidences is a significant moral issue, but it is not the only one. How competing interests are resolved concerning confidentiality varies between different legal systems and changes over time in any legal system in response to pressing social issues, changes in public morality and the persuasive powers of those affected.

This means that any client's desires for total simplicity, straightforwardness and certainty with regard to confidentiality are unlikely to be met. There will always be a degree of uncertainty about how confidentiality in therapy will be managed in response to competing moral and legal principles. Nonetheless it is reasonable for clients to desire basic information about how their confidences will be protected, and in most cases the management of confidentiality proves to be more straightforward in practice than the potential complexity of law developed to consider all eventualities would suggest. In the next section, we outline in general terms the general legal principles that are applicable in England, Wales and Scotland and increasingly across Europe.

2.3 What level of protection of confidences can clients expect in reality?

The psychological therapies have a longstanding concern with protecting client confidences, but therapists' legal obligations with regard to confidentiality are essentially the same as those of any professional who acquires sensitive personal information about others during the course of their work. In this respect therapists are no different from medics, dentists, nurses, accountants, ministers of religion, social workers or teachers with regard to confidentiality.

The current law provides a considerable degree of protection for confidences disclosed in therapy. First, there is a strong legal entitlement to a duty of confidentiality that protects personal information acquired during therapy and attendance at therapy from unauthorised disclosure. The entitlement to confidentiality exists as part of the therapist's duty of care to their client, even if the therapist is silent on this point. It is a right that can be legally enforced and protected by legal orders, payment of damages, and by professional and organisational disciplinary procedures. However, confidentiality is never protected as an absolute right in English and Scottish law. The right to confidentiality is enforced as a matter of benefit to society. Legally this is expressed as being in the 'public interest' and therefore may be overridden where the public interest would justify this.

Second, confidentiality is a matter of contractual agreement between client and therapist, in a contract which may include terms imposed by the parties, agencies, organisations and government guidance.

Third, there is a strong professional and legal assumption that clients ought to be informed in general terms about any limitations to confidentiality and that disclosures of confidentiality ought to be managed on the basis of the client's informed consent. Typical limitations to confidentiality include:

- Prevention of serious physical harm to clients or others.
- Any legal requirements to breach confidentiality, including court orders and statutory obligations.
- Any disclosures required to enhance the quality of service offered by the therapist, e.g. obtaining professional supervision and support or sharing information with colleagues in a team setting. For further discussion see Chapter 7.

Fourth, a client's right to control personal information held about them has been strengthened by data protection legislation that requires a client's explicit consent to the compilation of most types of records of sensitive personal information. It also gives the client the right to see any records that have been made and to ensure that they are kept safely (see Section 5). The right to privacy granted by the Human Rights Act 1998 may also strengthen a client's claim to confidentiality.

Fifth, clients are generally entitled to be informed of any breaches of confidentiality, regardless of whether these were accidental or deliberately made following careful consideration, unless there are grounds of public interest or legal obligations that prevent the client being informed (see Chapter 5). Where clients are entitled to information about a disclosure of confidential information, they should be told what was disclosed, to whom and when, as soon as is reasonably possible after the event.

Sixth and finally, although it is not strictly a legal requirement, most therapists will want to know about any specific concerns about confidentiality that might inhibit a client's participation in therapy in order to examine whether these can be resolved by mutual agreement.

Exactly how therapists meet these legal requirements in practice will vary. Some will address confidentiality through discussion and spoken agreement with the client. Spoken agreements are legally valid but are vulnerable to misunderstanding and are potentially weak as legal evidence in the event of any dispute. Some therapists provide information leaflets or a letter stating their terms of working, including how confidentiality will be managed, and often the limitations of confidentiality are set out alongside other terms and conditions of the therapeutic alliance. Other therapists may provide statements about the general responsibilities held respectively by a client and therapist which will include issues concerning confidentiality and professional boundaries, etc. It may be helpful to provide information in writing (or other format suitable for the client) at or before the client's initial appointment, to allow the client time to reflect and think of any questions they may wish to ask about the terms of working, before therapy begins.

Some therapists choose to place greater emphasis on outlining most eventualities at the beginning of the therapeutic relationship, whereas others choose to raise issues as they become relevant to the way therapy is unfolding. No matter which approach has been adopted, written agreements and records of the terms of the therapeutic alliance provide better evidence of what was being offered at the time and support both clients and therapists in their recall of what was agreed.

In this chapter we have addressed some typical concerns over confidentiality from the clients' perspective. We have sought to establish why absolute confidentiality is not legally enforceable and why some aspects of confidentiality may seem complex in the existing legal framework. We have concluded with a statement of what clients might reasonably expect from legally conscientious therapists. In the next chapters we examine the legal basis of managing confidences in greater depth, with particular attention to the legal issues and principles that ought to underpin the therapist's practice.

3 Confidentiality as a Legal Responsibility – Obligations of the Therapist

I want to be a psychotherapist and be listening for what will heal. Instead I find the current state of the law is so complex and unpredictable in its consequences that at least part of my mind is listening for potential difficulties over confidentiality. It gets in the way.

When we first started counselling people affected by HIV and AIDS, the moral panic was at its height. Our clients were frightened and felt very vulnerable to public prejudice, often with good cause. We became so concerned with issues of confidentiality that it was almost becoming the primary purpose of our service until we pulled ourselves up short and asked what are we here for? We are not offering consultation in confidentiality but psychological support and therapy.

I don't experience many problems with confidentiality. I am clear with my clients about what I can offer and the limitations of what I can keep confidential. If they want a service that's the way I do it. Occasionally some clients want more confidentiality than I offer and they have to choose whether to work with me on my terms or look elsewhere.

Keep it simple. I offer absolute confidentiality and would be prepared to go to prison to protect this.

The most difficult issue I experience is clients asking me to disclose information on their behalf when I don't think it is in their interests to do so or feel that it will damage our therapeutic relationship.

I just don't feel secure in my practice on this topic. I have tried to alert clients to all the potential restrictions on confidentiality before we start but often it is irrelevant and looks more like a legal seminar, which frustrates them and me. If I keep it simple, I can find myself being given information by inadequately informed clients who tell me things without realising that they have opened up ethical and legal dilemmas for both of us. With this client group, they can be exposing themselves to potentially serious consequences outside of therapy.

I feel the reputation of our service depends on being confidential, especially in a situation like this where everyone knows everyone else. If we don't get that right, there won't be any clients.

These are some of the comments about confidentiality that we have heard from therapists. This chapter looks at the law underpinning the duties and obligations of confidentiality, and how the principles of confidentiality might apply in the work of a therapist. We then explore the circumstances in which a therapist might perceive the need to breach confidentiality, putting this into the context of current legislation and guidance.

3.1. The duty of confidentiality: legal background and responsibilities

Therapy is governed and informed by the relevant law and also by professional regulations, guidance and disciplinary procedures. When we talk about the law, we are referring to different forms of law: statute law (i.e. the law made by parliament) and common law (i.e. the law laid down by court decisions interpreting statute law). Law can also be divided into that part that covers criminal actions (the criminal law) and the law that protects civil rights and duties and redresses civil wrongs (civil law).

Sometimes therapists may commit criminal acts, for example they may physically or sexually assault clients or colleagues, and they will then be subject to prosecution and punishment under the criminal law. However, other legal cases involving therapists are likely to involve allegations of breach of contract and/or professional negligence, and these are civil law cases. Some situations may involve both criminal and civil law, for example in a situation where a client is subjected to sexual harassment by a therapist, this may be both a criminal offence and also a ground for complaint and redress for breach of professional standards of conduct. Confidentiality is enforceable in the civil law courts in several ways. The civil law offers redress for acts of professional negligence, which would include a non-defensible breach of confidentiality: that is, a breach of confidentiality which was made without appropriate consent, and without a court order; or a breach of confidence which was not made in the public interest. The civil law also covers the enforcement of contractual rights and duties in therapy contracts. For more detailed discussion of the legal system and how civil law relates to contracts and to the business of providing therapy, please see *Essential Law for Counsellors and Psychotherapists* (Mitchels and Bond, 2010).

Confidentiality is about managing information in ways that keep it secure, and control unauthorised disclosure. It is particularly concerned with protecting information that is identifiable with a specific person, typically because the person is named, but the law will also protect the confidences of people whose identity can be deduced from the available information, perhaps because the listener knows some of the circumstances of the person being referred to. Thoroughly anonymised or generalised information in which the identity of specific people cannot be discerned is not protected by the law of confidentiality.

Confidentiality is a wide-ranging duty that applies to anyone in their personal or professional life. So therapists are not unique in their legal obligations, but the nature of therapy work makes this a particularly sensitive issue. In this chapter we concentrate on those aspects of the law that are most likely to be encountered in counselling, psychotherapy, coaching and psychology. This is one of the most rapidly developing areas of law and there have been very significant developments in case law (i.e. the law created by the courts), and also in developments of legislation, particularly the Human Rights Act 1998 and the Data Protection Act 1998. One of the consequences of these developments, particularly the strengthening of the relationship between confidentiality and privacy, has been to simplify and widen the circumstances in which a legal obligation of confidentiality will arise. The duty of confidentiality extends beyond our clients. In one of the most comprehensive studies of the law of professional–client confidentiality, Rosemary Pattenden provides a useful summary of the impact of these developments:

> A professional (like anyone else) who somehow acquires confidential personal information may be saddled with an obligation of confidentiality toward X, the subject of the information, whether there was a direct, indirect or no contact with X. All that is necessary is that the professional was aware, or a reasonable person in her position would have been aware, that the information is private to X. (2003: 13)

As a result of these developments, therapists have wider obligations than simply protecting private information disclosed directly by their clients. Information given by someone about a potential client in the process of making a referral is also covered by a duty of confidentiality even though this is an indirect communication about the person concerned. The knowledge that someone might require or is seeking therapy is a private matter, so care needs to be taken in replying to enquiries (e.g. unauthorised disclosures may be made inadvertently to the wrong person through a misdirected email, telephone or mobile message). Similarly, information sent in error about a client to the wrong therapist will create a duty of confidentiality in the recipient, even though there has been no contact between the recipient therapist and client nor is any future contact intended. A legally wise response to this situation would be to notify the sender of the error, assuring them that the information is being treated as confidential, and to ask their guidance on whether they would like it securely returned or destroyed.

The critical question in determining whether a duty of confidentiality has been created depends on the answer to whether there is a reasonable expectation of privacy. Lord Woolf examined how the right to privacy is protected by the common law (i.e. the law laid down in court decisions) relating to confidentiality following the Human Rights Act 1998 and brought these two elements together in a statement about how a duty of confidentiality arises:

> A duty of confidence will arise whenever the party subject to the duty is in a situation where he either knows or ought to know that the other person can reasonably expect his privacy to be protected. (*A v B plc and C ('Flitcroft')* [2002])

We will take this statement as the basis for examining the extent of therapists' obligations in terms of confidentiality. It becomes apparent that any disclosure of personal information to a therapist satisfies this test on several grounds, including the following:

1. *The circumstances in which the information was disclosed*: Counselling and psychotherapy are strongly associated with a robust ethic of client confidentiality. The ethical requirements and guidance offered by the leading professional bodies also stress confidentiality (BACP, 2013: 6 paras 20–24; BPS, 2006: 1.2; IACP, 2005: 1.5), and the long-standing attentiveness of therapists to issues of confidentiality has created a strong public expectation of confidentiality.

2. *The nature of the information itself*: Knowing that someone is receiving counselling or psychotherapy is potentially sufficiently sensitive to be protected by privacy because of its association with someone requiring or seeking help who might not wish this information to be known. The content of the therapy may also focus on what are properly regarded as private issues concerning personal relationships, and psychological and physical well-being. For nearly thirty years, the law has taken the view that 'certain kinds of information are categorised as private and ought not to be disclosed' (Law Commission, 1981: para. 2.3). In a leading case on confidentiality, *Attorney General v Guardian Newspapers (No 2)* [1988] took the view that some information is 'obviously confidetial.' The extra level of statutory protection during police searches which is offered to 'personal records,' a term defined in s. 12 of the Police and Criminal Evidence Act 1984 as meaning:

   'documentary and other records concerning an individual (whether living or dead) who can be identified from them and relating—

   (a) to his physical or mental health;
   (b) to spiritual counselling or assistance given or to be given to him; or
   (c) to counselling or assistance given or to be given to him, for the purposes of his personal welfare, by any voluntary organisation or by any individual who—

      (i) by reason of his office or occupation has responsibilities for his personal welfare; or
      (ii) by reason of an order of a court has responsibilities for his supervision.'

   provides a strong indication of how the English law has recognised the confidential nature of various forms of therapy for nearly thirty years.

3. *Personal information disclosed in a relationship of trust*: The existence of a relationship of trust may no longer be required to establish a claim to confidentiality or privacy because a duty of confidentiality can also arise outside a relationship of trust. However, where disclosures of personal information take place in the context of a relationship of trust, the legal presumption of confidentiality is extremely strong. In a New Zealand case, which carries persuasive weight in British courts, Judge Anderson stated:

   It should be so obvious as to go without saying that when a person seeking psychological support who consults, even gratuitously as here, a professional psychologist acting in such capacity for psychological advice then the usual confidentiality of a psychologist/patient relationship must apply. (*JD v Ross* [1998])

For all these reasons, counsellors and psychotherapists owe their clients a legal duty of confidentiality. Any personally identifiable information is to be protected. It does not appear to matter whether the disclosure of information is favourable or unfavourable to the person concerned. Any unauthorised disclosure may be damaging to a client. Disclosures of unfavourable information may damage someone's reputation, with all the consequences that might follow in their personal, work and social opportunities. Even information that is not considered harmful may become damaging to the person concerned due to the reactions of others, for reasons of timing, or by exciting jealousy, rivalry or other problematic reactions. The act of unauthorised disclosure alone may unsettle the relationship between therapist and client as well as the client's peace of mind. The Supreme Court of India observed that disclosure of confidences 'has the tendency to disturb a person's tranquility. It may generate more complexes in him and he may, thereafter, have a disturbed life all through' (*Mr X v Hospital Z* [1998]).

This general duty of confidentiality established by the decisions of the courts is further reinforced by the Data Protection Act 1998 and the Human Rights Act 1998 where these apply. These Acts will be considered separately in Chapter 6.

3.2 Exceptions to the duty of confidentiality

Although the law and ethical practice impose a general duty of confidentiality on therapists with regard to personal information about their clients, especially information considered private, there are a number of exceptions to this general duty.

Client information may lawfully be disclosed by a therapist only when:

- the client consents to or requests disclosure,
- the law requires disclosure, or
- the law permits disclosure.

3.2.1 Consent (where the client consents to or requests disclosure)

If a client consents to disclosure, the duty of non-disclosure ceases to exist. Seeking a client's explicit consent is legally and ethically the most satisfactory way of resolving dilemmas over confidentiality. The consent may be total or, more likely, quite specific in what information may be communicated, when and to whom. Anything that is not included in the explicit terms of the client's consent remains protected by an obligation of confidentiality.

Therapists are increasingly working in teams, agencies, or in co-operation with other agencies or organisations. This raises the question of whether clients need to give explicit consent to communications in the team on a confidential basis (see Chapter 7 for a further discussion of sharing information between professionals). Ethically, the optimum practice is generally considered to be seeking the client's explicit consent for these communications and clarifying where the boundary of the obligation of confidentiality lies – typically in an identified team, group of workers or in the agency. This is widely thought to be most respectful of clients and is a way of establishing the conditions in which to encourage open and candid communications by the client. It also provides an opportunity to establish the client's attitude to confidentiality and whether there are any issues that might otherwise be unknown to the therapist that ought to be taken into consideration. For example, a client might wish to restrict what may be communicated to a certain member of the team (e.g. someone who may be the client's relative, neighbour or social acquaintance). This attentiveness to consent is consistent with the personal dimension of the therapist–client relationship in which the therapist is not easily interchangeable with colleagues from one session to another in the way that is possible with physical care, such as giving injections or changing dressings. Where roles are interchangeable, there is a stronger case for establishing an expectation that there will be communication in the team in order to improve the quality of care offered and to provide a seamless service; but, even in these circumstances, clients can legally limit what is communicated about them (or to whom it may be communicated) by insisting on their right to confidentiality and privacy.

Where therapists work in multidisciplinary settings, such as a GP's surgery, a social care agency or educational institution, they may find themselves working in a context where the client's explicit consent is given at the outset: for example, on completion of a form when becoming a patient at the surgery, or a child starting at a school and so on; or the client's implicit consent may be considered by the agency to be adequate for disclosure on a confidential basis between colleagues in that setting. Provided the client concerned is aware of this practice of disclosure and has been given the opportunity to object to it, implicit consent is legally sufficient to legitimise the communication of confidential information. Recent developments in information sharing as matter of public policy are considered in Chapter 7.

3.2.2 Law requires disclosure (where court orders or statutes require disclosure)

Court orders

The law offers protection to someone who is legally required to disclose confidences, for example in response to a court order. Orders of the court must be obeyed and the penalty for disobedience is punishment for contempt of court. Orders may be made for a therapist to attend court as a witness, and/or to disclose therapy notes and records, or to provide a report for the court. The therapist may wish to attend a directions hearing to discuss issues of confidentiality of therapy information with the court, and to request appropriate directions. See Bond and Sandhu (2005) for further details of how to handle requests for confidential information by solicitors, other professionals, and the courts.

Statutory duty of disclosure: terrorist activities

There is a general duty to report information which assists in the prevention of terrorist activities. The Terrorism Act 2000, s. 38B, which applies to England, Wales, Scotland and Northern Ireland, makes it a criminal offence for a person to fail to disclose, without reasonable excuse, any information which the person either knows or believes might help prevent another person carrying out an act of terrorism or which might help in bringing a terrorist to justice in the UK. It is, in our view, unlikely that professional confidentiality would ever be regarded in these circumstances as a reasonable excuse by a court. The punishment on conviction ranges from a fine to a maximum of five years imprisonment on indictment.

Section 39 of the Terrorism Act 2000 creates a separate offence popularly known as 'tipping off'. This offence is committed 'where a person knows or has reasonable cause to suspect that a constable is conducting or proposes to conduct a terrorist investigation' and he

(a) discloses to another anything which is likely to prejudice the investigation, or
(b) interferes with material which is likely to be relevant to the investigation.

This criminal offence might include acts such as interfering with evidence by destroying records or artefacts, or warning or tipping off the person(s) under investigation. The maximum penalty on indictment for tipping off is five years' imprisonment, a fine, or both. Alteration or destruction of therapy notes which may provide potential evidence, or tipping off a client under investigation for terrorist activities might therefore come under this provision.

In addition to (and separate from) the obligations described above under s. 38B of the Terrorism Act 2000, there is a different duty under s. 19 of that Act for all citizens to report any information which they have gained through the course of a trade, profession, business or employment, concerning specified activities related to money and property used to assist terrorist activities. The duty to report any such relevant information learned at home was therefore not included in the Terrorism Act 2000. However, a duty does remain to report information about fundraising for the purposes of terrorism (s. 15), the use of money or property for the purposes of terrorism (s. 16), any funding arrangements for the purposes of terrorism (s. 17) or money laundering terrorist property (s. 18). The duty to disclose information (s. 19) arises where a person

(a) believes or suspects that another person has committed an offence under any of ss. 15 to 18, and
(b) bases his belief or suspicion on information which comes to his attention in the course of a trade, profession, business or in the course of his employment.

The person commits an offence if he does not disclose to a constable as soon as is reasonably practicable

(a) his belief or suspicion, and
(b) the information on which it is based.

There is a defence to a charge under s. 2 for someone who has a reasonable excuse for not making a disclosure, or for anyone in employment who has used a system established by their employer for making this type of report. Although therapists are much less likely to receive this type of information than someone working in banking or financial services, it is significant that the duty to inform would cover therapists where the information is acquired 'in the course of a trade, profession, business or employment'.

Statutory duty of disclosure: drug trafficking and money laundering

Recent developments in the law relating to the reporting of drug trafficking and money laundering for any crime have increased the obligations of people working in legal and financial services. Psychotherapists and counsellors are now less likely to acquire the kind of information that is required to be reported under the Drug Trafficking Act 1994, Proceeds of Crime Act 2002, or the Money Laundering Regulations 2007. If in doubt, seek legal advice. In certain cases, disclosure of this type of information may be justified on the balance of public interest (see below).

Statutory duty of disclosure: Serious Crime Act 2007 (SCA)

In relation to a wide range of 'serious offences' (defined in the SCA), the courts can make a 'Serious Crime Prevention Order' in England, Wales or Northern Ireland. Serious crimes include drugs offences, customs and excise, immigration and people trafficking offences, sexual offences, fraud, counterfeiting, terrorism, and offences of violence. This list is not exhaustive. A Serious Crime Prevention Order may contain a wide variety of prohibitions, restrictions or requirements in relation to, for example, finances and business dealings, working arrangements, travel, access to and use of specified premises, employment and communication. A particular requirement which could apply to therapy is a requirement on a person to answer questions, or provide information or documents (either specified or described in an order), at a time or frequency or at a place, or in a particular form or manner, to a law enforcement officer. Such a requirement could relate to disclosure of information or production of counselling records. This piece of legislation is so complex that legal advice or consultation with the therapist's insurers is advisable if a therapist receives a request for disclosure under the SCA. Insurers will often assist the insured with advice (or payment for advice) on managing disclosures.

Statutory services, court orders and child protection

A statutory duty to report or to provide information to the authorities when requested to do may arise when a therapist is working in association with the statutory services such as health or social care, or education. Recent developments in child protection law and guidance have increased many therapists' obligations with regard to the protection of children. An example of this is compliance with an order of the court to disclose the whereabouts of a missing child under s. 50 (3) (c) of the Children Act 1989.

Where therapists know that they are working in circumstances where they have a specific obligation to pass on information, or they sense that a client is about to give information during therapy that could create an obligation on the therapist to pass the information on to others, there is an ethical case for alerting the client to the consequences of their impending disclosure before it is made. This is most respectful of clients' autonomy and demonstrates a concern to be trustworthy and therefore is ethically desirable. However, in some circumstances it is not advisable, or even may be illegal to alert the client in advance (see the note in the next paragraph). The mere fact of the client's disclosure having taken place is sufficient to create a legal obligation to disclose the required information, but no more than the information required.

Note: Alerting a client to the possible need for disclosure of acts in relation to terrorism may be illegal, if it could amount to 'tipping off' where this is forbidden. Also, therapists should exercise caution and/or take appropriate advice before giving such a warning to clients in any situation involving child protection, since this may in some cases adversely affect a child's welfare or compromise a child protection investigation, with potentially serious consequences for a child.

3.2.3 Balance of public interest (where the law permits disclosure)

Arguably, the most important exception to the duty of confidentiality arises where there is a public interest in the disclosure of the information, which outweighs the public interest in preserving the client's confidentiality. In common law, the obligation of confidentiality arises because there is a public interest in ensuring that people's confidential information is respected, but this is not an absolute right that persists in all circumstances. There are times when confidentiality has to give way to broader public interest. One key case of relevance to therapy illustrates how the courts view the professional's role in such decisions and how it undertakes the difficult task of balancing the competing interests.

The case of *W v Edgell and others* [1990] concerned someone who suffered from paranoid schizophrenia. In 1974, W had shot and killed five people and injured two others. In 1986, he applied to a mental health review tribunal to be released from a secure mental health hospital in which he had been detained. The Secretary of State blocked W's release. W's solicitors commissioned an independent assessment and report from Dr Edgell, a consultant psychiatrist. Dr Edgell reported that W had a long-term and ongoing interest in home-made bombs and that he considered that W remained a danger to the public. W's solicitors withdrew his application for release. Even though Dr Edgell was bound by contractual terms of confidentiality when commissioned to undertake this work, he was sufficiently concerned about the potential dangers posed by W to have discussed the case and his concerns with the medical director of the hospital. As a result of these discussions, which were a breach of confidence owed to W and his solicitor, it was agreed that both the hospital and the Secretary of State should receive a copy of the report, further extending the breaches of confidence. When W learned that the report had been passed to the hospital and the tribunal, through the Secretary of State, he started legal actions against Dr Edgell and all the recipients of the report seeking:

- a court order to restrain them from using or disclosing the report;
- the return of all copies of the report; and
- damages for breach of the duty of confidence.

W's case failed in the High Court and his appeal was dismissed by the Court of Appeal.

In his judgement, Lord Justice Bingham reviewed decisions in previous cases and stated: 'The decided cases very clearly establish (1) that the law recognises an important public interest in maintaining professional duties of confidence, but (2) that the law treats such duties not as absolute but as liable to be overridden where there is held to be a stronger public interest in disclosure.' All the judgements viewed the potential seriousness of the dangers as justifying Dr Edgell's breach of confidentiality and his concern that those responsible for providing treatment and managing the care and custody of W should be aware of significant information gathered during his assessment. In many ways the past history and severity of the dangers posed by W made this a relatively easy balancing act. Despite the introduction of the Human Rights Act, a case based on similar circumstances today would be likely to reach the same conclusions in favour of disclosure.

Therapists are often faced with less clear-cut circumstances. Dilemmas over confidentiality concerning harm to other people can arise with clients who have no previous history of harming anyone but are proposing to harm someone in retaliation for some real harm caused to them, or in response to a psychological fantasy. The fact that the therapist is having difficulty containing his or her own anxiety is not a sufficient reason to breach a client's confidentiality. This might justify additional professional support provided on a confidential basis, but may not justify a breach of confidentiality likely to have significant consequences for the client. In making decisions on confidentiality (see Box 3.1), it may be useful to distinguish between situations when circumstances are of such seriousness that they justify a breach of confidence and situations where the balance of public interest appears to justify disclosure, and to understand the process of how such a decision ought to be undertaken.

There are many different versions of what circumstances ought to be taken into account, both in case law and professional guidance, especially for health workers. What follows is a carefully considered collation of that guidance bearing in mind the high levels of significance attached to the privacy and confidentiality concerning personal information in counselling, psychotherapy and psychology.

Box 3.1   Circumstances that might justify breaching confidentiality

- Real risk of serious harm.
- The threat appears imminent.
- Disclosure is likely to be effective in limiting the harm or preventing the harm occurring.

Criteria that might justify breaching confidentiality

- **Real risk**: A client who is actively planning something with a precise schedule, or who has advanced further in their intent by making physical preparations to cause harm, is moving beyond fantasy and into a preparation or action stage and, to this extent, could now be posing a real risk to themselves and/or others. Similarly, a client in the grip of uncontrollable rage or psychosis, or who has suppressed their inhibitions by intoxication, could be considered to pose a real risk depending on the other circumstances in the case.

  A client who has reported experiencing past similar intentions to harm others, but has not done so, might represent a lower risk. Whether or not they constitute real risk would depend on how this situation differs from earlier ones. For example, is this situation more severe or part of a pattern of escalating behaviour?

- **Serious harm**: A threat to life, inflicting serious physical harm, rape and child abuse would all be examples of serious harm. The risk of a car accident, accident at work, or the spread of serious disease could amount to serious harm. Suicide not only poses serious harm to self but the method chosen may create a risk of serious harm to others.

  The prevention of psychological distress or lower levels of harm without any associated serious physical injury, criminal activity or child protection issue, may not necessarily justify a breach of confidentiality in English law, especially for adults and young people who have sufficient understanding, maturity and intelligence to make them capable of giving valid consent. The prevention of psychological harm without other associated harms is best resolved by consent.

- **Imminent**: The risk or threat of harm must be sufficiently imminent that those bound by confidentiality are unlikely to be able to take other effective preventative action, for example reducing the risk in the course of therapy, and there is little possibility of the risk or threat subsiding with the passage of time, because time is running out.

- **Effective**: There has to be a reasonable probability that the breach of confidence will minimise or prevent the risk or threat of serious harm.

  The nature of the circumstances in which the risk is discovered will determine the extent to which a therapist can make a carefully considered judgement. For example, courts will accept that someone acting in an urgent situation, under the pressure of an immediately imminent risk, may have less opportunity to investigate any of these criteria than someone who has longer to consult colleagues or others with relevant expertise on an anonymous or confidential basis.

  If the therapist considers that the balance of public interest favours disclosure, the next step is to consider how to undertake this in ways that are consistent with the public interest in preserving confidentiality by avoiding unnecessary damage to the client's privacy by:

  o selecting the information to be disclosed: disclosure of information should be limited to that necessary in order to avert the risk;
  o selecting the recipient(s) of the information: disclosure should only be made to a person or agency that is capable of minimising or preventing the harm; and
  o recording the disclosure in the client records (see Box 7.2).

- **Seeking the client's consent**: A client's consent provides the best protection both of a client's rights and those of the therapist, unless seeking such consent enhances the risk of harm, will inhibit effective investigation of a serious crime, or the circumstances prevent this. There needs to be a sound reason for not informing a client in advance of an intention to breach confidentiality. If the client refuses consent, their reasons ought to be considered and, if possible, taken into account. General Medical Council guidance to doctors is of interest for therapists, directing:

37. Personal information may, therefore, be disclosed in the public interest, without patients' consent, and in exceptional cases where patients have withheld consent, if the benefits to an individual or to society of the disclosure outweigh both the public and the patient's interest in keeping the information confidential. You must weigh the harms that are likely to arise from non-disclosure of information against the possible harm both to the patient, and to the overall trust between doctors and patients, arising from the release of that information.

38. Before considering whether a disclosure of personal information would be justified in the public interest, you must be satisfied that identifiable information is necessary for the purpose, or that it is not reasonably practicable to anonymise or code it. In such cases, you should still seek the patient's consent unless it is not practicable to do so, for example because:

(a) the patient is not competent to give consent, in which case you should consult the patient's welfare attorney, court-appointed deputy, guardian or the patient's relatives, friends or carers;

(b) you have reason to believe that seeking consent would put you or others at risk of serious harm;

(c) seeking consent would be likely to undermine the purpose of the disclosure, for example, by prejudicing the prevention or detection of serious crime; or

(d) action must be taken quickly, for example, in the detection or control of outbreaks of some communicable diseases, and there is insufficient time to contact the patient.

39. You should inform the patient that a disclosure will be made in the public interest, even if you have not sought consent, unless to do so is impracticable, would put you or others at risk of serious harm, or would prejudice the purpose of the disclosure. You must document in the patient's record your reasons for disclosing information without consent and any steps you have taken to seek the patient's consent, to inform them about the disclosure, or your reasons for not doing so.

(GMC, 2009: 37–39)

Please note that the GMC updates its guidance regularly, for example see the recent updated GMC guidance on *Good Medical Practice* (2006) and the GMC *Guidance for Doctors on Protecting Children and Young People* (GMC, 2012) at www. gmc-uk.org.

Communicate the information on a confidential basis

Written communications should be marked 'Confidential' or 'In confidence'. Oral communications should be preceded by a clear statement that what is being disclosed is confidential. If the therapist is unfamiliar with the practice of the person or agency receiving the information, it is reasonable to ask how the information will be protected or treated in advance of disclosing it.

Make a record of the decision-making process as soon as practically possible. This is now a standard requirement in most statutory services and serves to mark the seriousness with which someone's privacy and confidentiality is regarded, as well as providing the essential basis for any review by the courts or other agencies of the decision-making process. The possibility of a client complaining or initiating litigation following a breach of confidentiality makes this a respectful and prudent practice for all therapists.

Notify the client of the communication of confidential information, specifically, what has been communicated to whom, unless there are good reasons for not doing so (e.g. situations that make it inadvisable to seek consent; see note above at page 25, para 2 and also Box 7.2. Where the disclosure concerns serious crime, the law may forbid notifying the person concerned and to do so may be an offence known as 'tipping off' (see above at para 3 on page 23).

The courts are interested in whether the therapist has taken reasonable care in weighing up where the public interest lies and will take account of the circumstances in which the decision had to be made. They do not expect that all therapists will necessarily agree with the decision. Courts are concerned that the specific decision and actions by the people concerned have been taken with a reasonable level of conscientiousness and respect for the obligation of confidentiality. In situations where there is real risk of physical harm to another, courts should not be over-zealous in proving the therapist wrong (Brazier, 2003: 68).

There is a noticeable difference between the legal reasoning in British and American cases that is reflected in guidance offered by professional bodies. This may be a source of some confusion, as many American textbooks on therapy are read by British therapists. One of the recurrent sources of confusion concerns whether therapists have a duty to warn a third party of dangers posed by one of their clients. In the USA, a client, Poddar, was being seen in a university health centre by a clinical psychologist, Ms Tarasoff. Poddar told his therapist that he intended to murder Ms Tarasoff when she returned from a trip to Brazil because he felt rejected by her. The therapist knew of his previous history of violence, that he had also armed himself with a gun, and took his threat seriously. The psychologist consulted with colleagues, unsuccessfully attempted to have Poddar institutionalised, and notified the university police, who briefly detained him but released him because he appeared rational. No one warned the intended victim of the danger she was in. Poddar brutally murdered Ms Tarasoff. Her parents initiated the case of *Tarasoff v The Regents of the University of California* [1974], which is now widely cited in therapeutic literature as establishing a duty to warn third parties. This is an outdated interpretation of this case. The judgement was reconsidered in *Tarasoff II* [1976], which changed the duty from one of having to warn the potential victim to one of taking reasonable steps to protect the person at risk of harm. This revised duty allows the circumstances to be taken into account and could be met in a variety of ways, including warning the person at risk, informing others who are likely to warn the victim, or notifying the police of a potential danger. This duty to act to protect someone from risk of physical harm by a client is stronger in American law than on this side of the Atlantic. The consensus amongst legal commentators is that *Tarasoff* would not be followed in English courts (Jackson, 2006: 342; Pattenden, 2003: 695; Pattinson, 2006: 197).

There is no positive duty in English and Scottish law to warn third parties or to take reasonable steps to protect a potential victim in similar circumstances to *Tarasoff*. However, British courts would probably regard any breach of confidentiality as justified on the balance of public interest if a therapist did warn a potential victim in similar circumstances or if the therapist sought the assistance of appropriate authorities to prevent the harm. In this respect, British therapists retain more opportunities to exercise their professional judgement than their American colleagues.

However, remember that we owe a duty of care to our clients, and so if one client poses a threat to the health or welfare of another client, as we have a duty of care to both clients, we also have a responsibility to act in such a way that the welfare of both clients is protected. If, therefore, one client poses a real and immediate threat to another (such as one of a couple who we are counselling threatening violence to the other) there is a responsibility to take appropriate action to remove or reduce the risk of harm. Situations such as this can be met by appropriate counselling agreements in which the limits of confidentiality and the responsibilities of the therapist are clearly set out.

3.3 The prevention and detection of serious crime

Apart from the statutory provisions of the Serious Crime Act 2007, under which a court may make a Serious Crime Prevention Order requiring certain actions or disclosure of information or records (discussed on page 30 at 3.3), the prevention and detection of serious crime also constitutes justification for breaches of confidentiality. The big difference between the two is that under a Serious Crime Prevention Order the therapist is responding to a court direction, whereas in other situations, the therapist has to make up their own mind whether or not to breach confidentiality in the public interest.

The prevention and detection of serious crime is a wider category than prevention of serious harm to others, considered in the previous section. Apart from the lists of serious crimes now contained in the Serious Crime Act 2007, the definition of serious crime in the context of justification for disclosure of confidential information seems to have been left to the courts and public to define, as a matter of common sense. The Department of Health has offered the following guidance, which is reflected in the Serious Crime Act 2007 and in the GMS guidance on *Confidentiality* (GMC, 2009):

> Murder, manslaughter, rape, treason, kidnapping, child abuse or other cases where individuals have suffered serious harm may all warrant breaching confidentiality. Serious

harm to the security of the state or to public order and crimes that involve substantial financial gain and loss will generally fall within this category. In contrast, theft, fraud or damage to property where loss or damage is less substantial would generally not warrant breach of confidence. (DH, 2003a: 35)

See also the NHS *Confidentiality: NHS Code of Practice: Supplementary Guidance: Public Interest Disclosures* (DH, 2010b), which contains a useful flow chart for decision making. The 2003 guidance cited above is reflected and discussed in the 2010 document (pp. 8–11).

See in particular the following paragraphs, which may be useful for reflection:

12. Is disclosure necessary to prevent, detect or prosecute serious crime? Confidential patient information can be disclosed in the public interest where that information can be used to prevent, detect, or prosecute, a serious crime. "Serious crime" is not clearly defined in law but will include crimes that cause serious physical or psychological harm to individuals. This will certainly include murder, manslaughter, rape, treason, kidnapping, and child abuse or neglect causing significant harm and will likely include other crimes which carry a five-year minimum prison sentence but may also include other acts that have a high impact on the victim.

13. On the other hand, theft, fraud or damage to property where loss or damage is not substantial are less likely to constitute a serious crime and as such may not warrant breach of confidential information, though proportionality is important here. It may, for example, be possible to disclose some information about an individual's involvement in crime without disclosing any clinical information.

14. In the grey area between these two extremes a judgement is required to assess whether the crime is sufficiently serious to warrant disclosure. The wider context is particularly important here. Sometimes crime may be considered as serious where there is a prolonged period of incidents even though none of them might be serious on its own (e.g. as sometimes occurs with child neglect). Serious fraud or theft involving significant NHS resources would be likely to harm individuals waiting for treatment. A comparatively minor prescription fraud might be serious if prescriptions for controlled drugs are being forged.

15. In some circumstances there may not be sufficient information available to determine whether or not a disclosure may serve to prevent or detect a serious crime. It may help to first hold an anonymised discussion with colleagues to establish whether concerns are justified and greater sharing of information is required may be appropriate.

16. Note that the public interest defence is separate from, and additional to, specific statutory requirements for disclosure in relation to crime. There is a legal duty to report financial assistance of terrorism, and legislation requires health professionals to release, where requested by police:

The names of patients treated after a car accident, to assist in the investigation of alleged dangerous driving;

Medical records / information, human tissue or fluid, if the request is backed by a court order or search warrant;

Medical records / information where there are reasonable grounds for believing the records are evidence in relation to an offence and it is necessary for police to seize them in order to prevent loss or alteration of evidence.

(DH, 2010b, 8–10)

We recommend downloading a full copy (see References for the URL) of this guidance for therapists who work in statutory sectors and in particular with or for the NHS.

3.4 The Human Rights Act 1998

The Human Rights Act applies across the United Kingdom, to all 'public authorities', a term which is not defined but includes the courts and tribunals, and therefore has a pervasive influence in all areas of society. There are similar measures in place across most of the European Union and where human rights are protected by the European Court of Human Rights (ECtHR) in terms of the European Convention on Human Rights (ECHR). Article 8 of the ECHR (as set out in Schedule 1 to the Human Rights Act) establishes the 'right to respect for private and family life'. This is not an absolute right. Articles 8.1 and 8.2 ought to be read alongside each other as the second qualifies the rights asserted in the first:

> Article 8.1 Everyone has the right to respect for his private and family life, his home, and his correspondence.

> Article 8.2 There shall be no interference by a public authority with the exercise of this right except such as is in accordance with the law and is necessary in a democratic society in the interests of national security, public safety or the economic wellbeing of the country, for the prevention of disorder or crime, for the protection of health or morals, or for the protection of the rights and freedoms of others.

Although we are not aware of any cases specifically involving privacy in counselling or psychotherapeutic consultations and their records, we would suggest that they are covered both by the wording of Article 8 and by analogy with medical cases. It has not proved especially difficult for individuals to establish that any disclosure of their medical records constitutes a prima facie violation of Article 8 (Jackson, 2006: 323).

The courts have approached cases from the viewpoint of weighing competing interests and deciding where the balance ought to lie. In *Z v Finland* [1998] the ECtHR balanced a wife's right to privacy concerning her medical records against the police need to access those records as part of an investigation into sexual offences by her husband. Specifically, they wanted to discover when he became aware of his positive HIV status. The court decided that the personal and community interest protecting the confidentiality of medical records may be outweighed by the interest in the investigation and prosecution of crime. However, it was not considered proportionate to reveal her identity to the public in a Court of

Appeal judgement. Similarly in *MS v Sweden* [1999], the court considered that the prevention of benefit fraud outweighed the protection of the privacy of medical records.

As many therapists work in agencies with accountability to management, a case concerning the investigation of a GP may be of interest. The case of *A Health Authority v X* [2001] concerned the investigation by a health authority into a doctor for suspected over-prescribing, incomplete medical records, inappropriate delegation of his responsibilities and failing to obtain adequate medical consent before performing medical procedures. Some patients withheld their consent to disclosure of their medical records. Again the court decided in favour of disclosure, as Lord Justice Thorpe observed, 'as it invariably does, save in exceptional cases'. The proper administration of criminal justice and the proper administration of professional disciplinary hearings justified the release of the records, with conditions of confidentiality imposed on those who received them.

All the Articles in the ECHR have to be held in balance with each other. For example, in a case concerning the treatment of a celebrity, her rights to privacy under Article 8 had to be balanced with the right to freedom of expression under Article 10, which is frequently used by the press to support their right to publish. In *Campbell v Mirror Group Newspapers Ltd* [2004] the court was asked to consider the rights of a celebrity, the well-known fashion model Naomi Campbell. A newspaper had published a story about her drug addiction, her receipt of treatment and her attendance at Narcotics Anonymous. The story was illustrated with photographs of her attending a Narcotics Anonymous meeting. At the final appeal, Naomi Campbell accepted that the press was entitled to contradict her previous claims that she was not a drug addict and that the disclosure of her addiction was in the public interest. However, she disputed the right of the press to publish photographs and information about her attendance at Narcotics Anonymous. The House of Lords agreed with her in a majority verdict of 3:2.

Naomi Campbell's case was brought for breach of confidence and compensation under the Data Protection Act and illustrates how this legislation may also be used to protect confidentiality. We will consider this legislation in greater detail in Chapter 6.

3.5 Protecting clients from self-harm and suicidal intent

Determining what is ethical and lawful when working with suicidal clients poses some of the most difficult dilemmas that are routinely encountered by therapists and mental health workers. For a discussion of the wider ethical and legal issues, see Bond (2010: 101–19).

In this section we will consider whether there is a duty to breach confidentiality in order to obtain assistance for a suicidal client; whether it is legally defensible to breach confidentiality to obtain assistance; and the difference between adult and child clients in this regard. Detailed consideration of the relationship between consent and mental capacity is set out in Chapter 11.

Unlike American law, there is no general legal duty in England to report suicidal risk or serious self-harm. English law has a long tradition that any adult with mental capacity may refuse treatment for physical illness for good reason, irrational reasons or no reasons, even if the consequence is life threatening. This often puts doctors in a difficult position if they have a limited opportunity to give a treatment for a life-threatening medical condition but the patient is hesitating beyond the time when successful medical treatment can be given. To give treatment by force against a person's express wishes may constitute a physical assault and other legal wrongs.

Similarly, if an adult client, with mental capacity, is contemplating suicide and actively forbids a therapist to seek additional help, the therapist is under a general legal obligation to respect the client's confidence, unless the therapist and client have agreed on limits to confidentiality in the therapeutic contract: for example, it has been agreed between therapist and client that the therapist may refer the client to an appropriate person or agency and disclose confidential information if the therapist believes that the client or others are at immediate risk of serious harm.

Where a client is contemplating suicide, there is no general legal duty to breach a confidence in order to rescue the client unless the therapist is working in an organisational or institutional setting such as a prison, mental health unit or other service in which there may be an obligation to protect someone from self-destruction. However, the therapist may also perceive a potential risk of serious harm to others from the client's proposed method of suicide, justifying disclosure in the greater public interest.

However, the therapist also has to consider the possibility of a risk of harm to others. An intent to kill oneself is insufficient to indicate mental illness without the presence of other symptoms indicating an associated mental illness. The symptoms of mental illnesses (such as major depression, post-traumatic stress disorder, schizophrenia, psychosis, etc.) when there is also a risk of serious harm to the client or others might justify a referral for assessment or treatment under the mental health legislation, even if this requires a limited breach of confidentiality. The Adults with Incapacity (Scotland) Act 2000 and the Mental Capacity Act 2005 set out new criteria concerning the legal capacity for adults to give consent to treatment and the circumstances when others may give consent for health care on their behalf; for discussion, see Chapter 11.

People under the age of 18 have a legal entitlement to privacy and confidentiality. However, the law permits the High Court to assume a greater level of responsibility to ensure the safety and welfare of children and young people until they reach adulthood, and therefore it may give a 'Direction of Lawfulness' for medical staff to provide necessary treatment, for example in cases of young people at risk of serious harm from eating disorders such as anorexia or life threatening physical illnesses. Chapter 11 explores the issues of mental capacity, consent and confidentiality in relation to the rights of children and young people under the age of 18. From their 18th birthday onwards, a person with appropriate mental capacity is entitled to refuse medical treatment, even when this may result in their death.

The complexity of the law with regard to self-harm and suicide has resulted in therapists attempting to make the situation more manageable and to establish a right to consult with others or make a referral if the client is considered to be suicidal or at risk of serious self-harm, or there is a risk of serious harm to others. For example, it is widespread practice in this field for a therapy contract to offer high levels of confidentiality except where the therapist is legally required to provide information, or where the client consents, or where there is a risk of serious harm to the client or others. In practice, this limitation of confidentiality may be used as a prior condition to receiving therapy. The client may indicate acceptance of these terms by the act of signing a therapy contract with a limitation of confidentiality clause in it, or simply by commencing therapy on the basis of a verbal agreement, accepting these terms, unless anything has clearly been communicated by the client to the contrary. Even though a therapist reserves the right to seek assistance for a client at risk of serious self-harm, there is still a matter of judgement about when to exercise this right and how to do so with the minimum of damage to a client's rights to privacy and confidentiality. Although this practice appears to be widespread and supported by the relevant professional bodies, we do not know of any instances where it has been considered by the courts.

Practitioners are well advised to give very careful consideration to the relevant circumstances if they are considering breaching confidentiality in order to protect an adult from self-inflicted harm, against the express wishes of that person. The balance of public interest in favour of acting is stronger where the proposed self-harm could also cause physical harm to others: for example, crashing a car on a public road or jumping from a height where there is the risk of causing serious harm to others. In other situations, if the therapist has not already obtained the client's agreement to a limitation on confidentiality prior to commencing therapy, the therapist is legally best advised to actively seek the client's consent whenever possible, prior to obtaining additional assistance even if this involves additional time and effort (see the discussion in Chapter 4).

With clients who have given their consent (or implied their agreement) to the counsellor acting in their best interests if they or others are at risk of harm, discuss with the client, consider and ideally discuss in supervision:

- What has the client given me permission to do?
- Does that permission include referral?

A therapist who knows or has reasonable cause to suspect that a client is likely to harm himself or others but will not give consent for referral must carefully consider the possible consequences for their client of referral or non-referral without client consent. Suggestions for issues to consider if the client is unable to give consent or refuses to give consent for referral can be found at the end of Chapter 14 at 14.7.

3.6 Making referrals

Therapists' professional responsibility requires that they must act within the area of their personal expertise, and should consider their own limitations; see, for example, BACP's *Ethical Framework* (2013: 2). The implication of this is that when they reach the limits of their expertise, consideration should be given to referral on where appropriate and with the client's consent. If the client does not consent to referral on, then if the client or others may be at risk of harm, the therapist should address the issues raised at the end of Chapter 14 at 14.7.

In practice, most therapists probably would only want to make a referral without the express consent of the client in circumstances where the client had lost mental capacity, was no longer connecting with the therapist psychologically, or for any other reason there was a risk of serious harm to the client or others, and/or the counsellor had reached the limits of their expertise or felt that the client was in need of additional assistance or support over and above that which the counsellor alone could provide.

3.7 Being explicit with clients about confidentiality

Given that therapy is a relationship of trust, in which fidelity, beneficence, candour and client autonomy are essential, the best way round the problem is to meet the issues head on and discuss confidentiality and its potential limitations openly with clients and to reach a mutually acceptable agreement as part of the therapeutic contract at the outset of therapy. Many therapists seem very afraid of doing this.

Some counselling organisations have a process in which there is an assessment or introductory meeting which is held before counselling work commences with a nominated therapist. We have been told by some of these counselling organisations that they fear that if they entered into detailed discussions about limitations on confidentiality with clients at that first pre-therapy meeting (which may be referred to as an introductory or assessment session), they might risk losing new clients, so at that first meeting, some organisations may avoid any discussion of confidentiality, leaving it to the counsellor subsequently allocated to discuss and negotiate any limitations on confidentiality later on in the course of therapy. This and other similar practices are open to potential criticism. Delay in discussion of confidentiality and failure to establish a clear agreement about it with the client at the outset of therapy may leave the client in the vulnerable position of disclosing sensitive personal confidences, with no clearly established boundaries about what will happen to that information if, for example, the client or others are at risk of serious harm. The therapist, too, is potentially vulnerable without the sound basis of explicit client consent should any further action or referral prove necessary.

We would recommend that therapists consider establishing a system in which the issue of confidentiality is discussed in a practical way at the outset with each new client, before therapy commences, and that a clear agreement is made with the client about disclosure and referral on, either as part of an assessment process or as part of a therapeutic contract.

A general consent condition may be agreed with the client for the therapist to have permission to disclose information (or refer on) to appropriate agencies if, for example, there is a risk of serious harm to the client or to others. Therapists may then interpret such a generalised permission as an adequate basis for taking positive steps to seek assistance for the person concerned unless the person actively refuses such assistance. The practical usefulness of such a condition may be that it makes a refusal of such assistance less likely, especially if the client's confidences are as well protected as the circumstances allow. However, therapists should be mindful that the existence of a widespread practice does not in itself make it lawful or immune from legal challenge. Such a general consent, if verbal and unwritten, could be interpreted in many ways and would be very difficult to substantiate and prove in a court case. A distressed client coming into counselling for an initial assessment or a first session is unlikely to recall word for word any explanation that they were given about disclosure, and their understanding of what precisely was agreed may very well be woolly and unclear. They may, for instance, be unsure as to whether a general consent to disclose actually implies or includes consent to go ahead and make a referral and to which person or agency a referral would be made.

For the avoidance of doubt, it is best to discuss the therapist's terms of working openly and directly with the client and to agree these issues, including confidentiality, at the outset of the therapeutic alliance, creating, wherever possible, a clear and unequivocal understanding with the client about the therapist's role and responsibilities, including those of disclosure and referral. The client will then be in the best possible position to consider these issues and to give explicit and informed consent as part of the therapeutic contract. Again, legally speaking, for the avoidance of doubt, consents agreed with the client should be clearly expressed in writing (or another format, such as an audio recording, suitable for the client's needs), so that the client can have a copy to retain and study at leisure and to ensure that both the client and the therapist have a clear understanding and a record of their agreement.

Some therapists provide information about their terms of working with clients in the form of an information letter or leaflet (or in another format suitable for their client group). This can be provided in advance of therapy, and the therapist may then refer to the information given when they are negotiating the therapy contract. It has the advantage of allowing potential clients to consider the terms in advance, and also to have them in a permanent form for reference. The therapy contract might be shortened by referring to the information leaflet, and discussion of terms at the commencement of therapy can then be less intrusive.

A contract can be ended, or the terms of a contract can be varied by mutual agreement, and so a client could at any time during therapy verbally or in writing ask to alter the therapy agreement, for example, a client may wish to withdraw their consent to disclosure (so ending the existing therapeutic contract) and then the issue of disclosure and referral would have to be revisited, and a new therapeutic contract agreed.

3.8 Therapists acting from self-interest

Therapists are not permitted to use information provided in confidence by clients for their own gain, for example to use information about a potentially lucrative sale of a business or house. However, the law does recognise some legitimate self-interest as grounds for limited disclosure of information in order to protect therapists' rights. The information disclosed should be restricted to that which is necessary to achieve the permitted purpose and disclosed in confidence.

For example, therapists may disclose the information required to claim unpaid fees; defend themselves against defamatory statements; or prepare a defence in a disciplinary hearing. Some therapists have been stalked or harassed by a client. Legal advice to them has usually suggested that they send a letter through a solicitor saying that if the problematic behaviour persists they will regard themselves as freed from the obligation of confidentiality in order to take reasonable preventative action. The client may be warned that any repetition of the problematic behaviour will be taken to imply consent to disclosure. Any breach of confidence in such circumstances should be restricted to that which is required to protect the therapist's legitimate interests or rights. For example, in a professional conduct hearing, disclosing everything known to the therapist about a client is likely to be a breach of confidence in both ethics and law, whereas restricting disclosures to those that relate to the accusations under consideration would be legally defensible.

No advance warning to clients is required if the therapist is concerned that the client is about to commit a serious crime against the therapist. A breach of confidence that is restricted to the information required in order to obtain assistance is legally defensible, for example in cases of stalking, where the risk is protracted. Some therapists have suffered serious physical assault by clients and, exceptionally, some have been murdered. Concern about confidentiality ought not to delay the seeking of appropriate assistance where there is a real risk of serious harm or a serious crime being committed against the therapist.

3.9 Possible outcomes of litigation for breach of confidentiality

The courts do take violations of someone's confidences or privacy very seriously. A court may:

- impose a court order (e.g. an injunction or interdict) in order to prevent a breach of confidence, if the possibility of this occurring is known in advance;
- award damages to compensate someone for their losses and harm arising from the breach; or

- award aggravated or exemplary damages which go beyond that required for mere compensation, in order to show judicial disapproval of the behaviour of someone who has breached confidentiality (this does not apply in Scotland).

Imprisonment has been threatened as a possible consequence of a non-defensible breach of confidentiality (for example disclosure with malicious intent), if the disclosure is public and may cause damage to the person's reputation or work. This is very different from a disclosure justifiable in the public interest to protect a person from a real risk of serious harm.

   In some situations, clients may prefer to pursue action for breach of confidence under data protection legislation (see Chapter 5) or a complaint for breach of professional conduct with the applicable professional body. Both these courses of action will usually expose the client to a lower level of financial risk than a court case where they could be required to invest large sums of money and face the possibility of paying the other side's costs if the case is lost.

3.10 Significance of consent

The best solutions to issues concerning confidentiality will nearly always be disclosures made with the client's consent. Consent provides the best protection of everyone's interests and is worth the investment of time and effort. However, the law concerning consent is quite complex because of the different possible circumstances and mental capacity of the person giving consent. Under statutory law, there are distinctions between an adult who has mental capacity and one who does not, and mental capacity is vital for valid consent (see the Glossary and Chapter 11 for definitions and discussion). The law concerning mental capacity and consent also distinguishes between adults and children, see Chapter 12 for consent issues relating to children and young people.

Part II

Record Keeping and the Law

4 Record Keeping – Basic Responsibilities

Does the law say that I have to keep case records?

Is it considered good practice to keep case records, and what would happen if I did not want to comply?

What should I include in my notes? Is there anything that I should leave out?

I had a client who absolutely refused to allow me to keep notes. I refused to take her on as my agency requires note taking. I am still not sure that that this was fair to the client or what happened to her.

A client was in therapy for PTSD after an accident. The accident triggered other memories and she disclosed a history of severe child abuse which she worked through in the course of her therapy. This was recorded in her notes. When her personal injury case came up in court, the lawyers asked to see the therapy notes. She did not want her family or the other parties in the case to know about her past. I did not know what to do and I really wished that I had not kept such detailed notes.

I am quite puzzled about what to do about keeping notes. I usually keep brief factual notes with a few reminders of things that I might need for my session with the client. Is this good enough?

I don't keep notes of sessions as I work in shared premises and can't be sure of adequately protecting them when I am not there. I used to take my records to and from home where I could lock them away. Unfortunately, as I was returning home after seeing several clients, my car was stolen with all the notes locked in the boot. (I was just paying for the petrol.) It was an awful experience telling those clients. I decided that their distress was so much greater than any benefits of keeping records.

This chapter addresses the issues raised by therapists above, and explores the basic responsibilities of record keeping, including the rationale for keeping records, issues to consider if a client does not want notes kept, ownership of client notes, what client records might contain, and the perennial dilemma of what to do with process notes. Chapter 5 explains data protection, and Chapter 6 explores the legal issues relevant to deciding how long client records should be kept.

4.1 Current practice

Current practice by therapists over record keeping is very varied. Some therapists keep extensive notes that combine the information communicated by the client (i.e. client material) and the therapist's professional comments and interpretations of what has been communicated. Some practitioners include reflections on their own subjective responses to the client's communications in order to distinguish their client's material from their own and inform their interpretations. This element of therapists' records is sometimes referred to as 'process notes', which are an essential component of some approaches to therapy. Box 4.1 gives examples of various approaches to keeping records and process notes.

Box 4.1   Examples of therapists' different approaches to note keeping

- Full notes which combine process and content (e.g. similar to the full notes that a trainee might be expected to take as the basis for an in-depth case study, or for detailed discussion with a trainer or supervisor).
- Shorter notes that focus almost exclusively on the content of the client's communications, key events in the session and any therapeutic plans or strategies. These may also be combined with keeping a separate set of process or supervision notes (see 4.8).
- Separate notes may be kept relating to reflections on the therapist's subjective responses in the therapy (process notes).
- Separate supervision notes.
- Some practitioners may not make or keep any notes at all (see para. 4.2).

This diversity of record keeping practice is the inevitable outcome of different approaches to therapy and different ways in which therapists exercise their professional care for their clients. For some, note taking is an essential activity that provides time for reflection and a useful support to assist in accurately recalling earlier sessions. Others place more emphasis on what the client takes from sessions and brings back with them to the next, and therefore are less concerned with maintaining an independent record. Some are concerned that the details in any records held may have the potential to drag the client back to experiences that therapy has helped the client to leave behind, for example if the records were stolen or required in legal proceedings. Therapists walk a tightrope between providing effective care, with all the different interpretations of what this could be, and protecting a client's privacy.

The context also matters. Some settings, such as clinics, place greater emphasis on record keeping than other types of service which offer community support or personal development. Therapists who work across a range of practice contexts may have experienced a wide range of expectations and practice regarding record keeping and how these vary according to context, not least the availability of resources to make and store them securely. So it is not surprising that different therapists may reach different conclusions about how best to keep records to support their work or they may vary their practice for different aspects of their work. Such diversity in practice creates the potential for many different legal concerns about record keeping. Chapter 5 deals with data protection and freedom of information, Chapter 6 with how long to keep records, and Part III of the book looks at a variety of situations and dilemmas in relation to disclosure.

4.2 Are therapists obliged to keep notes?

4.2.1 Law

There is no specific overarching legal requirement at the moment that every therapist should keep records of all their work with clients. However, there is a growing expectation from the courts and other professionals that therapy records are kept. As we will see below, the legal and practice necessity of keeping accurate records is to some extent dependent on factors including professional expectations, the therapy work context, the therapist's modality and client needs, and certain specific legal and agency requirements relevant to the therapy work. There are also certain situations, for example in forensic work and in therapy with children and vulnerable adult witnesses, where there is a clear expectation that records of the therapy will be kept. This is discussed further below in 4.2.2, and Chapter 13 looks specifically at working with victims and pre-trial therapy with vulnerable adults and children.

4.2.2 Ethics

Since the circumstances of the provision of therapy are many and varied, some professional bodies are cautious about creating an ethical requirement to keep therapy records in all circumstances. The British Psychological Society, in 2006, required that psychologists 'should keep appropriate records' as an expression of the ethical principle of respect (BPS, 2006: s. 1.2). However, the Health & Care Professions Council now makes record keeping an absolute duty for practitioner psychologists and its other registrants: see *Standards of Conduct, Performance and Ethics*, 'You must keep accurate records' (HCPC, 2012: 10).

   Similarly, the British Association for Counselling and Psychotherapy encourages practitioners 'to keep appropriate records of their work with clients unless there are adequate reasons for not keeping records' (BACP, 2013: 6, paras 20–24). This ethical statement assumes that it is generally desirable to keep records in line with public expectations of professionals, but recognises that there may be some circumstances in which keeping no records may be justifiable. Such circumstances are likely to be very rare. Since the inception of voluntary registration and the BACP Register in 2013, therapists are likely to be expected to keep records as a matter of their general professional responsibilities, in line with the general expectation of other professionals in the health care system. The courts will generally expect that therapists will keep appropriate records, and in any court case, a therapist appearing as a witness in court is likely to be asked for justification of any failure to keep records, because accurate recording provides the evidential basis for professional accountability, and courts will look to therapy records for an accurate account of the events of therapy. The same rationale is likely to apply to a disciplinary or complaints procedure, in which a lack of accurate therapy records could constitute a disadvantage for the therapist concerned.

Keeping appropriate records enhances the quality of work undertaken by the therapist by providing an opportunity for reflection when compiling the notes and recording treatment plans and a point of reference to assist the therapist's recall of significant moments during therapy.

4.2.3 Legal requirements to keep records

See Chapter 3 for a discussion of the legal requirement for confidentiality generally in relation to client information. In relation specifically to therapy records, although there may be no general legal requirement that notes should be kept in all circumstances, a legal obligation to keep notes might arise in a number of ways, such as:

- a requirement of the therapist's contract of employment in an agency or organisation;
- a term of a contract agreed with a client who is contributing towards the cost of his or her own therapy;
- a term of a contract agreed with an organisation (e.g. an insurance company, which is paying for work with a client);
- a statutory duty imposed on public bodies or agencies within which the therapist is working; or
- an obligation to the courts when the therapist is working with witnesses; see the current guidance on working with victims and witnesses. For example, the Crown Prosecution Service (England and Wales) requires that 'Records of therapy (which includes videos and tapes as well as notes) and other contacts with the witness must be maintained so that they can be produced if required by the court' (CPS, 2001: s. 11.4). This requirement concerns the provision of therapy for vulnerable or intimidated adult witnesses. There are comparable stipulations for therapists working with child witnesses (CPS, 2001: ss 3.7–3.14). The Scottish Government has also issued guidance for therapists in Scotland, in the form of its publications *Interviewing Child Witnesses in Scotland* and *Code of Practice to Facilitate the Provision of Therapeutic Support to Child Witnesses in Court Proceedings* (Scottish Executive, 2008a, 2008b). Both of these publications are available on the Scottish Government's website at www.scotland.gov.uk.

Recording any breaches of confidentiality is a requirement in some agencies and a wise precaution when working in private practice or as a volunteer. Such a record should include:

- date of the disclosure;
- a note of the information that has been disclosed;

- person to whom disclosure made;
- method of disclosure (e.g. letter, phone call etc.);
- whether or not the client has consented;
- any evidence of consent; and
- the justification for the disclosure if it has not been authorised by the client affected.

4.3 Can a therapist refuse to work with a client who does not want notes kept?

A therapist who is either under a legal obligation to keep records or is ethically committed to doing so may decline to work with a client who refuses to permit the keeping of records.

Some therapists may decide to see clients without keeping any records, if they have the discretion to exercise this choice. The ethical reasons that they may have for doing so might include the deterrent effect of record keeping on some potential clients, for example those people who live at the margins of society and mistrust the authorities. In some circumstances, the therapist may have no secure way of protecting records from unauthorised access where they are known to be vulnerable to burglary. In some cases, this may be an exceptional arrangement for a particular client who will accept therapy only on the basis that records are not kept.

The presumption in favour of keeping records means that in any court context, therapists can expect to be asked by lawyers and courts why they have not kept records. The therapist should make their decision upon the basis of best practice in the prevailing situation, and formally record that decision and the reasons for it. It is wise to have written confirmation that a client has agreed to or required that no records are kept, especially where this is an exceptional arrangement in a service that normally keeps records. In agencies and organisations where not keeping records is routine practice, it is wise to ensure that this practice is included in any agency policy statements or service agreements, and communicated in information to clients and other interested parties in order to avoid misunderstandings. The absence of records will not prevent the therapist being required to give evidence in legal proceedings. On the contrary, anecdotal evidence from therapists indicates that the absence of notes makes it more likely that a therapist will be required to appear in person as a witness for cross-examination. The court has no other way of obtaining the evidence. Where notes exist, it is possible that the submission of those notes or the alternative provision of a comprehensive report based on those notes (which, if possible has been read and approved by the client as accurate) may obviate the need to attend court.

4.4 What are the basic legal obligations when records are kept?

Most countries in the European Economic Area (EEA) have already produced legislation or are in the process of producing legislation which regulates almost all aspects of storage, use and disclosure of clients' records by professionals. This creates a shared framework for the management of records across Europe and requires additional safeguards for communications beyond the EEA. This legislation serves two purposes:

- to protect the privacy of people; and
- to ensure that people about whom information has been collected can check the accuracy of that information.

The Data Protection Act 1998 (see www.ico.gov.uk) and the Freedom of Information Act 2000 are examples of legislation to protect sensitive personal data. For details of these statutory provisions, see Chapter 5. Briefly, most of the information held by therapists will be regarded as 'sensitive personal data'. Sensitive personal data contains information about:

- racial or ethnic origin;
- political opinions;
- religious beliefs or beliefs of a similar nature;
- trade union membership;
- physical or mental health condition;
- sex life;
- criminality, alleged or proven; and
- criminal proceedings, their disposal and sentencing.

The legal right to process sensitive personal information requires greater attention to the data subject's rights. The most significant of these rights is that the recording and use of sensitive personal data require the client's explicit consent. The client has to actively state that they are agreeing to a record being kept and used in the knowledge of the purpose(s) for which the record is being made, how it will be used and any limitations on confidentiality. This should be the routine practice of therapists who hold computerised records or who hold manual records in any form of organised filing system.

The Data Protection Act includes eight principles that guide the legal use of all records of personal data.

Personal data shall be:

1. Processed fairly and lawfully.

2. Obtained only for one or more specified and lawful purposes, and shall not be processed in any manner incompatible with that purpose or those purposes.

3. Adequate, relevant and not excessive.

4. Accurate and, where necessary, kept up to date.

5. Not be kept longer than necessary.

6. The clients' rights must be respected.

7. Take appropriate security measures.

8. Personal data shall not be transferred outside the European Economic Area (All EU Member States plus Iceland, Liechtenstein and Norway).

This may be an issue for clients who move outside the EEA and desire a referral or for therapists whose work requires them to move between the EEA and other countries. A client's consent permits the transfer of personal data.

When working internationally outside the EEA, there are considerable variations in how each country approaches data protection. As the legal penalties and costs for breach can be considerable, this is an important issue for consideration in how you establish any services outside the EEA. For the latest guidance, search for reputable recent guidance under <data protection international> or <data protection + country>. A useful starting point is DLA Piper (2014) *Data Protection Laws of the World*.

4.5 Clients' right of access to their own notes

The sixth principle of data protection requirement gives the subject of personal data a right to access to the information which is being held about them. This right is referred to as a 'subject access right' to all computerised records and data held in structured manual files. The aim is to enable any citizens to know what information is being processed about them. A written request, proof of identity (if required) and payment of the prescribed fee entitles the data subject to be informed about what data are being processed, for what purpose, to whom it has been or may be disclosed, and to be provided with a copy of those data. This information should be provided within forty days.

Any therapist who is concerned about the client's response to seeing the records may offer to be present and explain the records or to arrange for another suitably qualified person to be present, but cannot insist on this. Nor can the release of records be made conditional on the client paying any outstanding fees. The client is entitled to unconditional access.

A client who considers that there is an inaccuracy in the record may ask for it to be corrected with the agreement of the therapist. If there is disagreement about what would be a correct record, it is good practice to include a record of the client's objections in the notes.

If the therapist is concerned that access to the notes would cause serious harm to the physical or mental health of the data subject and that the notes constitute a health record, it may be possible to refuse or defer access with the authorisation of the health professional who is currently or was most recently responsible for the clinical care of the person concerned (Data Protection (Subjects Access Modification) (Health) Order 2000: s. 7). The legal presumption in favour of access to personal data makes this an exceptional provision that ought not to be sought or granted lightly.

A client may have a contractual right to see her notes even when there is no statutory right of access to the therapeutic notes (for example because they are 'unstructured' and thus fall outside the requirements of the Data Protection Act). The therapist and client may have agreed access to the notes as part of the therapeutic contract between them. The client may insist on their production as part of the disclosure of documents for a court case, possibly by the use of a court order. In the last resort, it may simply be unconscionable in the eyes of equity, a long-standing set of legal principles, to withhold access.

4.6 Access to notes by others

4.6.1 By other members of the client's family

Adults can insist that a professional protects the confidences contained in records from other members of the family unless the professional is legally required to disclose them, for example as part of the disclosed documents required by the court in family proceedings. Where children or young persons are considered to be sufficiently 'competent' to give their consent to receiving therapy on a confidential basis *and* both the young person concerned and the therapist agree that it is best that the parents are not informed, then the information may be lawfully withheld from someone with parental responsibility (*Gillick v West Norfolk and West Wisbech Area Health Authority* [1985]). Similarly, information may be withheld from other family members. Possible exceptions to this general principle arise where the disclosure would protect others from serious harm or where a young person's life or safety is at serious risk.

A young person who is not competent to give consent to therapy cannot be assured of total confidentiality with regard to those with parental responsibility. The therapist ought to take into account the best interests of the young person and also be aware of the generally positive view that courts take of involving parents unless there are good reasons for not doing so, for example increasing the risk of further abuse. If the therapist is concerned that the child may be subject to abuse, then refer to the government guidance issued under the Children Act 1989 and the Children Act 2004 listed at the end of this book, including *What to Do if You are Worried a Child is Being Abused* (DfES, 2006a); *Information Sharing: Practitioner's Guide* (DfES, 2006b); *Working Together to Safeguard Children: A guide to Inter-Agency Working to Safeguard and Promote the Welfare of Children* (DfES, 2013); and *Confidentiality: NHS Code of Practice* (DH, 2003a) and its accompanying Guidance (DH, 2010b); see also Chapter 12.

4.6.2 After a client's death

In England there is no statutory protection of confidences about someone following their death, nor may a breach of confidence following the death of the confider be actionable (Pattenden, 2003: 639). Despite this lack of legal protection, the normal ethical requirement for health workers and psychological therapists is that respect for confidentiality continues after the death of the person concerned. This is an example where professional ethics aim at a higher standard than strictly required by law. For the powers of the Coroner to order disclosure of notes in proceedings before the Coroner's Court, see Chapter 7 at 7.2.1.

4.6.3 Other clients, when several clients are being seen at the same time

Information can be disclosed to more than one person at the same time on the basis that it will be treated as confidential by all the recipients. The laws concerning confidentiality would apply. Therapists should have a clear confidentiality sharing agreement in place when working with teams, groups, families and couples and so on.

4.6.4 By journalists and members of the public

The Freedom of Information Act 2000 is a major piece of legislation that requires public bodies and companies functioning as public bodies to respond to requests for information. This legislation has proved invaluable to journalists wanting to discover information held by public bodies, particularly non-personal information such as public policy decisions. Individual citizens can also request information of this type. However, personal information is exempt from this legislation and should be sought under the data protection procedures through the data subject.

4.6.5 By police

The police are not normally permitted access to counselling records (unless the client explicitly consents, or they are acting under a court order). Section 11 of the Police and Criminal Evidence Act (PACE) 1984, as amended, excludes material from a search, stating that:

(1) Subject to the following provisions of this section, in this Act "excluded material" means—

personal records which a person has acquired or created in the course of any trade, business, profession or other occupation or for the purposes of any paid or unpaid office and which he holds in confidence.

Section 12 of PACE gives further detail of the definition of personal records:

In this part of this Act "personal records" means documentary and other records concerning an individual (whether living or dead) who can be identified from them and relating—

(a) to his physical or mental health;

(b) to spiritual counselling or assistance given or to be given to him; or

(c) to counselling or assistance given or to be given to him, for the purposes of his personal welfare, by any voluntary organisation or by any individual who—

   (i) by reason of his office or occupation has responsibilities for his personal welfare; or

   (ii) by reason of an order of a court has responsibilities for his supervision.

This definition specifically includes counselling records, giving them additional protection. This protection is not absolute. Police may obtain a court order which, when granted, will entitle them to access to the client's records. If the police are investigating a 'serious arrestable offence' they may obtain a warrant from a circuit judge, a more demanding process than the usual search warrants issued by magistrates.

In addition, under the Serious Crime Act 2007, police or other law enforcement officers can apply for a Serious Crime Prevention Order requiring a person, including a therapist, to disclose information or records (see Chapter 3 at pages 30–31 at 3.3).

4.6.6 By lawyers

Lawyers have no greater rights of access to therapists' notes than any other citizen. Typically, they ask for access to their client's notes on the basis of their client's consent, but they may seek a court order that entitles them to access to the notes of their client or possibly to the client notes of another person. Full details about how to respond to a lawyer's request for therapeutic notes can be found in an earlier volume in this series, *Therapists in Court* (Bond and Sandhu, 2005).

4.6.7 By courts

The courts, at all levels, carry the power to order the disclosure of therapists' records and may order the therapist to appear as a witness. Child protection and road traffic legislation give courts additional powers of ordering disclosure, and the Serious Crime Act 2007 created additional powers for courts, for example to make a Serious Crime Prevention Order which may require disclosure of information or records (see Chapter 3 at pages 30–31 at 3.3). For discussion of working with children and vulnerable witnesses in court, see Chapter 13, and for details about working in the context of judicial process alongside lawyers and the courts see *Therapists in Court* (Bond and Sandhu, 2005).

4.7 Who owns therapy notes?

The question 'Who owns the notes?' is usually asked in therapeutic contexts because there is concern over the control of the contents of the notes. The question may arise in organisational contexts because someone more senior in an organisation is seeking access to the contents of the client notes. We are aware of this question being asked in health care, education and employee assistance schemes. Behind the question lies an assumption that ownership determines who has control of access to the contents of the notes. This is a mistaken assumption because the law distinguishes between ownership and authorised use of those notes. Ownership of records is usually governed by ownership of the material they are recorded on. Use of records (including confidentiality) is usually governed by the therapeutic contract. It is therefore possible to physically own the notes but to be constrained from having access to them or being able to use them because they are held on the trust that they are confidential. For example, a company may employ a therapist, pay the therapist's salary and provide the stationery or computing facilities to compile the client records. It therefore owns the records in law. However, the company may have required that (and typically will have required that) those records are treated as confidential to the therapist or to the staff who work in that section of the company and the therapist will have worked with clients on this basis. No matter how senior the member of staff, it would usually be a breach of confidentiality for someone outside the 'circle of confidentiality' agreed between the client and therapist to seek access to those notes. Conversely, where there is an agreement that the contents of sessions are made known to or are accessible by other members of an organisation, then the therapist may be required to establish a client's consent to this prior to offering therapy. Both the therapist and agency have a vested interest in striking a balance between deterring clients from accepting a service because client information will be made too freely available and being too restrictive when communicating information. Any changes in practice should be prospective rather than retrospective and will require client consent. Therapists need to ensure consistency between what is agreed with clients and their employer if they are to avoid potential liabilities for either breach of confidentiality or breach of their terms of employment.

In private practice, the notes will usually belong to the therapist unless there is a contractual agreement to the contrary. If the therapist gives the notes to the client as a client-held record, it is wise to clarify whether the therapist retains ownership or is content for the client to hold both ownership and possession. Ownership of patient-held records in the health service is typically retained by the NHS.

When clients ask about the ownership of notes, they are typically concerned about control over the personal information they contain. In English law, there is no ownership of information, because once it is imparted by one person to another it belongs equally to them both. The clients' best protection lies in their legal right to privacy and confidentiality, which is governed by the common law, contract law, and the law of tort (see Chapters 2 and 3). Clients can create additional protection for themselves by reaching agreement with the therapist on issues about confidentiality and privacy which can be clarified and preferably recorded in the therapeutic contract.

4.8 Process notes

Process notes (by which we mean a therapist's reflections on their own process and that of the client relevant to the therapy) are a feature of some areas of professional practice and integral to some approaches to therapy. We make a distinction here between process notes made for the purposes of the therapy (and from which the client may be identifiable); and those purely personal reflections which, for example, a trainee therapist might keep in their personal journal, and from which the client cannot be identified.

Process notes have raised some interesting legal questions over the years but there is no case law from which to give authoritative answers. The perennial questions from therapists are:

- Do I have to give my clients access to my process notes?

and

- Am I required to include my process notes if a court requires that I submit all my counselling records concerning a named client?

There is sufficient uncertainty over the answers to each of these questions for a variety of opinions to exist. We will add our opinion by answering each question in turn. In practice, what happens will depend on the circumstances of a specific case. Nonetheless, it is helpful to consider the general legal principles that are likely to be applied.

The distinctive feature about process notes is that they contain information about the subjective processes of the therapist. Some therapists appear to be wary about releasing these notes to legal scrutiny on two accounts. First, these are subjective notes that are being used in a legal culture where objectivity rules, and therefore, are potentially likely to be misunderstood and sometimes even ridiculed. Sometimes they are merely tolerated. But this tolerance is often in short supply in an adversarial system with rigorous testing of the evidence by both sides. The therapist may be making reference to her own life story or subjective processes as a basis for understanding her client better. Sometimes this personal reflection strengthens the empathy for another person's experience. On other occasions it is used as a way of separating out the therapist's sense of herself from her client's experience so that she can hear another person's experience more clearly. The therapist's sense of herself is a key point of reference in understanding many aspects of the client in most of the psychoanalytic and humanistic approaches to therapy. As a consequence, the process notes are an essential component of some therapeutic approaches but are often more revealing of the therapist than the client. This has led some therapists to ask whether they can withhold them from scrutiny by their client and courts.

When pressed hard, some therapists will argue that they are very uneasy about releasing information gained in the privacy of therapy into a potentially public contest between opposing parties in the courtroom. This unease exists even when the case involves a client and events concerning a third party in which the therapist has no direct involvement other than being a witness to the psychological consequences of the event for the client. In such circumstances, it is argued that it is unfair to the therapist and a violation of her privacy to include those parts of records that are primarily about herself.

Similarly, therapists are reluctant to give clients access to private personal material that they may have included in their notes but used only indirectly in communications with their client to inform their interventions. Again some therapists argue that this is an invasion of their own privacy and makes them vulnerable to those clients who may be persistently intrusive or predatory.

Our sense from being involved in workshops throughout the UK is that there is a widespread and considerable sense of unease amongst therapists about the disclosure of process notes. It is one of the most contentious issues for therapists about their involvement in any legal processes. What we are about to say is unlikely to ease these concerns.

Under data protection legislation (see Chapter 5), in specified circumstances, a person is entitled to have access to personal information held about them. In our view, if the process notes identify the client, or contain information from which the client may be identifiable from their circumstances etc., or if they are contained in the named client's file, or contain named references to a client in another file (such as a supervision file), we consider that when data protection legislation applies, the client is entitled access to these process notes in response to a data subject's access request. A client may also be entitled to records where their identity is not explicitly named but which can be inferred. A brief passage from a most thorough study of confidentiality indicates the strength of the duty to disclose:

> Maintaining dual records – one version for the client and another for the use of the professional – is illegal. Files have to be disclosed no matter how damaging to the professional. Thus the Department of Trade had to disclose records that described the applicant as a 'prat' and an 'out-and-out nutter'. (Pattenden, 2003: 650)

Current trends in the discovery of documents as part of the process of litigation are against the protection of process notes in order to protect the privacy of the therapist, or the client. The law has progressively moved over the last few decades towards a requirement that everything that is discoverable ought to be made available to all the parties in a court case unless the court directs otherwise. This openness of evidence is believed to comply with the right to a fair trial under Article 6 of the European Convention on Human Rights, also providing the best chance of an out of court settlement in civil cases and increasing the likelihood of a fair and decisive hearing should the case be heard in court. It lowers the risk of new evidence being found after the case has been decided. From this perspective, the balance of public interest in ensuring justice outweighs the privacy of both client and therapist. These developments reduce the opportunities for withholding therapeutic documents from court proceedings. However, many documents or parts of documents will not be used if they are not considered relevant to the issues that the court has to address in a particular case. Article 8 of the European

Convention on Human Rights establishes the right to respect for private and family life. Where there are significant issues of privacy involved for either the client or the therapist, the therapist could request leave to attend a Directions Hearing, in which a judge can be asked to review the evidence and decide what is relevant and therefore should be made available for use in the case, making appropriate directions regarding the evidence. A more complete account of the legal issues and process can be found in *Therapists in Court* (Bond and Sandhu, 2005: 19). The therapist may incur legal costs in asking a judge to review documents.

Probably the best way of avoiding or minimising the difficulties posed by process notes is to review one's record keeping practices. Active weeding out of process notes that are not an essential part of the client record and are no longer relevant to the therapeutic process and securely destroying these is a viable option. This destruction must take place *before* a legal request for disclosure is received. Ideally, it should be a routine practice as part of a record keeping policy. Destroying evidence after receipt of a legal request or court order to disclose it is a serious offence.

It may also be worth considering whether any of the material included in the process notes goes beyond what is directly relevant to the work with the client and might be better written in a personal journal with no reference to a particular client. Provided that the client is not identifiable from the process notes, it is highly probable that this material would not need to be disclosed to either the client or the courts. The usual test for whether something must be disclosed is based on whether the material is linked to a named client or whether the identity of the client can be inferred from information in the notes. The adoption of these practices reduces the possibility of process notes being problematic but does not totally eliminate the risk for process notes that remain in existence because they continue to serve a therapeutic purpose. The personal journal is not totally immune to discovery. It could be required in cases that directly involve the therapist, such as criminal or civil offences committed against clients, because of the insights such a journal might offer into the therapist's motives and psychology. However, for ethically conscientious therapists, rethinking the management of process notes is probably the best way to strike a balance between the professional benefits of keeping a record of the subjective therapist's processes while minimising unwanted or damaging disclosures. It is salutary to realise that if a document exists, it is vulnerable to disclosure. There are probably no documents in existence that have total immunity to disclosure in current law.

There is an alternative line of argument in favour of keeping process notes on the same basis as any other notes about a client because they form part of the therapeutic process. If therapists could be confident that these notes would be treated respectfully within the legal process, then this would cause less concern. During the preparation of this book we have met a small number of therapists who have either chosen not to weed out this aspect of their records or have been required to disclose records including their process notes, and that these records have been treated respectfully in court. Being able to explain the purpose of the process notes in clear and non-technical language greatly helps in earning the respect of the court. When writing their records, therapists should constantly ask themselves:

- Can I explain clearly and stand by all that I have written down in my client records and process notes?
- If I should be asked to explain them in court, could I do so with confidence that they accurately reflect my work with the client and also convey a reasonable standard of therapeutic practice?

If the answer is negative to either of the questions above, it is the therapist's practice that needs to be changed, not the record.

5   Data Protection, Freedom of Information and Technology

Personal information (data) should be protected, that is, treated with respect and confidentially, and the legal issues applicable to the holding of personal data is governed by the Data Protection Act 1998, the Freedom of Information Act 2000, and other relevant subsidiary legislation. The law relating to data protection is administered by the Information Commissioner, and the Information Commissioner's office (ICO) provides information, advice and support through telephone, email and postal contact with the office, publications and its website at www.ico.gov.uk. The postal address and contact details for the ICO are at the end of this book.

Useful ICO publications include:

How do I Handle Subject Access Requests? (2013)

A Practical Guide to IT Security (2012b)

Anonymisation: Managing Data Protection Risk – Code of Practice (2012a)

Advice on How to Safeguard Your Personal Information (2011c)

Data Sharing Code of Practice (2011b)

The Employment Practices Code (2011)

Privacy Notices Code of Practice (2010a)

A Complete Guide to Notification (2010b)

5.1 Notification

This is the formal, legal requirement under the Data Protection Act 1998 to notify the Information Commissioner's Office (ICO) that personal data are being held on computers, laptops and other electronic forms of data processing and recording. The requirement to notify applies to all personal data records held on automated electronic forms of equipment used for data processing and recording. Notification leads to *registration* of the data holder under the Data Protection Act for the payment of an annual fee. See *A Complete Guide to Notification* published by the ICO in 2010. This booklet provides clarification of the law and practical suggestions for how when and how a data controller should notify the ICO office, and it is available in printed copy or online at www.ico.gov.uk.

Notification is required when sensitive personal data is processed by means of any automated form. There are some exceptions, listed in *A Complete Guide to Notification* (2010b: s. 6), which also has a questionnaire to help data controllers decide whether they might be exempt from notification or not.

Failure to notify when required to do so by data protection law is an offence punishable by a fine. Notification carries with it an obligation to observe all other requirements concerning data protection.

5.2 Registration

Registration of the data holder under the Data Protection Act 1998 is the entry of the data holder's name and details on the *Data Protection Register* for the payment of an annual fee. The Register is accessible and searchable online at www.ico.gov.uk. The *Data Protection Act 1998 Legal Guidance* (ICO, 2001) provides clarification of how the Register operates and the duties and responsibilities of those who are registered, and is available at www.ico.gov.uk.

5.3 Data

The legislation is particularly concerned with the regulation of personal data: that is, data which relate to a living individual who can be identified from the data on their own or when combined with other data held by the data controller. It will be seen that the identifiability of the person to whom the data refers is key to the definition. The Commissioner recognises that an individual may be 'identified' without necessarily knowing the name and address of that particular individual.

'Data' as defined in the legislation also includes 'an expression of opinion about the individual and any indication of the intentions of the data controller or any other person in respect of the individual.' Therapy notes and the comments and thoughts of a therapist about the client or their therapy are therefore likely to fall within this definition of data.

In the context of the Internet, many email addresses are personal data where the email address clearly identifies a particular individual: the ICO gave an example that the email address (elizabethfrance@dataprotection.gov.uk) could constitute personal data about the (former) Information Commissioner, Elizabeth France.

If personal information is held on automated electronic equipment (widely defined to include everything from mainframe computers, home PCs, laptops, pads and tablets linking to cloud storage, mobile phones etc.), then, unless there is an exemption, the data controller has a duty to notify the ICO in order to be included in the online register for an annual fee (see paras 5.1 and 5.2). Further details may be obtained from *A Complete Guide to Notification* (ICO, 2010b) or from the website www.ico.gov.uk.

Some holders of personal data are exempt, but therapists and providers of pastoral care who hold their records on computers are not usually excluded. A reasonably user friendly nine-step check on whether or not there is a duty to notify can be found in *A Complete Guide to Notification* (ICO, 2010b) or on the ICO website (see www.ico.gov.uk).

5.4 Access

Access to personal data held in records (by the person about whom they are held) is governed by the Data Protection Act 1998 and the Freedom of Information Act 2000, together with relevant subsidiary legislation.

All personal data held by public bodies, whether computerised or manual, structured or unstructured, are accessible, subject to certain statutory safeguards, to the person about whom the records are held (the data subject). This includes health, education and social services records, irrespective of how and when they were made.

Privately held personal records are not subject to the Freedom of Information Act 2000, but they are subject to the data protection legislation (and therefore accessible) if they fall into the category of 'a relevant filing system'. There may also be contractual or equitable rights of access in situations where a statute does not apply. For a discussion of access and its legal implications, see the *Data Sharing Code of Practice* (2011b) available from www.ico.org.uk, and also see section 5.8 below.

5.5 Disclosure

By 'disclosure' we mean in this book the sharing of information with another party or organisation: for example, the disclosure of client records to a court, a public authority, or to a relative. The Freedom of Information Act 2000 brings personal data which are held by public authorities within the Data Protection Act 1998. Personal data held by all registered data controllers under the Data Protection Act are protected by the legislation from unauthorised disclosure; please refer to the *Privacy Notices Code of Practice* (ICO, 2010a) and the *Data Sharing Code of Practice* (2011b) available from www.ico.org.uk.

Personal data held by therapists outside the Data Protection Act are subject to the therapist/client contract, possibly also to agency practice, and always to professional guidance on best practice within the law relating to confidentiality.

5.6 What are the basic legal obligations when records are kept?

Most countries in the European Economic Area (EEA) have already produced legislation or are in the process of producing legislation which regulates almost all aspects of storage, use and disclosure of clients' records by professionals. This creates a shared framework for the management of records across Europe and requires additional safeguards for communications beyond the EEA. This legislation serves two purposes:

- to protect the privacy of people; and
- to ensure that people about whom information has been collected can check the accuracy of that information.

In this section we will restrict our attention to legal requirements in Europe and in particular to the implications of the Data Protection Act 1998 and Freedom of Information Act 2000. The law is complicated because it is drafted to cover all types of data, but we have tried to concentrate on those aspects that are particularly relevant to therapists. Where there are no statutory requirements, legal obligations may arise from common law, a contract of employment and any other legally enforceable contracts.

One of the reasons for developing this legislative framework was the recognition of the potential power for good and harm posed by computerisation and the ways that this increases the availability of information about people. The legislation is particularly concerned with the regulation of personal data: that is, data which relate to a living individual who can be identified from the data on their own or when combined with other data held by the data controller. If the personal information is held on automated electronic systems, widely defined to include everything from mainframe computers, laptops, pads and tablets, mobile phones and so on, there is a duty to notify the ICO in order to be included in the online Register for an annual fee (further details may be obtained from the ICO or from the website www.ico.gov.uk). Some holders of personal data are exempt but therapists and providers of pastoral care who hold their records on computers are not usually excluded: see *A Complete Guide to Notification* (ICO, 2010b) which contains a reasonably user friendly nine-step check on whether or not there is a duty to notify. This can be found on the ICO website www.ico.gov.uk. Failure to notify when required to do so is an offence punishable by a fine. Notification carries with it an obligation to observe all other requirements concerning data protection.

5.6.1 Does the data protection legislation apply to me if I keep only paper records?

Personal records that are only held on paper do not require notification, *but* note that other aspects of the data protection legislation may in some situations apply equally to computerised and paper-based records. The situation with regard to paper-based records is complex, as data protection requirements only apply to manual records that are organised and accessed manually in a 'relevant filing system'. The current diversity of practice in record keeping by therapists means that some are covered by the legislation but others are not. A 'relevant filing system' is defined as 'any set of information' that is structured, either by reference to individuals or by reference to criteria relating to individuals in such a way that specific information relating to a particular individual is readily accessible (see Box 5.1). In other words, can data about specific individuals be located by a straightforward search? A card index of clients' names organised alphabetically containing their contact details would be a relevant filing system. A client's file that is divided into sections such as name and contact details; reasons for seeking therapy/original referral; information given to client about the therapy and contractual agreements; summary appointments made and sessions attended; correspondence sorted by source; notes of sessions and so on would constitute a relevant filing system. If the sections are easily identifiable and separated by dividers, someone who is unfamiliar with the contents of the file would have little difficulty in finding, upon request, correspondence from the client's employer, the reason for the referral, or how regularly the client attends sessions. However, many therapeutic records are not so well organised because information is simply added to the file as it comes to hand, and the file therefore contains a mixture of data stored in chronological order.

Box 5.1 How can I distinguish between 'relevant filing systems' and other types of manual records?

The Data Commissioner recommends applying the 'temp test'. This involves considering whether a temporary administrative assistant (a 'temp') would be able to extract information about an individual without any particular information on the type of work involved or the documents within the files. This test assumes that the temp is reasonably competent and requires only a short induction, explanation and/or operating manually in order for them to access the information. It is not a relevant filing system if the temp requires detailed knowledge of the type of work, the types of records held, or unusual features of records in order to operate it.

The Commissioner offers the following example:

John Smith is your employee. He requests details of the leave he has taken in the last six months. You have a collection of personnel files.

(a) If there is a file entitled 'leave' containing alphabetical dividers the temp would have no difficulty in finding the leave record of John Smith behind the 'S' divider. This is a relevant filing system.
(b) If there is a file entitled 'John Smith' which is subdivided into categories such as 'contact details', 'sickness', 'pension' and 'leave' the temp would have no difficulty in finding the leave record of John Smith. This is a relevant filing system.
(c) If there is a file entitled 'John Smith' in a system that only contains the leave record of employees, with leave recorded on standard forms filed in date order within the respective files for each employee, the temp would have no difficulty in finding the record of John Smith's leave taken. This is a relevant filing system.
(d) If there is a file entitled 'John Smith' but there is no subdivision of its contents, documents are randomly dropped into the file or are filed in chronological order regardless of the subject matter, the temp would have to leaf through the file contents to obtain the information required. This is not a relevant filing system.
(e) If there is a file entitled 'John Smith' with subdividers that classify the contents of the file in a vague or ambiguous way (such as 'correspondence', 'comments' and

'miscellaneous'), established members of staff only know through experience and knowledge of the particular practice and custom of filing in that system that, for example, leave details are recorded on the back page of a report that is filed in the 'miscellaneous' section. However, the temp would have to leaf through the file contents to obtain the information required because it is not clear from the structure of the file, or from any operating manual, where the relevant information will be held. That would only become clear were the temp provided with additional information specific to that particular workplace and system. This is not a relevant filing system.

For further guidance, see the 'Durant' case and its impact on the interpretation of the Data Protection Act 1998.

Current guidance about what constitutes a 'relevant filing system' specifically excludes records that are simply a chronological record compiled of documents and notes as they come to hand or any other form of haphazard filing. One of the consequences of this is that a client's rights over data held about him or her are better protected by seeing a therapist who keeps electronically stored records or maintains a well-ordered filing system rather than someone who does not keep organised records. Note that records which are created on a PC or laptop and then stored in cloud storage by the author or by another organisation operating a system 'in the cloud' will be covered by the Data Protection Act, as the data are being 'processed' in the meaning of the Act.

A client who works with a therapist who keeps records that fall short of a 'relevant filing system' means that the client *cannot*:

- require information about the type of data held;
- ensure that personally sensitive information is held on the basis of explicit consent;
- be confident of the legal right to obtain a copy of his or her own records;
- use readily available rights under this legislation as a way of protecting privacy and confidentiality of records; or
- enlist the support of the ICO to investigate a potential suspected abuse of the records.

But remember that such therapists are increasingly rare and most therapists will keep a relevant filing system.

Clients are legally best protected against the abuse of their records if they fall under the terms of the data protection legislation. In many ways the burden on the therapist is no greater than that already imposed by their professional bodies. The duties imposed by the Data Protection Act are no more onerous than the duties of good record keeping, with which most of us already comply (see the eight principles of Data Protection in section 5.7).

If a therapist is inadequately resourced by their employer or agency, or legally challenged about their records, there may be some benefits in strengthening the legal basis for preventing unauthorised intrusion and the data protection legislation may help by providing a legal justification for data protection legislation compliant record keeping policies and practice.

The value to service users in having access to their own notes, particularly in order to correct inaccuracies, was recognised by Parliament when it amended the Freedom of Information Act 2000 to bring all unstructured personal data held by public authorities, particularly health, education and social services, within the scope of the Data Protection Act. This has the effect of requiring that *all* written records, including therapists' records made in these settings, should conform to data protection requirements including the data subjects' right to see a copy of their own records where these have been retained, even if they were compiled many years or decades before the request. Detailed guidance on the specific requirements and exemptions for these agencies can usually be obtained from a specialist within the organisation.

Data protection legislation distinguishes between 'personal data' and 'sensitive personal data' which require higher standards. Most therapists will hold both types of information. Personal data do not have to be about someone's private life, but may be information about someone whose identity can be inferred even if the person is not named. It includes any expression of opinion about the individual and any intentions by the record keeper or others towards that person. Personal data might include someone's name, home or work address, income, educational or employment history, provided this information does not imply sensitive personal information, for example that they receive residential psychiatric care, or a religious belief or political affiliation. (See below for what is classified as sensitive personal information.) The legal basis for holding personal data requires that, before collecting the data, the client should be informed of the identity of the 'data controller'; the purpose for which the data are being collected; and how the data will be used or processed; the client also ought to be informed if the purpose changes after it has been collected (unless this is for the prevention or detection of crime).

The communication of personal data is permitted to protect the vital interests of the data subject. 'Vital interests' do not appear to have been legally defined but the language implies something of substantial interest to the person concerned and therefore excludes trivial matters. A client's consent permits the processing of data that would otherwise be in breach of data protection.

Most of the information held by therapists will be regarded as 'sensitive personal data', which includes information about:

- racial or ethnic origin;
- political opinions;
- religious beliefs or beliefs of a similar nature;
- trade union membership;
- physical or mental health condition;
- sex life;
- criminality, alleged or proven; and
- criminal proceedings, their disposal and sentencing.

The legal right to process sensitive personal information requires greater attention to the data subject's rights. The most significant of these rights is that the recording and use of sensitive personal data require the client's explicit consent. The client has to actively state that they are agreeing to a record being kept and used in the knowledge of the purpose(s) for which the record is being made, how it will be used and any limitations on confidentiality. This should be the routine practice of therapists who hold computerised records or manual records in an organised filing system (see *Privacy Notices Code of Practice*, ICO, 2010a).

The Data Protection (Processing of Sensitive Personal Data) Order 2000 does permit the keeping of records and their use without explicit consent if it is both in the 'substantial public interest' and for the purpose of discharging 'any function which is designed for the provision of confidential counselling, advice, support or any other services'. We know of no reported cases to guide the interpretation of these requirements. In our view a therapist who relied on these requirements would be required to show that: (1) the circumstances prevented obtaining explicit consent or made it inadvisable to do so; (2) a substantial public good was being served; and (3) the sensitive personal data were adequately protected by confidentiality. In such circumstances, it might be reasonable to rely on implied consent or to defer seeking explicit consent until the circumstances permit this. It would not permit recording sensitive personal data against the client's explicit wishes. Communicating sensitive personal data, whether or not they are part of any records, without a client's consent or other legal justification would usually be a breach of the right to privacy under the Human Rights Act 1998 and a common law breach of the client's entitlement to confidentiality. Depending on the circumstances, making an unauthorised disclosure may also create a liability for breach of contract or professional negligence.

5.7 The eight principles of data processing in the Data Protection Act

The Data Protection Act 1998 includes eight principles that guide the legal use of all records of personal data. These require that personal data shall be:

1. Processed fairly and lawfully.

Therapists must give clients information as to how they will use information about them. Information should not be obtained by deception and it should be used in accordance with any duties of confidentiality.

2. Obtained only for one or more specified and lawful purposes, and shall not be processed in any manner incompatible with that purpose or those purposes.

There is an obligation to inform the client about the purpose for which the data are being recorded. Where a therapist is considering disclosing information to a third party, she must consider how the recipient intends to use the data. If the therapist is aware that the information will be used in any way that is inconsistent with the original purpose, then the disclosure should not take place without the prior informed consent of the client.

3. Adequate, relevant and not excessive.
4. Accurate and, where necessary, kept up to date.
5. Not be kept longer than necessary.

The test for these three principles is what is required in order to achieve a therapeutic purpose? When parts of the notes become irrelevant, are found to be inaccurate, or are no longer required to provide therapy, they should be securely destroyed. Where contact with the client continues over a substantial period of time, these principles encourage a periodical review of the records and 'weeding out' what is no longer required. Chapter 8 provides a case study of how an agency developed its policy to satisfy these principles. Extending the retention of data beyond what is reasonable to provide therapy requires additional explicit consent if sensitive personal data are to be held for those purposes. We return to this issue in Chapter 6.

The next three principles introduced new rights for the client.

6. The clients' rights must be respected.

The primary function of this principle is to give the clients the right to information about personal data held that relate to them and to a copy of those records. The next section in this chapter provides more detail about these rights.

7. Take appropriate security measures.

This creates a requirement to take appropriate technical and organisational measures against unauthorised or unlawful processing of personal information and against accidental loss or destruction of or damage to notes and records prepared by therapists and other staff. Appropriate safeguards may require:

- Technical security (IT systems).
- Physical security of premises, for instance sensitive information kept in secure locked storage. This includes protecting records from accidental discovery or deliberate interference by others with legitimate access to the premises, such as cleaning or maintenance staff.
- Reasonable precautions against unauthorised access by trespassers and burglars.
- Staff selection and training, for example the training of any secretarial or reception staff in confidentiality. Making confidentiality concerning clients a condition of employment is increasingly common practice in this sector and is consistent with this requirement.

8. Personal data shall not be transferred outside the European Economic Area (All EU Member States plus Iceland, Liechtenstein and Norway).

This may be an issue for clients who move outside the EEA and desire a referral or for therapists whose work requires them to move between the EEA and other countries. A client's consent permits the transfer of personal data.

Other countries outside the European data protection requirements will frequently have their own legally enforceable obligations.

5.8 Clients' right of access to their own notes

The sixth principle of data protection requirement gives the subject of personal data a right to access to the information which is being held about them. This right is referred to as a 'subject access right' to all computerised records and data held in structured manual files. The aim is to enable any citizens to know what information is being processed about them. A written request, proof of identity (if required) and payment of the prescribed fee entitles the data subject to be informed about what data are being processed, for what purpose, to whom it has been or may be disclosed, and to be provided with a copy of those data. This information should be provided within forty days: see *Data Sharing Code of Practice* (ICO, 2011b) and *How do I Handle Subject Access Requests?* (ICO, 2013).

Any therapist who is concerned about the client's response to seeing the records may offer to be present and explain the records or to arrange for another suitably qualified person to be present, but cannot insist on this. Nor can the release of records be made conditional on the client paying any outstanding fees. The client is entitled to unconditional access.

A client who considers that there is an inaccuracy in the record may ask for it to be corrected with the agreement of the therapist. If there is disagreement about what would be a correct record, it is good practice to include a record of the client's objections in the notes. It is best practice not to rewrite the original notes but to record the objection at the time it was raised and to record any revised version of the notes against the date on which the new version was agreed. Many computerised record systems will not allow you to return to earlier entries to make changes in order to protect their integrity so it is always possible to see when any corrections or alterations have been made.

If the therapist is concerned that access to the notes would cause serious harm to the physical or mental health of the data subject and that the notes constitute a health record, it may be possible to refuse or defer access with the authorisation of the health professional who is currently or was most recently responsible for the clinical care of the person concerned (Data Protection (Subjects Access Modification) (Health) Order 2000: s. 7). The legal presumption in favour of access to personal data makes this an exceptional provision that ought not to be sought or granted lightly.

A client may have rights to see her notes even when there is no statutory right of access to the therapeutic notes because they are 'unstructured' and thus fall outside the requirements of the Data Protection Act. For example, the therapist and client may have agreed access to the notes as part of the contract between them. The client may insist on their production as part of the disclosure of documents for a court case, possibly by the use of a court order. In the last resort, it may simply be unconscionable in the eyes of equity, a longstanding set of legal principles, to withhold access.

5.9 Access to notes by others

This section is about access to notes by 'third parties' (i.e. people other than clients) who are mentioned and identified or identifiable in client records.

Those who process sensitive personal data (and mental or physical health comes in this category) should have obtained the client's explicit consent to process the data (i.e. to keep records). Clients may speak about and name others in the course of therapy, and usually those other persons will be unaware that their personal information may be mentioned in records. Therapists are therefore unlikely to have obtained the consent of any others than their client for keeping records. If other people are specifically named in the therapy records or identifiable from the content (e.g. the client speaks about 'my husband Jim') then the person named, if they are made aware that they have been named and that sensitive personal data is held about them, may seek to know what is written about them in the therapy record.

The *Data Protection Act 1998 Legal Guidance* recognises this problem. It provides that:

> A particular problem arises for data controllers who may find that in complying with a subject access request they will disclose information relating to an individual other than the data subject who can be identified from that information, including the situation where the information enables that other individual to be identified as the source of the information.

> The Act recognises this problem and sets out only two circumstances in which the data controller is obliged to comply with the subject access request in such circumstances, namely:

> where the other individual has consented to the disclosure of the information;

> or

> where it is reasonable in all the circumstances to comply with the request without the consent of the other individual. (ICO, 2001: s. 4.1.4)

The Act assists in interpreting whether it is reasonable in all the circumstances to:

> comply with the request without the consent of the other individual concerned. In deciding this question regard shall be had, in particular, to –

> any duty of confidentiality owed to the other individual;

> any steps taken by the data controller with a view to seeking the consent of the other individual;

whether the other individual is capable of giving consent; and

any express refusal of consent by the other individual. (ICO 2001 para. 4.1.4)

See also the *Data Sharing Code of Practice* (ICO, 2011b) and *How do I Handle Subject Access Requests?* (ICO, 2013) available from www.ico.org.uk.

Where the information requested consists of certain records or reports relating to the physical or mental health or condition of the data subject, education or social work, there are special rules regarding subject access and third-party information. These rules are set out in *The Data Sharing Code of Practice* (2011b) available from www.ico.org.uk.

Access to client records by others (e.g. family, relatives after death, under court orders, etc.) is explored in Chapter 4.

5.10 Data protection and technology

As new technology is increasingly used in the delivery of counselling, psychotherapy and coaching, there will be corresponding implications for professional practice ethics. Technology also offers new opportunities for research and professional practice and will raise new legal and ethical challenges. The law in this area is rapidly developing and our space is limited, so we have addressed below some of the questions most frequently asked of us and practitioners should refer to specialist publications for other areas of technology relevant to their practice. See also *A Practical Guide to IT Security* (ICO, 2012b).

The questions we are asked most frequently refer to online counselling, emails and various types of recordings. We have addressed these below.

5.10.1 Emails, mobile phones, Skype and online delivery of counselling and psychotherapy

Emails, Skype, and all other online methods of delivery of counselling and psychotherapy are using electronic data processing and so all are subject to the data protection regulations, for the reasons set out earlier in this chapter. Therapists using these methods to store or transmit client data should register as data processors, and comply with all current data protection legislation. Even if a therapist is not using online therapy working but communicates with their clients by email, through websites or by any form of text messaging, data protection registration should also be considered and advice taken from the ICO where necessary. Remember too, that mobile phones have the capacity for electronic storage of sensitive data and online work, and so may also be covered by the data protection legislation if they are used for storage of clients' personal data and communication with clients and/or used in therapy.

If in doubt, contact the Information Commissioner's Office to check, and see the ICO publication *A Practical Guide to IT Security* (ICO, 2012b).

Just as we have a duty of care for security of our paper records and diaries, we also have a duty of care to maintain security of portable hardware which is kept in an office or during travel and so on (i.e. having reasonable security for our offices, and not leaving a laptop in a car, taxi or on the train!). This is a specialist area of work and the law is fast developing in response to changes in technology. We cannot give a detailed exposition of the law in relation to online working because it may cover different countries or continents, and it is in rapid development. It is wise to check with the ICO (www.ico.gov.uk) whether the Data Protection Act applies to your work in other geographical areas, and be aware that other jurisdiction laws may apply to online work with clients abroad.

The general principles of maintaining security and safe storage of records apply equally to online work, and online security for communication and for storage of records should be maintained by reasonable means, for example use of password protection of computers and laptops and encryption of electronic sensitive data. We have a duty of care to clients to take all reasonable security precautions for online and mobile information including diaries, contact lists, client records and other data relating to clients. For practical guidance on how to use encryption and passwords, see www.ico.gov.uk.

Remember that security is a matter of taking reasonable care. Password protection is the absolute basic necessity for PCs, computers, mobile phones and portable electronic devices on which sensitive personal client data is stored. If a portable device is stolen, data on it should be inaccessible to the thief, protected by means of password and where possible a system that can automatically delete the data on a stolen or lost device. Of course a determined person can access data by illegally breaking security codes, but we cannot be expected to take more than reasonable security precautions. The ICO advises that when we have kept electronically stored data for as long as necessary (see Chapter 6 for exploration of how long to keep records of counselling and psychotherapy), we should securely destroy or delete it.

Many therapists and organisations now use 'cloud storage' and this too, should be secure. Some counselling and other organisations (e.g. Employee Assistance Providers etc.) may require therapists to upload data such as client records to them via a website link. The organisation and the therapist have a duty of care to the client to check that the website connection, links and storage are secure (i.e. password protected or secured in some other way). *Note*: therapists should be careful to check their contract with such organisations, as some try to make the therapist contractually responsible for maintaining security of data, when in practice, once the data is uploaded, the therapist can then do nothing more to protect it.

5.10.2 Tape, audio and video recordings

Recordings of any sort are made and stored electronically, and so are covered by the data protection legislation. There is therefore the issue of registration to be considered and the duties under the Data Protection Act discussed earlier in this chapter, and also an additional duty of care to the client for secure storage of the data, and consents should be sought for the sharing of information on the recordings. It is wise therefore to check with the ICO (www.ico.gov.uk) whether the Data Protection Act applies to your work.

- Consider why the recording is being made. Who asked for it and who will benefit from it? For example, is it to assist the counsellor in training, supervision or educational purposes, or just as an aide memoire?
- Is the recording intended as an aid to therapy for both client and therapist?
- What therapeutic issues might there be about the making of recordings ? For example, does the client have an issue with former abuse that involved some sort of recording or photography?
- Is the client fearful of recordings and potential disclosures, for example that the recording may be produced in court?

Remember that the whole of our client notes and records may be required in court proceedings, including any recordings made. If a therapist proposes to record sessions, there is an ethical and legal duty of care to the client, which includes making the client fully aware of the purpose of recording, and what may happen to the recording. In all cases, the client should first give explicit consent to the recording being made, with full knowledge of its potential uses. The client should also be made aware of (and explicitly agree to) where the recording is stored, who has access to it, and the length of time that it will be kept.

Who owns the recordings?
Legally, ownership of a recording (whatever form it takes) vests in the person who owns the physical medium on which the recording exists (e.g. the tape, CD, DVD, iPad, mobile phone or other device etc.) unless otherwise specifically agreed. However, the *content* of the recording is regulated according to the contractual agreement between the parties who made the recording (e.g. client and therapist, or two counsellors in training etc.).

Where should recordings be kept?
Clients and counsellors may agree between themselves about labelling, storage, security and confidentiality, unless they are both bound by agency policies.

Can the client refuse consent to make a recording?
The client has a contractual right to refuse recording, provided that they have mental capacity (see Chapters 11 and 12).

Does the client have the legal right to listen to their own recordings? Who else has the right to listen to them?
Recordings are part of the client record and therefore subject to disclosure to the client and to others where required by the law. They are also subject to the terms of the therapeutic contract.

Can clients request to keep their recordings, or to destroy their recordings if they so wish?

This depends on the legal ownership of the recordings and any statutory or contractual duty to retain records for any specific length of time. If they are owned by the client, then the client may do with them as they wish (unless otherwise agreed with the therapist). If there is an agency or statutory duty that applies to the recording, for example if it forms part of a mental health record, then those provisions govern what happens to the record.

Therapists and clients should discuss and agree in their therapeutic contract what they will do with any recordings that they make. For discussion of contracts, see Mitchels and Bond (2010), and for information sharing among professionals, see Chapters 7, 8 and 9 of this book. Where explicit consent is required for the making, storage and use of recordings, this should form part of the client or the supervision contract, and, for the avoidance of doubt, the client's explicit consent should be obtained where appropriate and necessary.

A final word – the Information Commissioner's Office (ICO) now seems to assume that most therapists will use some form of digital processing for making appointments, records and other communications with clients and colleagues in the provision of their therapy services. 'Processing' is wider than clinical notes, as we have seen above, so communications within a counselling or psychotherapy service – particularly appointments or other data related to providing and receiving therapy services – could consitiue 'sensitive personal data.' This arguably increases the gravity of the decision whether or not to register, as even the processing of non-sensitive personal data requires registration. Failure to register when required to do so is an offence of strict liability with unlimited fines. Not being registered is sufficient to have committed the offence regardless of intentions. Failure to update or amend registration is also an offence but not of strict liability. The self-assessment for registration has very limited exceptions – see http://ico.org.uk/for_organisations/data_protection/registration/self-assessment. The best advice for anyone wondering whether they need to be registered is to ask the ICO or complete this series of questions. It only takes a few minutes.

6 How Long Do We Keep Records?

Everyone seems to do something different! Can I choose my own time to keep records?

Do I need to tell my clients how long I will keep their records?

I am really unsure how long to keep my records after I stop seeing my client. The books and articles I have read seem to advise different times and don't seem to be able to agree with each other.

I stop keeping records as soon as I think that my client won't return. I shred them and dispose of them safely. Is this OK?

My lawyer advised that I should keep my client records for seven years, but I know other therapists who are keeping their records for shorter lengths of time based on legal advice and I met someone the other day who keeps hers for ten years. Surely the law can't be so vague?

This chapter explores the issues relevant to deciding how long to retain client records. There is no 'one size fits all' simple answer to the question of 'How long should I keep client records?'. Therapists who ask for legal advice may receive very different answers, depending on the context of their work and types of clients. However, there is one firm answer to part of the question: whatever length of time we choose, we need to tell our clients how long their records will be kept. The reason for this is explained later in the chapter.

The appropriate length of time to keep records depends largely on the therapist's assessment of three separate issues:

- An assessment of the purposes to which the records might be put.
- The time limits applicable to different types of legal action and between jurisdictions.
- Time limits for professional complaints and disciplinary procedures.

There is no time limit on bringing criminal cases (some cases are brought many years after the crime, perhaps because new evidence has been discovered), but the law sets certain time limits for bringing different kinds of cases in civil law. Time starts running at specified points, such as when the cause of action arose, or when it was first discovered. For example, a legal case may be brought against a therapist, or a client may want access to therapy notes to provide evidence in a case brought by the client against a third party. It might be reasonable to assume that after expiry of the legal time limits, any records are redundant and can be safely destroyed, but as we see in the next paragraph, some time limits may be quite fluid.

6.1 Time limits for bringing legal actions

There are few time limits on prosecution for criminal actions, while serious criminal offences (such as rape, sexual abuse of children, arson and murder) have no time limit imposed. In criminal cases, the public interest, the gravity of the offence and the duration of time since its commission, coupled with the nature and weight of the available evidence, may influence the decision whether to pursue a criminal prosecution or not. The more serious the case, the more likely it is to be pursued.

The law imposes time limits on the bringing of different types of civil cases before the courts. We have set these out in Figure 6.1. Since strict general rules might operate unfairly in specific situations, some exceptions have been embodied in statute and developed in case law. For example, in the group of cases referred to as *A v Hoare and Others* [2008], the House of Lords (now called the Supreme Court) considered and revised the law on the discretionary extension of time limits in claims for personal injury based on allegations of past sexual abuse. The Supreme Court in this case allowed civil cases to be brought against perpetrators of sexual abuse many years (e.g. in one case 12 years) after the events alleged.

In a similar way, many professional bodies impose time limits on the bringing of claims and complaints against their members. We have considered a number of situations here, but the list is not exhaustive. The law and professional practice in this field is complex, and where consideration is being given to bringing a legal action or making a formal complaint, legal advice or advice from the relevant professional organisation based on the specific circumstances of the case should be sought.

Civil claims in England and Wales are currently regulated by the Limitation Act 1980, as amended. In Scotland they are governed by the Prescription and Limitation (Scotland) Acts 1973 and 1984. In the Law Commission Consultation Paper dated 6 January 1998, the Commission recommended that 'there should be an initial period of limitation of three years that would start from the date the plaintiff discovers, or ought reasonably to discover that he has a legal claim against the defendant … the initial limitation period would be extended where the plaintiff was under a disability, that is, where the plaintiff lacks the capacity to make or communicate decisions, or is under eighteen.' In *Kapadia v London Borough of Lambeth* [2000] (CA), the time limit was extended to six years in respect of a person with depression, which the court in those circumstances construed as a disability within the meaning of these recommendations.

In the case of fraud, concealment or mistake, the limitation periods may be postponed: see s. 32 of the Limitations Act 1980.

To provide a general idea of the time limits currently operative in law, Figure 6.1 presents in briefest outline the basic time limits specified for England and Wales by the Limitation Act 1980.

---

12 years

- Specialty contracts (e.g. under seal) (Limitation Act 1980 s. 8).
- Recovery of land (Limitation Act 1980 ss. 15 and 17).

6 years

- Tort (other than personal injury or death) (Limitation Act 1980 s. 2, but the Latent Damage Act 1986 provides for extension up to a maximum of 15 years if the claimant had no means of knowing that an act or omission might have given rise to the circumstances in respect of which the claim is made).
- Arrears of rent (Limitation Act 1980 s. 19).
- Contract (simple) (Limitation Act 1980 s. 5).
- Enforcement of judgments (Limitation Act 1980 s. 24).

3 years

- Tort: Personal injury or death (through negligence, nuisance or breach of duty) (Limitation Act 1980 s. 11). This may be extended in some cases by the discretion of the court (Limitation Act 1980 s. 14 and s. 33). See the recent case of *A v Hoare and Others* [2008] UKHL 6 in which the House of Lords discussed the use of this discretion in cases based on allegations of past sexual abuse.

2 years

- Contribution towards a judgment or arbitration award (Limitation Act 1980 s. 10).

1 year

- Defamation or Malicious Falsehood (Limitation Act 1980 s. 4A).

Figure 6.1 *Time limits for civil cases (under review at the time of going to press)*

If someone feels aggrieved by the actions of a therapist, they may prefer to make their complaint within a professional conduct or disciplinary procedure. Professional conduct hearings are time-consuming and may create emotional stress for all concerned, but they generally involve less financial investment and risk to the complainant than court proceedings. The sanctions that may be imposed in disciplinary proceedings, for example retraining or supervised practice, may be desirable. It is therefore wise to take the time limits for professional complaints into consideration in determining how long to keep records.

6.2 Time limits for complaints to organisations with responsibility for overseeing professional conduct

We made enquiries of a number of professional organisations to ascertain what, if any, time limits were imposed on complaints against their members. We found that the British Psychological Society (BPS), the United Kingdom Council for Psychotherapy (UKCP), the Health Professions Council (HPC) and the Commission for

Social Care Inspection (CSCI) impose no time limits on the making of complaints against their members. However, these organisations recognised that the passage of time may have an impact on the availability and reliability of relevant evidence and therefore may influence the way in which complaints are handled. As a guide, Table 6.1 gives an overview of the limitation periods for different types of legal actions.

Table 6.1 *Limitation periods for different types of legal actions*

Type of legal action	England and Wales	Scotland
Breach of contract	Complaint to Employment Tribunal for breach of contract of employment: three months from date on which employment ended. Actions for breach of contract in the civil courts: up to six years from the date on which cause of action accrued – s. 5 Limitation Act 1980.	As in England. Up to five years from the date on which the cause of action accrued – Section 6 and Schedule 1 of the Prescription and Limitation (Scotland) Act 1973.
Action in tort for damages for personal injury caused by negligence, nuisance or breach of professional duty of care	Under s.11 of the Limitation Act 1980, no case may be brought more than three years from the date of the precipitating event, or the 'date of knowledge' of the person injured (i.e. that event caused damage). Actions by children: three years from 18th birthday. Time limits for personal injury cases may be judicially extended in some circumstances: see s. 14 (below) and s. 33 of the Limitation Act 1980. See also the recent case of *A v Hoare and Others* [2008] UKHL 6 in which the House of Lords considered the use of this discretion in cases based on allegations of past sexual abuse. In the case of disability, s. 28 Limitation Act 1980 allows an extension of time from cessation of disability or death. See also s. 14A Limitation Act 1980 for specific forms of negligence where facts were not known at date of accrual. See also s. 14B Limitation Act 1980 for specific forms of negligence not involving personal injury.	Under the Prescription and Limitation (Scotland) Acts 1973 and 1984, no case may be brought more than three years from the date of the precipitating event, or the date on which the pursuer had knowledge of the relevant facts, or on which, in the opinion of the court, it was reasonably practicable for him to gain that knowledge. Time limits may be judicially extended – s. 19A, Prescription and Limitation (Scotland) Act 1973.

Type of legal action	England and Wales	Scotland
Damages in Tort (other than personal injury or death)	Under s. 2, Limitation Act 1980, no actions shall be brought after the expiration of six years from the date on which the cause of action occurred, or the 'date of knowledge', i.e. that event caused damage. Actions by children: six years from 18th birthday. No judicial discretion to allow in late cases. For recent examples see *Allen v British Rail Engineering* [2001] and *London Borough of Southwark v Afolabi* [2003]. In case of disability, s. 28 Limitation Act 1980 allows the extension of time from cessation of disability or death.	As for personal injury above under the Prescription and Limitation (Scotland) Acts 1973 and 1984. *Malcom v Dundee City Council* [2007] CSOH 38, Court of Session on 22 February 2007, is a recent Scottish example, in which the Court refused to exercise discretion to extend time. However, this case did not relate to assault, but was raised under the Protection from Harassment Act 1997.
Applications for compensation for Criminal Injury	Criminal Injuries Compensation Authority (CICA) claims – 2 year limitation applies from date of injury.	As in England and Wales.
Criminal cases	No general time limits to bring a prosecution. Some statutes impose limits. Take legal advice regarding specific offences.	As in England and Wales.
Applications to UK courts under the Human Rights Act 1988	One year limit imposed by the Human Rights Act 1998 s. 7(5) for bringing proceedings against a public authority.	As in England and Wales.
Actions for libel or slander	One year from the date on which the cause of action occurred. See s. 4A Limitation Act 1980 as amended by s. 5 of the Defamation Act 1996. In case of disability, s. 28 (4A) Limitation Act 1980 allows the extension of time from cessation of disability or death.	Three years from the date when the right of action accrued, subject to disregarding any time during which the person alleged to have been defamed was under a legal disability – s. 18A, Prescription and Limitation (Scotland) Act 1973. Time limits may be judicially extended – s. 19A, Prescription and Limitation (Scotland) Act 1973.

The British Association for Counselling and Psychotherapy (BACP) has a policy relating to complaints against members which is set out in the *Ethical Framework* (BACP, 2013), in which complaints against members can be lodged either:

- within a reasonable time of the alleged professional misconduct; *or*
- within three years of the ending of the professional relationship; *or*
- within three years of the date when the complainant reasonably became aware of the alleged professional misconduct.

The complainant must provide a written explanation as to when/how they became aware, and this will be considered by the Pre-Hearing Assessment Panel which will decide if the explanation given is good and/or sufficient.

The General Medical Council (GMC) operates a five-year limit on all complaints unless the Registrar considers that it would be in the public interest to investigate: see *The General Medical Council (Fitness to Practise) Rules Order of Council* 2004:

> No allegation shall proceed further if, at the time it is first made or first comes to the attention of the General Council, more than five years have elapsed since the most recent events giving rise to the allegation, unless the Registrar considers that it is in the public interest, in the exceptional circumstances of the case, for it to proceed. (2004b: s. 4 (5))

For further details see the GMC website www.gmc-uk.org. The impact of the general consensus amongst organisations overseeing professional conduct to impose no time limit on the making of complaints is that, if a therapist is looking to self-protection, he may be inclined to retain records indefinitely. This is in contrast to the provisions of the Data Protection Act 1998 which provides that sensitive personal data should be kept only as long as is necessary. We are not aware of any court cases on this issue. Since the Human Rights Act 1998 applies equally to therapists and to clients, when forming a policy about keeping records it seems both legally and morally just that the needs and rights of both should be respected and protected.

6.3 Policy and practice in record keeping

Consideration of legal implications requires attending to the balance between private and public interests. Personal values and philosophy also need to be taken into account. In an area of such complexity, and one where it is impossible to anticipate all eventualities, there is always the possibility of a cause of action emerging long after the event, a case going wrong, or being challenged over exceptional issues that do not fit a practitioner's or agency's values. These will usually be rare events, but cannot be totally avoided by busy therapists. One way of preparing for being challenged on the exceptional case and testing your values related to record keeping is to ask yourself:

- When I am challenged on my policy and practice over record keeping, which would I prefer to be known for – being over-zealous in attending to my clients' rights or attending to my own need to be self-protective?
- In a situation where I may be damned for whatever I do, which I would prefer to stand for?
- Where do I consider the balance between the private and public interests to lie?

Lawyers experienced in defending professionals against negligence and other civil claims will usually advise keeping records for as long as necessary to ensure that time has expired for these types of action. Insurers who provide cover for professional liability may prefer records to be as full as possible and kept for as long as possible to provide the best possible protection for therapists in case they are sued or subject to professional disciplinary proceedings. These opinions are directed at providing the professional with the maximum protection. On the other hand, lawyers grounded in human rights or data protection are more likely to give priority to the clients' interests, especially their privacy, and therefore minimise the length of time for which records ought to be kept.

Therapists have to find a balance between differing legal views in order to develop a position that is appropriate to the circumstances of their work. The data protection requirements are an attempt to reconcile these opposing tensions.

Our recommended way forward in situations where there may be a foreseeable tension between the client's, the therapist's and any agency's interests in how long records are kept, is to discuss these issues with the client and to agree upon appropriate action. The therapist or their employing organisation may have a firm policy which the client may choose to accept or reject.

In any event, it is always wise to let clients know how long their records will be kept. Once records are destroyed they cannot be brought back. If a period for retaining records is agreed on with the client, then the therapist or agency should stick to the agreed time, even if this is affected by the therapist's intended move to another location or retirement from practice. If the client should need or wish to have their records in existence for longer periods than the therapist or agency plans to keep them, then, if the client is aware of the issue, they have an opportunity to discuss this with the therapist and together they can negotiate and agree a way forward.

See Chapter 10 by Cindy Bedor for a full discussion by an experienced practitioner about the development of policy and practice in different organisations.

Part III

Confidentiality and Disclosures:
Information Sharing

7 Sharing Information Between Professionals

How do I balance my therapeutic relationship with the client with my professional responsibilities?

If a client tells me about something criminal that they have done, or about to do, must I report it?

What if I find out that my colleague has done something criminal?

My fourteen-year-old client told me that her (much older) boyfriend got her drunk at a party and then had sex with her – should I share this information?

My colleague, a fellow therapist, confessed that he has been very emotionally labile recently, very quickly angry, and has lost his temper with family and staff. I'm worried about his contact with young and vulnerable clients – what should I do?

Do I have to produce my notes when a solicitor writes and asks for them?

The family are arguing over contact. Their case is now in the county court and the solicitor for the children's mother has asked to talk with me over the phone. She also said that she wants me to go and give evidence about father's alcohol dependency. Do I have to do as she asks?

My client is a witness for the prosecution in a criminal trial next month. The defence have warned me that they might want me to go to court. I don't want the defendant to see all of my client notes – can I refuse?

These are just some of the questions that we are asked by the hundreds of therapists with whom we are in contact. At any time in the course of their work, therapists might come across every type of human behaviour – our clients can be unimaginably courageous, virtuous or criminal. If we are lucky, we are not faced with too many legal and ethical dilemmas, but the situations that seem to trouble us most are usually those that pose moral dilemmas and those that involve some sort of criminal activity.

A particularly difficult situation to resolve is the activity of a client or colleague which we feel we should share with other professionals. We found in the last edition of this book that the treatment of information sharing between professionals was so complex that in this new edition, we have taken a wider approach, and we have written specifically in Chapter 8 on disclosure in situations of supervision and training, in Chapter 9 in research and audit, in Chapter 12 child abuse, and in Chapter 15 we explore issues concerning vulnerable adults and adult witnesses and victims of abuse. We also explore several 'whistle-blowing' dilemmas in the context of the workplace and other professional settings in Chapter 15.

This chapter takes a generalised approach to information sharing between professionals and provides guidance on ways of thinking through the decisions that may have to be made. We have also created a Disclosure Checklist to assist therapists to think through dilemmas (see section 15.6 and Box 14.2).

7.1 When should I share information with other professionals?

7.1.1 Team sharing of information

Many therapists work as part of a team, for example as part of a GP surgery or health care team. The client or patient will probably have agreed to information sharing amongst members of the team (either in general principle or explicitly about specified matters), and the sharing may be general, specific or perhaps on a 'need to know' basis. Such agreements are often part of the procedure of accepting a patient into the care of a hospital or other health care team.

Other therapists may work in agency or organisational settings where there are clear policies and procedures for information sharing: for example, in schools, residential care, prisons, institutions, and other Home Office work, adoption agencies, and social care. Information sharing is made easier for both therapist and client when there are clear policies and procedures to follow. Those therapists who are working alone or outside an agency or organisational setting may have to decide how and when to share information with other professionals.

Counselling is now a self-regulated profession (see 7.1.2 below and the BACP website www.bacp.org.uk), but counselling and psychotherapy are not yet government regulated professions with restrictions on the uses of the title 'counsellor' or 'psychotherapist'. However, counselling and psychotherapy are business activities which are subject to various forms of overt (and also less immediately obvious) government control (e.g. the law against terrorism and serious crimes), and the direct effects of the treatment recommendations by NICE (recently renamed the National Institute for Health and Care Excellence but retaining the original abbreviation; see www.nice.org.uk).

Those therapists working in the health care services must comply with wider regulation and standards: for example, the provision of Access to Health Records Act 1990 under the Data Protection Act 1998, the Freedom of Information Act 2000, and internal government agency procedures for the protection of vulnerable adults and children (see Chapters 11, 12 and 13).

7.1.2 Regulation and the sharing of information

Government regulation aims to protect the public who use certain services by providing formal benchmarks for professional standards and by providing a degree of quality control of practitioners providing those services. The British Association for Counselling and Psychotherapy (BACP) has entered into agreement with the government for self-regulation from 2013 onwards through the creation of a BACP Register of members. Registrants have a certain standard of qualification and experience, and agree to adhere to the requirements of self-regulation. One of these requirements is to comply with the current version of BACP's *Ethical Framework for Good Practice in Counselling and Psychotherapy* (2013). This sets standards for therapist–client relationships, including confidentiality and principles of practice which govern good practice and information sharing (see the *Ethical Framework* for information sharing).

There are three situations when information may legally and ethically be shared:

- when the client consents or specifically requests information to be shared;
- when the law requires information to be shared (e.g. statute, court order etc.); or
- when the balance of public interest outweighs the client's wishes and justifies disclosure (e.g. where there is a real and imminent risk that the client may cause serious harm to self or others).

7.1.3 Dealing with requests for disclosure of client notes and records

Detailed information about responding to requests for disclosure of notes and records for court purposes can be found in *Therapists in Court* (Bond and Sandhu, 2005).

Confidential information about clients should be disclosed only where:

- the law requires (e.g. terrorism);
- the law permits, in the public interest (e.g. serious crimes, child protection etc.); or
- the client consents.

We wrote about making referrals and disclosure of information about clients, including capacity and consent, and discussion of specific situations where disclosure may be requested, in *Confidentiality and Record Keeping* (Bond and Mitchels, 2008). If notes and records are by the Data Protection Acts and/or the Freedom of Information Act 2000, then clients may be entitled to access the information held about them (see Chapter 3 and Bond and Mitchels, 2008).

When considering whether to disclose information, the checklists in Boxes 7.1 and 7.2 provide a guide to thinking through the relevant issues.

Box 7.1   Issues to be considered in dilemmas over confidentiality

With all clients, including those who have refused consent, consider these issues, discuss with the client if appropriate, and ideally discuss them in supervision:

- Is there a real risk here?
- Who is at risk?

(Continued)

(Continued)

- What is the likelihood of serious harm occurring in this case?
- Is this serious harm imminent?
- If I refer and/or disclose information, what is likely to happen?
- If I do not refer, what is likely to happen?
- Do the likely consequences of non-referral include a real risk of serious harm to the client or others?
- If so, are the likely consequences of non-referral preventable?
- What would have to happen to prevent serious harm to client or others?
- Is there anything I (or anyone else) can do to assist in preventing this harm to my client or others?
- What steps would need to be taken to implement such assistance?
- How could the client be helped to accept assistance/the proposed action?
- Does my client have the mental capacity to give explicit informed consent (or refusal of consent) at this moment in time?
- If the client does not have mental capacity, then what are my professional responsibilities to the client and in the public interest?
- If the client has mental capacity, but does not consent to my proposed action (e.g. referral to a GP), what would be my legal and professional situation if I went ahead and did it anyway? What safeguards can I put in place to protect confidentiality and the client's rights?

Box 7.2   Decisions and disclosures checklists

Part 1 The information: sources, reliability and consent issues

- Is this information founded on information from a reasonable and/or reliable source?
- What is the likelihood of serious harm in this case?
- Is this serious harm imminent?
- If I refer/disclose this information, what is likely to happen as a consequence?
- If I do not refer, would the likely consequences of non-referral include any serious harm to the client or others?
- If so, are the likely consequences of non-referral preventable? What would have to happen to prevent serious harm to my client or others?
- Is there anything I (or anyone else) can do to assist in preventing this harm to my client or others?
- What steps would need to be taken to implement such assistance?
- How could the client be helped to accept assistance/or to support the proposed action?
- Does my client have the mental capacity to give explicit informed consent (or refusal of consent) at this moment in time?

- If the client does not have mental capacity to make their own decisions, then what are my professional responsibilities to the client and in the public interest?
- If the client has mental capacity to make the decision, but does not consent to my proposed action (e.g. referral to a GP, or to the police, or to social services etc.), does the public interest justify the intended disclosure or referral?

Part 2 Legal and ethical issues in making a good disclosure

1. Am I acting within the law?
2. Am I acting in the guidelines of my Code of Ethics (e.g. the BACP's current *Ethical Framework*)? What would be my professional situation if I go ahead and make the referral without client consent?
3. Is this information regulated by the Data Protection Act 1998 (DPA) or the Freedom of Information Act 2000 (FOIA); (e.g. do the records comprise client-identifiable sensitive personal data held electronically or in a relevant filing system?
4. Were the notes made by a professional working for a public body in health, education or social care?
5. What are the relevant rights of the person concerned under the Human Rights Act 1998 (HRA)?
6. If working in the health community, is disclosure compliant with the Caldicott Principles and guidance (DH, 2010a)?
7. Is there a legitimate requirement to share this information: e.g. statutory duty or a court order?
8. What is the purpose of sharing the information? (See Part 1 above)
9. If the information concerns a child, young person, or vulnerable adult, is sharing it in their best interests?
10. Is the information confidential? If so, do you have consent to share it?
11. If consent is refused, or there are good reasons not to seek consent, does the public interest necessitate sharing the information?
12. Is the decision and rationale for sharing the information recorded? (See Part 3 below)
13. What is the most appropriate way to share this information? (See Part 3 below)

Part 3 Guidance in making a good disclosure

1. Inform the client, *except* in circumstances where telling the client:

- is illegal (tipping off), or
- will cause or increase any risk of harm to the client or others, or
- may prejudice a police or inter-agency investigation of a serious crime.

2. Limit the information disclosed to the minimum necessary in order to avert the risk.
3. Select the recipient(s) of the information: disclosure should only be made to a person or agency that is capable of minimising or preventing the harm.

(Continued)

(Continued)

4. Mark written or emailed communication 'Confidential' or 'In confidence.' Oral communications should be preceded by a clear statement that what is being disclosed is confidential.
5. If the therapist is unfamiliar with the practice of the person or agency receiving the information, it is reasonable to ask how the information will be protected or treated in advance of disclosing it.

Part 4 Recording the disclosure

Make a note as soon as possible of the following:

- the information provided
- to whom it is given
- the date the disclosure was made
- how the information was given
- whether the client agreed to the disclosure, and if not, why the disclosure was made without client consent.

7.2 Notes as part of evidence in court proceedings, and court reports

For detailed information on responding to requests for disclosure and giving evidence in court, please see *Therapists in Court* (Bond and Sandhu, 2005). Below are brief notes, which we hope will be useful.

Criminal cases are tried in the magistrates' court or the Crown Court, depending on the type of case and its severity, and in some cases the prosecution and defence may make representations to the court about where the case should be heard. Cases may begin in the magistrates court and be committed to the Crown Court for trial. The criminal prosecution and appeals system is briefly explained in Mitchels and Bond, 2008: Ch. 1.

Therapists might be asked to give evidence in criminal cases by the prosecution or by the defence. Usually a request comes via the police or Crown Prosecution Service, or it may come from a defendant or solicitors. If a therapist receives a court request for therapy notes, see sections 4.6 and 4.8 and also refer to (Bond and Sandhu, 2005) on responding to a request to provide evidence in a criminal court. For general guidance on being a witness in any court, see section 7.3, and for pretrial working with vulnerable witnesses and children, see Chapter 13.

Therapy with children or adults who may be a witness in court proceedings may be subject to certain controls: see Achieving Best Evidence in Criminal Proceedings: Guidance on Interviewing Victims and Child Witnesses and Using Special Measures (Home Office, 2007; MoJ, 2011b) and also the current guidance from the Crown Prosecution Service (England and Wales) (2005) *The CPS: Provision of Therapy for Vulnerable or Intimidated Adult Witnesses Prior to a Criminal Trial: Practice Guidance*, available at www.cps.gov.uk. See Chapter 13 of this book for details of the Department of Public Prosecution's *Code of Practice for Victims of Crime and supporting public information materials* (*The Witness Charter: Standards of Care for Witnesses in the Criminal Justice System*, MoJ, 2013; and *Working with Victims and Witnesses*, MoJ, 2013), all available online at http://www.justice.gov.uk.

7.2.1 The Coroner's Court

Therapy notes or a report may sometimes be required for use in the Coroner's Court. The Coroner has a specific judicial role and a judicial responsibility to inquire into certain types of death occurring in their jurisdiction. New legislation came into force on 23 July 2013, governing the procedures and rules that Coroners should follow. See www.judiciary.gov.uk for a copy of the Chief Coroner's Guidance on the new law. The new legislation includes:

- Coroners and Justice Act 2009 (in force from 23 July 2013)
- The Coroners (Investigations) Regulations 2013
- The Coroners (Inquests) Rules 2013
- The Coroners Allowances, Fees and Expenses Regulations 2013

The Coroner may have the assistance of a police officer in gathering evidence for an investigation and may use administrative staff in organising inquests. A request for information may come from the Coroner via the Coroner's Office, or via a police officer assisting a Coroner's inquiry. A therapist may respond to a request for information by disclosing information: with client consent, or in response to a statutory duty or a court order, or when the client's wishes or interests are overridden by the public interest. The Coroner has the power to make an order for disclosure of information or for disclosure of documents to be used in evidence. An order made by the Coroner under the new legislation must be obeyed, and there are judicial penalties for non-compliance (see Schedule 5 of the Coroners and Justice Act 2009).

Relatives of a deceased client have no automatic right of access to the client's records, but the usual guidance regarding disclosure will apply (see Box 7.2). If therapy records or reports are put in evidence in a Coroner's inquiry or inquest, then be aware that they may be disclosed to interested parties with the consent of the Coroner.

7.3 Giving evidence in court

When therapists give evidence in any legal proceedings, they may either be regarded as an 'expert witness' or they may be treated as an ordinary witness of fact. The court will decide whether a therapist is to be treated as an expert in a particular case. Usually, court directions will be made in relation to the evidence, and the leave of the court is required before an expert witness is instructed in family cases. Expert witnesses have special privileges; they are usually provided with all the documents in the case, and they are allowed to sit in the court and hear the case as it progresses in order to evaluate the evidence given, and if necessary, comment on it and advise the court. Witnesses of fact must remain outside the courtroom until they are called in. Experts are also usually paid by one or more of the parties to attend court. The overriding duty of an expert witness is to the court (and to justice) and not to the party who instructed them to attend. Reports of expert witnesses in family cases must follow the guidance on expert evidence set out by the President of the Family Division in *Re TG (A Child) [2013] EWCA Civ 5 (at http://www.bailii.org)*. These are a short set of Practice Directions (25A-F) replacing earlier versions. For further notes see www.judiciary.gov.uk. In other types of case, experts are usually instructed by solicitors who will advise on form and procedure.

No matter what the status of the witness, certain guidelines are helpful:

- *Do not go beyond the remit of your expertise*: Experts should never go beyond the remit of their instructions or their expertise. Never agree to give expert evidence on a matter in which you do not have experience and expertise. There have been cases in which, regrettably, this has happened, to the detriment of a party, the child, justice, or someone who is directly connected with or affected by the case. The Court of Appeal gave helpful guidance for experts and lawyers in *R v Cannings* [2004].
- *Agree the fees, who is to pay, and when payment is to be made, first*: If you expect to be paid for court attendance, discuss fees and expenses with the party who is requesting your evidence. In family cases there are rules and guidance about payment protocols: see *Re TG (A Child) [2013]*. In other cases, the court rules may assist, but instruction and payment is a matter of contract between the parties and the witness. In criminal cases, instructions come from the Crown Prosecution Service or the defence lawyers. In civil cases, it will be one of the parties. If the party instructing you has public funding, they will need to get 'prior authority' from the Legal Services Commission to instruct you. If the matter is private, then the solicitor instructing you should also be responsible for agreeing and organising payment.
- *Ask for clear instructions in writing*: Always ask for a letter of instruction setting out the agreed terms of the instruction, and the issues on which you are asked to give evidence.

7.3.1 Preparation and court etiquette

Preparing for court

- Put all the therapy notes onto a treasury tag, or if using a ring binder, make absolutely sure that it will not 'ping' wide open unexpectedly and spill all the notes in a muddled heap on the floor!
- Make sure that all notes are there, including original scribbled notes and any neat copies made later.

- Organise the records and correspondence so you can find your way around them easily.
- Read through notes and any other material so that is fresh in mind.

At the courthouse

Arrive in good time. It might take ages to find a parking space, so allow for this. All cases are listed on a notice board at court, which will tell you which court you are in. Some cases are listed by number only. If you don't know the number, find a court usher (usually a person in a black gown with a clipboard, whose role is to make cases run smoothly by getting the right people and things into the right places at the right time). The usher will need to know your name and role, so that they are aware that you have arrived. Tell the usher where you are, if you are waiting to be called to give evidence but need to nip off to use the facilities or the canteen.

Find the solicitor instructing you (with the usher's help if necessary), and make contact. They will then guide you as to what is expected. If there is no solicitor, ask the usher.

Before going into court, things to remember

- Ensure that any parking ticket or meter covers the whole of the time you expect to be at court, or at least until lunchtime when you can feed it again. Nothing worse than a sudden anxiety in the middle of your evidence about getting a parking ticket.
- Visit the lavatory first if necessary – nerves may affect the bladder and you do not want to have to ask the court for a 'short break' soon after getting into the witness box.
- Turn off mobile phone or pager.
- Do not discuss the case at all outside court with anyone, except the solicitor instructing you, or with their approval.
- If a witness of fact, wait outside to be called in. If you are an expert witness, check first with the usher and then go into court and sit near to the solicitor or party instructing you.

In court

Try not to come into the court laden with unnecessary coats, bags, umbrellas and so on. When you go into the witness box, find a safe place inside the courtroom to put everything down first (except notes and reading glasses), as muddle in the witness box looks unprofessional.

Decide beforehand whether you will take the oath or affirm. The usher will ask which you prefer, when you go into the witness box.

Speak clearly and assertively. Take time to answer questions if necessary. If a question is unclear, seek clarification. When answering questions, turn your body slightly and address the answers directly to the magistrates or the judge. Turn back to the advocate for the next question. This makes it more difficult for advocates to interrupt. However, if interrupted in the middle of giving an answer, politely but firmly say that you will continue to answer the first question, then address the next one. Remember that the duty to the court is to 'tell the whole truth and nothing but the truth'.

The best and most important advice is to have confidence and remember that you are the therapist and therefore a professional with expertise in your own field. The court will not have the level of understanding that you have of your work. Be prepared to explain professional issues to the court. If you can explain your actions, your notes, and your views to the court, and justify them professionally, then there is nothing to fear from questions from a judge or advocates in cross-examination.

8 Sharing Information in Supervision and Training

My training organisation requires that we have supervision. I know my supervisor writes reports about my practice. I am not sure how much of what I say to her is confidential between us but I am nervous to ask.

I discuss my clients in supervision without revealing their names. Ought I to be telling my clients that this is what I do? I always tell them if I cannot protect their identity and seek their consent.

It is a normal part of our course to discuss clients as case studies. We are required to seek their consent. Is this legally necessary?

My client has produced some interesting drawings in therapy. I would like to show them to my supervisor and trainers to see what they think they are about. What do I need to do ethically and legally to allow this?

I am supervising a counsellor and becoming increasingly worried that personal difficulties in his life are causing problems in his work with clients. I am discussing my concerns with him and supporting him to make changes … but, if there is no improvement, am I allowed to raise my concerns with his employer?

8.1 Supervision

The respective duties of the supervisor and supervisee will depend in part on their professional modality, their contract of supervision, and the organisational setting within which they work (i.e. whether, for example, they work in an organisation in which they have a managerial relationship as well as a supervisory one). (See Clarkson, 1995; Feltham, 1999; Hackney and Goodyear, 1984; Hawkins and Shoet, 1996; Jacobs, 1996; Mearns, 2008; Page and Wosket, 1998; Tudor and Worrall, 2004; BACP, 2013).

As a Supervisor, you have to encompass many functions in your role. In part you are a counsellor giving support; also you are an educator helping the supervisee learn and develop, and in many situations you are also a manager with responsibilities both for what the supervisee is doing with and to the client, and also to the organisation within which you both work.

(Hawkins and Shoet, 1996: 37)

There are potential problems of combining the roles of supervision and management, of concern to BACP. If a line manager is also a supervisor, this can lead to difficulties, since a conflict of interests may arise between the needs of the organisation or institution (the priority of the line manager) and the needs of the counsellor [or the client]. If the counsellor has a personal or professional problem with their supervisor, they may have no resource for support and help, and their work may be compromised or at risk. For this reason, BACP's *Ethical Framework* states:

Supervising and managing

32. Practitioners are responsible for clarifying who holds responsibility for the work with the client.

33. There is a general obligation for all counsellors, psychotherapists, supervisors and trainers to receive supervision/consultative support independently of any managerial relationships.

34. Supervisors and managers have a responsibility to maintain and enhance good practice by practitioners, to protect clients from poor practice and to acquire the attitudes, skills and knowledge required by their role.

35. Supervisors and managers may form a triangular relationship with a counsellor or psychotherapist, particularly where services are being provided within an agency. All parties to this relationship have a responsibility to clarify their expectations of each other and, in particular, the steps that ought to be taken to address any concerns over client safety. The role of an independent supervisor is widely considered to be desirable in promoting good practice but, to be most effective, requires clarity in how such a role relates to line management and the division of tasks and responsibilities between a supervisor and any line manager.

(BACP, 2013: paras 32–35)

An example of the type of potential conflicts of interest that may arise might be in a voluntary or charitable organisation providing counselling services, where the counsellors, some of whom may be trainees on placement, and/or working on a voluntary basis, would like to receive supervision at low cost. They may be line-managed by a person in the organisation's management system. If that person also provides individual or group supervision, there may be scope for potential conflicts of interest, putting clients and therapists at risk. Some organisations may have in-house supervisors who are funded by the organisation and who perhaps are contractually bound to it, and also (to varying degrees) subject to the control of the Organisation. It is worth considering the many potential hazards of dual roles see *Dual Relationships in Counselling and Psychotherapy* (Syme, 2003) and also the BACP Information Sheet G3 *Dual Roles* (Jacobs, 2007).

In supervision, the supervisee's needs and interests are an essential focus of the work, but, as Page and Wosket (1998) rightly point out, the welfare of the supervisee's client is of primary importance in supervision, especially where the client is at risk. This is different from counselling, in which the work centres on the client and the client–counsellor relationship.

In supervision, practitioners need to create a balance between the legal and professional boundaries of supervision with the supervisee's obligations under their client contracts and the other overarching legal duties and responsibilities which apply to both the supervisor and supervisee (e.g. in criminal law, negligence, child protection etc.). Both need to be aware of overarching issues such as legal limitations, public interest, confidentiality and how to share information between professionals appropriately.

The supervisor has a contractual duty and responsibility to the supervisee. The supervisor has no direct contractual relationship with the supervisee's client(s), but holds the responsibility to oversee the supervisee's practice for the benefit of the supervisee's clients. Although a supervisor should not be overly prescriptive, but facilitative, there are times when authoritative action or advice about best practice, including ethics or law is necessary. For example, when a client is at risk and an inexperienced supervisee needs guidance or direction about when or how to make an appropriate disclosure or a referral when working with trainees or therapists who are inexperienced in specific issues for their current casework, the following advice is legally sound:

> [A] supervisor needs to be prepared to carry a more readily identifiable authority which includes monitoring the practice of the supervisee. This does involve assessment, judgment, and on occasion being prescriptive about what the other person should or should not do. (Page and Wosket, 1998: 22)

In the context of supervision, the supervisor has responsibility for monitoring and evaluating the quality of the counselling practice of the supervisee: for example, to watch for burn-out in highly stressful areas of work, with difficult or demanding clients, or where work levels are high. This responsibility is increased in a situation where supervision includes an element of management. Supervisees also have their own duty, within the supervisory relationship, to constantly monitor and evaluate their own practice (Proctor, 1986).

The supervisor and the supervisee have a contractual relationship with each other in which the supervisor has (amongst other responsibilities) a duty of care to the supervisee. The counsellor's own separate contractual relationship with their client also includes a duty of care (see Mitchels and Bond, 2010: Chapter 3 generally and section 3.10 for the supervisor's potential liability in tort).

The supervisor does not have a direct contractual relationship with the supervisee's client, but does have an ethical responsibility to attend to that client's welfare in supervision. This means in law that a supervisor may be sued for breach of contract by a supervisee, but not by the supervisee's client.

However, in the law of tort (see Mitchels and Bond, 2010: Ch. 3), if the chain of causation could be proved the supervisor could, in theory, potentially be accountable to the supervisee and their clients in the context of their role in relation to a client who has been brought to the supervision and in respect of whom the supervisor had provided therapeutically incorrect or unhelpful advice or guidance which was then acted upon by the supervisee to the detriment of the client. A claim of this sort against a supervisor would be difficult to establish in law, and so far as we are aware no such action has been brought in England and Wales.

We are, however, aware of supervisors being brought into the complaints procedure by a counsellor's professional organisation to discuss ethical responsibilities. In any legal case based on the alleged professional negligence of a supervisor, appropriate legal advice should be sought on the specific circumstances of that case. For further discussion see Mitchels and Bond (2010: Chapters 3 (Negligence), 4 (Contract), 6 (Insurance), and 9 (Employment)).

In employment or in training situations, the supervisor may be expected or specifically contractually bound to report any concern arising where the supervisee is unfit to work, or where the standard of the supervisee's work falls below that expected of a competent professional. Equally, a supervisor is held legally responsible to their supervisees and to any organisations concerned for the accuracy and professional competency of any reports made for accreditation, registration, fellowship or disciplinary purposes.

We have been asked, 'Do clients have the right to ask for records of supervision sessions?' This is a complex issue. In most cases clients are not identified in supervision, and therefore the notes of the supervisor about the therapeutic work of the supervisee cannot be directly related or traceable to a specific client, even though the work with that client may be discussed in general anonymous terms in supervision. However, if the client is clearly identified by the supervisee, or even if the client is identifiable (e.g. through discussion of the context of the client's life, work, family circumstances etc.), then the supervisor's notes may be linked with that client work, and in the event of a complaint or legal case, the supervisor's notes may be of material relevance to the issues of the case and it is possible that they may be requested as part of the evidence.

8.2 Supervisees in training

Supervision contracts are of great importance in setting out clearly the duties and responsibilities of the supervisor, the training organisation and the trainee. The supervision contract should also address, where relevant, the boundaries of confidentiality of the supervision work in relation to that training.

A recognised supervisor for a training organisation may be required to submit regular reports of the supervisee's progress, which may be shared with the supervisee and discussed in advance of submission. The supervisee may expect to read these reports and to be able to add their own comments. As noted above, the supervisor may also have accepted a contractual duty to share with the organisation any serious concerns about the trainee's work or health (mental or physical) which may interfere with the supervisee's ability to function effectively in counselling.

It is possible in law that a trainee who has suffered quantifiable damage of some sort could take legal action against their training organisation or their trainer, alleging, for example, that the trainer has breached their duty of care by paying inadequate attention to the trainee's academic or psychological needs, thereby causing damage or loss to the trainee. A training organisation in a contractual relationship with its trainees will have a duty of professional care which may include both the organisation and its trainers. The duty of care to trainees must be balanced by the trainers' other contractual and ethical responsibilities for assessment and reporting. See Mitchels and Bond (2010: Chs 3 and 4) for further discussion.

Supervisors of therapists in training are usually providing a high level of support to their supervisees, and may provide necessary professional guidance and advice. On occasions, there may be differences in opinion or practice issues arising between the training organisation and the supervisor which may need to be resolved. The needs of the supervisee's clients, and also to those of the trainee are vital concerns, which should be addressed in the context of current professional guidance, the current law, and the supervision contract. Where supervisees need to work with video or audio recordings of client sessions in supervision or in training, issues arise concerning the client's confidentiality when tapes are shared. Typical questions we are asked include:

- *Should I tell the client why the recording is being made?* The counsellor has an ethical duty to provide the client with an explanation about the purpose and any proposed use of any recordings. As a matter of good practice, the counsellor should seek the client's explicit consent for disclosure of recordings for therapeutic, educational or supervision purposes. If the Freedom of Information Act 2000 or the Data Protection legislation apply, then there is a legal duty to give an explanation of potential use and obtain explicit consent for making, keeping and sharing recordings.
- *Who owns the recordings?* Legally, ownership of the recording vests in the person who owns the physical medium on which the recording exists (e.g. the tape, CD, DVD etc.), unless otherwise specifically agreed. However, the *content* of the recording is regulated according to the contractual agreement between the parties who made the recording (i.e. client and therapist; two counsellors in training etc.).
- *Where should recordings be kept?* Clients and counsellors may agree between themselves about labelling, storage, security and confidentiality, unless they are both bound by agency policies.
- *Can the client refuse consent to make a recording?* The client has a contractual right to refuse recording, provided that they have mental capacity; see Chapter 4 of this book and Mitchels and Bond (2010: Ch. 4 (Contracts)).
- *Does the client have the legal right to listen to their own recordings? Who else has the right to listen to them?* Recordings are part of the client record and therefore subject to disclosure to the client and to others where required by the law. They are also subject to the terms of the therapeutic contract.
- *Can clients request to keep their recordings, or to destroy their recordings if they so wish?* This depends on the legal ownership of the recordings and any statutory or contractual duty to retain records for any specific length of time. If they are owned by

the client, then the client may do with them as they wish (unless otherwise agreed with the therapist). If there is an agency or statutory duty that applies to the recording (e.g. if it forms part of a mental health record), then those provisions govern what happens to the record.

Therapists and clients should discuss and agree in their therapeutic contract what they will do with any recordings that they make. For discussion of the law of contracts as it relates to therapy, see Mitchels and Bond (2010: Ch. 4). Where explicit consent is required for the making, storage and use of recordings, this should form part of the client or the supervision contract, and for the avoidance of doubt, the client's explicit consent should be obtained where appropriate and necessary.

Sharing Information in Research and Audit

As a counsellor working in a GP surgery, I have been asked to respond to an audit of the practice's range of services. I am not sure whether my clients are aware that this might include my work with them – what should I do?

Is it ethical to use client assessment questionnaires in research if their names are deleted?

I am doing field research on PTSD. Some of the questions that I might ask could trigger memories for the respondents – if I make sure that there is some psychological help available for them, is this OK?

I have been asked to help with some research, funded by a commercial firm producing drugs. How do I find out about professional codes of ethics in research, so that I can make sure that we are sticking to them?

This chapter explores the role of sharing information in the context of research, looking at the ethical and legal aspects to be considered, from the perspective of the researchers and their respective organisations, and also considering the needs and legal rights of those who are subjects of the research.

9.1 Ethics, research integrity and research conduct

We need to ensure the quality of our research, with a concern to avoid a lack of integrity due the exploitation or abuse of participants, falsification of data or other failings in the research process. Integrity, quality and transparency are often linked in guidance. *Integrity* relates to the degree of trust or confidence someone can place in the research if intending to rely up on it for further research or to inform practice. 'Transparency in research ethics' is defined by the Economic and Social Research Council (ESRC) as 'The full, accurate, and open disclosure of relevant information' (2012: 41). Transparency is a significant issue because it enables others to assess both the quality and integrity of the research as well as its applicability to their purposes.

Other issues sometimes raised as matters of *integrity* are protecting the independence of the research and being explicit over any conflicts of interest. It is important that provision is made for anyone with concerns about the research, especially participants, to know how to raise concerns or complaints and that they are proactively informed about how to do this.

9.2 Ensuring the welfare of research participants

The general rule in medical treatment is that no adult or child with the mental and legal capacity to make their own medical decisions may be given medical (and by analogy, psychological) treatment without their consent. Medical or other treatment without consent (save in emergencies) may incur liability for damages in tort (e.g. for assault) or constitute an offence in criminal law. Detention in hospital or any other place without appropriate consent could constitute false imprisonment. A similar rationale applies in the necessity for appropriate consent for medical research. For counsellors working in GP or hospital practices, explicit consent needs to be given to share sensitive personal information for research or audit purposes: see Chapter 5 on data protection, *Confidentiality* (GMC, 2009) and the *Data Sharing Code of Practice* (ICO, 2011b). Information can be anonymised for research purposes: see *Anonymisation: Managing Data Protection Risk – Code of Practice* (ICO, 2012a).

9.3 Guidance on researcher conduct

For academic research, information has to be shared, but carefully boundaried, if research is to be carried out both ethically and with due diligence. If research is led or overseen by a university, the use of that university's guidance on research ethics may provide useful information for identifying factors to be taken into account in developing guidelines for a piece of research. See also the reference books on counselling research (e.g. Cooper, 2008; McLeod, 2014).

9.4 Mental capacity and the protection of children and vulnerable adults as research participants

Practitioners undertaking research with vulnerable adults and children will need to have valid consent to enter into research agreements. Practitioners may benefit from reference to suitable relevant resources and guidance regarding how to apply the mental capacity legislation, and in the case of children, information on assessment for competence in accordance with the guidelines set out by Lord Fraser and others in the case *Gillick v West Norfolk and Wisbech AHA* [1986]. See Chapters 11 and 12 of this book for discussion of mental capacity and consent issues in working with children and adults.

9.5 Research cited in evidence in court, or in expert witness reports

Whether a witness is to be treated by the court as an expert is entirely a matter for the court to decide. This will depend on the nature of the case, and the extent of the expertise and experience of the particular witness which should be directly relevant to issues in the case. A witness should not put themselves forward as an expert in a case, but wait to be invited to do so by the court, usually at a Directions

Hearing, when the evidence for the case is being reviewed in advance of the hearing and witnesses ordered or requested to attend. The court may give directions concerning the evidence to be called, for example to request reports, counselling notes, or the attendance of a therapist as a witness.

Ordinary witnesses must stick to the facts. Expert witnesses may be invited by the courts to give facts and also to give their opinion on matters relevant to a case. If a counsellor or any other person is called as an expert witness to give evidence in court, they may also wish to cite relevant research in giving their evidence, for example as authority for a statement or a diagnosis, prognosis, treatment plan and so on. Witnesses should be extremely careful not to overstep the limits of their experience and expertise, and should be careful not to make wide or inaccurate statements, or to make statements unsupported by relevant evidence.

In an effort to be accurate in giving evidence, if citing research, witnesses should ensure that they thoroughly understand the research evidence, and to be prepared to explain it, and to explain any limitations on the relevance or accuracy of the research on which they intend to rely. They may be asked by the court to provide copies of research cited in court, for the parties and for the court, so this should be made known to the court in advance so that copies can be made available.

9.6 Citing online and journal research

Beware of citing online research unless the sources are known to be accurate and reliable. Some online resources such as Wikipedia and private websites are interesting, but the content may not be reliable or accurate. Academic journals usually print research which has been peer reviewed and is likely to have gone through a stricter process of publication. Be aware of the limitations of any research cited, for example, consider the research questions, the methodology (underpinning philosophy of the research), the research methods (e.g. sampling and analysis) and whether the research results are limited or whether they may be capable of generalisation. See Cooper (2008) and McLeod (2014) for further information relevant to research in therapy.

9.7 Sharing information in research and audit

Therapists working in GP surgeries, hospitals, social care and other government or organisational settings may be asked to share information in research for the purpose of audit, for the purpose of the advancement of health care in general, or to improve the service provided.

Practitioners should be aware of the requirements of the data protection legislation and the Freedom of Information Act (see Chapter 5) and also, if client information is to be used in audit, ensure that clients have given their explicit consent to the sharing of personal data. Usually such data is anonymised, and clients' identity and identifying factors are protected, but consent to share data is still required.

Recently, there has been much in the news concerning proposals for a wider sharing of patient information in health care in order to enhance knowledge and improve practice. In the light of concerns expressed that patient data may be more widely shared in the future, it would be useful to watch for news and future health care information to see how these proposals will operate. See the GMC website www.gmc-uk.org and current guidance *Confidentiality* (GMC, 2009) and *Seeking Patients' Consent: The Ethical Considerations* (GMC, 2000a).

Part IV

Confidentiality and Disclosures: Policy, Practice and Procedural Issues

10

Developing Agency Policy and Practice and Evaluating Organisational Policies on Confidentiality and Record Keeping

As a counsellor, I want to help the agency I work for to provide the best service that we can to our clients. Is there any guidance about the policies that we should have on confidentiality and keeping records, and to help us think our policies through?

I don't agree with one of the policies of my organisation. I have raised it with management, but they are not interested in hearing my views. Is there anything I can do?

My agency is bound by government guidance. As an independent practitioner, do I have to comply, too?

I have been let down by a lot of people I've trusted at work. It feels like everything I've worked for is just wasted. What I want from this counselling is good professional support, which I think I deserve to get from my employer, and what I need right now is a safe place to start to pick up the pieces of myself.

We thank Cindi Bedor, who has kindly contributed this chapter. Readers of the First Edition told us that they value Cindi's insights from her experience as a BACP accredited counsellor and as the manager of a counselling service. Cindi has extensive experience in organisational settings including workplace counselling, managing counselling and multi-disciplinary teams, and policy development, and currently as Head of Staff Counselling and EAP Manager for the Royal United Hospital NHS Trust in Bath. She has added to this chapter new legislation, relevant government policies and codes of practice.

The last comment quoted at the start of this chapter came from a client and may be expressing the hopes and expectations of many employees who come to a workplace counselling service. The quotation is a remarkable articulation of the particular qualities they might expect from their counselling, and those words hovered in my mind for many months as my team and I developed and wrote a procedure for maintaining client confidentiality and keeping records. The case study of that experience, which appeared in the First Edition of this book, described our journey and how we arrived at our destination of producing a clear, considered procedure for recording and maintaining client records, a procedure that felt very much alive and evolving within our daily practice. In addition, it was supported by the stakeholders of our service: our clients, managers, legal department representatives, and our data protection officer. The content of the procedure and the process by which we developed it ultimately awarded us greater assurance that we were meeting our responsibilities to our clients, our employer and the law, and we acquired some understanding about how we could be supported should something go wrong.

This chapter looks back on that process after the passing of several years, and reflects on what worked well then and what seems to have stood the test of time. We were keenly aware even then of the ground-breaking, frequently changing nature of the law and its application to client confidentiality, and indeed the legislative and cultural landscapes continue to pose new challenges to how therapists and services respond and grow. And as ever, these factors speak of the context and nature of the therapeutic work in which we are engaged.

The original case study was written from my perspective as manager of a counselling service which was sited alongside the occupational health service, and together we formed the Occupational Health and Counselling Service of Bristol City Council. As with many workplace counselling services, we had grown organically over ten years, from a small number of welfare officers into a team of twelve counsellors, reflecting the organisation's need for specialised employee support and a growing recognition of the value of therapy. The counselling team comprised experienced workplace counsellors with a diverse range of theoretical orientations, including cognitive behavioural therapy (CBT), psychodynamic psychotherapy, Gestalt, solution-focused and integrative therapy. Most of the counsellors worked part-time, in a range of venues around the city. They had been managed by the occupational health manager until my post was created and I became the first counsellor-manager of the service.

I viewed the diversity of theory and practice within our team as a real strength, and together we fruitfully tussled with the type and quantity of standardisation to introduce into our individual and collective practice. We all agreed that standardising client confidentiality and record keeping processes was a priority, yet it took a considerable time to harness the commitment, energy and focus needed to commence and stay with the process. With reflection, my challenges as the service manager, responsible for creating this procedure, were many. New in post and in a newly created role within a team accustomed to working independently, I needed to maintain the engaged and logistical momentum of team discussions, to find time for lengthy consultations as I sought expert advice, to hold the tensions and strong feelings generated by discussions within the team, to allow enough time for individual growth and team cohesion, and ultimately to represent adequately the rights, responsibilities, hearts, minds and intentions of all parties.

It was valuable experience for me to take into my current role, managing an in-house staff counselling and support service within an NHS acute hospital. With reflection, I can see how many of the principles underpinning my work as therapist and manager were strengthened by it, and equally how I have either refined or let go of some procedural aspects as I adapted to my new setting and as the legal, technological and cultural climate has changed. Revisiting now the original case study, I will consider aspects of the process and content in response to the current thinking and context.

10.1 Where and how do we start?

It is a rare thing to feel passionate about policies and procedures, and yet as we immersed ourselves in the process of exploring, questioning, researching and debating every facet of client confidentiality and record keeping practices, some exciting and unexpected things happened: we started talking together about what we really do with our clients, challenging assumptions and well-worn ways of working; at times we trod tentatively around the boundaries that distinguish between individual and collective priorities; we got stuck in our resistances to change; and ultimately we developed individually as practitioners and as a team. We started talking to professionals outside our discipline and service, to gain the views of our employing organisation's Legal Services Department, data protection officer and principal insurance officer. We consulted literature produced by the Information Commissioner's Office (ICO) and British Association for Counselling and Psychotherapy (BACP), and contacted counselling services similar to ours. There were few signposts at the time to direct us to our destination and our most meaningful discoveries were found in the journey.

I adopted a consultative approach to developing this particular procedure, to incorporate the enormous expertise held by therapists within the team, and more crucially to gain enough collective ownership of a key procedure for successful implementation. Admittedly, this approach required time and was more costly than it could have been had I merely written a draft procedure for circulation and comments. I believe the investment was rewarded many times over, as the process stimulated far more rigorous debate and challenge through our discussions. It also meant that we went to the heart of why, as individual therapists, we were there in the first place, and from there how we would define our collective purpose. As service manager, I gained more insight into how my team worked and this informed a stronger sense of governance. I now employ this approach for all key issues within my current service. It brings together therapists who work part-time, some of whom rarely see each other, it opens out the issue at hand more thoroughly and for deeper scrutiny, it keeps us connected to the meaning of the therapy we practice, and it creates the environment for sound decision making. From a management perspective, all of these benefits contribute to a better standard of clinical governance.

We had no written statement or procedure for marking and describing the parameters of client confidentiality and our record keeping practices. Uneasiness grew amongst our team with each new request for disclosure of information held in a client's file, and this anxiety was fuelled by reports of counsellors being summoned into the witness box. Our discomfort seemed to contain:

- *Concern* that our clients received from us a professional service of a high standard on a daily basis, and that we maintained this standard in the event that we were called into the courtroom. We had confidence in the quality of our day-to-day therapeutic work, but that confidence wavered at the thought of stepping into a legal and public environment unknown to us.
- *Awareness* that we assumed we were all working with similar interpretations of our responsibilities regarding confidentiality and record keeping, whilst suspecting that in practice we applied this in different ways. Several years ago this would have been very common within counselling services, and few therapists would have fully considered how responsibility and accountability were held within the service. As manager, I held responsibility for ensuring that our legal and professional obligations were met and I sought my own assurance of shared understanding and practice in this fundamental area. It remains true today that I would be expected by my employers and professional body to account for the application of ethical and legal principles and responsibilities within our service, and assurance that individually and collectively our team meets our responsibilities adequately is important to me.
- *Questions* about the legal and ethical aspects of our procedures, systems and practice – how would we know if we were working in line with current thinking and good practice? Would they be good enough if put to a legal test? What was really expected of us by our clients, peers, managers, professional bodies and the law? The core of this anxiety related to our work, and ourselves, *being seen* outside of the closed environment of the therapy room. I notice less of this anxiety now, perhaps due to increased guidance from our professional bodies and insurers, a greater awareness of legal issues and processes, and now most of us know of a therapist colleague who has been called to give evidence in court – and survived.
- *A sense* that, due to the workload demands upon us, we were unable to keep pace with the latest research, literature or legal cases regarding confidentiality. Certainly, amongst workplace counsellors, the demands continue to increase and there seems less time than ever to keep up-to-date with the huge spectrum of changes in theory, practice, cultural issues and trends. We can lose ourselves as we seek more expertise in one area of our practice, only to suddenly find we have clients who are texting us and we have not thought out the boundaries of confidentiality regarding text messaging!
- *Anxiety* and feelings of vulnerability – who would support and protect us should something go wrong or if we were called to appear in court? Much more support and guidance is available now, from professional bodies, insurers, clinical supervisors, legal and data protection departments within organisations, and peers who have been through the process.
- *A desire* to continue raising the standards of our service and our profession.
- *A general feeling* of being lost in the face of a very large and complex issue, not knowing where to begin, and feeling resistant to trying to understand an area outside our training and expertise.

Not knowing where to begin, we explored the expectations, needs and requirements of all parties – client, counsellor, supervisor, organisation and profession – and the findings of that exercise became our starting point. A few themes emerged to define our purpose and set the foundation for this procedure: responsibility, accountability, protection and trust. Each party involved in the counselling process required these in some way, and I noticed how frequently the themes were present in our discussions. I can see now how important it was that we fully feel, understand and acknowledge the way in which each party held these needs and expectations. It was not enough to simply 'write a procedure'. In addition, we needed to move from assumed to explicit understanding by naming the issues. Finally, we realised that the procedure we wrote must be clear and accessible to anyone, and especially to those outside our profession.

And yet a question remained: how could we be responsible and accountable, offer protection, act in a trustworthy manner and be clear about all of this when each client, and certainly each disclosure request, is different and takes us into unknown, or at least unclear, territory? Our confidentiality procedure had to allow a place for unforeseen events and be flexible enough to contain necessary ethical decision-making processes.

10.2 Understanding the legal, defensive and managerial issues

The time came to navigate our way through the literature into the realm of confidentiality and the law. We were aware of the conflicting views regarding note keeping of client sessions, and the making of 'official' and 'process' notes. One view at the time was that no notes should be made; another opinion was that therapists could be deemed negligent if they did not keep notes. Many therapists held the belief, instilled through their training, that their process notes were their own private property and could therefore contain any material that they believed facilitated their work with their client. This contrasted with another view that process notes were the property of the employing counselling service and therefore belonged in the client's file. This issue stimulated our most energetic discussions. No clear, definitive guidance was available to us at the time and we discovered how important our notes were to us, how strongly we defended our unique ways of making and using them – and our perceived right to do this – and it was a struggle to find an agreed compromise.

Consulting further afield, a wide range of procedures and practice were described by other services I contacted, and most had no written procedure but clearly had agreed working practices that each therapist employed in their own way, especially so in the making and keeping of process notes.

Other resources consulted at this point included the BACP *Ethical Framework* and Information Sheets, the Data Protection Act 1998, the Caldicott Principles (see Glossary and Chapter 7 for definition and further details), and literature and internet searches relating to confidentiality and record keeping.

Our organisation's data protection officer agreed to offer advice regarding our compliance with the Data Protection Act (DPA), and this dialogue greatly enhanced collaboration between the counselling service and our employing organisation. The meaning of a 'relevant filing system' was clarified, as was the impact on practice of the Data Protection Act and the Freedom of Information Act (see Chapter 5 for details). Our real challenge, it seemed, was to balance the requirements of data protection; our notes should be 'adequate and relevant' but 'not excessive', and our decisions regarding our use of process notes should take both these requirements into account. This remains a cornerstone of good, ethical and legal practice today, and at times it can prove as challenging a balance to strike as it was then.

It was the express view of our data protection officer at that time in the past that our clients had a right to refuse to allow us to make and keep notes, and that it was our responsibility to inform them of this right. This came as quite a surprise to us. It raised many questions about informed consent and clinical efficacy, especially with clients deemed traumatised or at risk, and it brought anxiety that, whilst protecting clients' rights, in the context of a profession that generally expects a certain level of note taking as part of good practice, the therapists were unprotected from accusations of negligent therapeutic practice. Thinking we had no choice, we did find a way of integrating this aspect of the DPA into our procedure and practice, but it was an uncomfortable practice for us all.

Overall, our legal services department, principal insurer, data protection officer and senior managers preferred the most comprehensive collection of data possible, including a signed confidentiality and data protection statement. For the most part, we chose to comply with their preferences, apart from keeping overly lengthy session notes. Looking back now, I can see how paper-heavy and unwieldy the procedure had become in our efforts to meet our legal commitments.

10.3 From past to present

Much has changed in the past few years regarding the making and keeping of client notes. Professional guidance (see BACP's *Ethical Framework*, 2013: 5) expects that in the case of therapy practice, notes will be made, unless unusual circumstances arise, and the making of notes would cause extreme distress to the client or others. This professional expectation is more likely to be embodied in implementation of the DPA. Our clients would be expected to present a justifiable reason for refusing our data collection and note keeping, and a process for both client and counsellor to follow is outlined in Part II, s. 10 of the DPA. The descriptions of a 'relevant filing system' and 'sensitive personal data', and Schedules 1 and 2 of the DPA remain helpful and relevant to the creation of a client file within a counselling service. How the data is used and stored, and how it is accessed by clients or shared with other parties remain within the jurisdiction of the Act.

Updated and clear guidance is available from BACP, in the *Ethical Framework for Good Practice in Counselling and Psychotherapy* (2013), the BACP Registration Criteria and Information Sheets P12 'Making notes and records of counselling and psychotherapy sessions' (2010) and G1 'Access to records of counselling and psychotherapy' (2009), about good practice in making, keeping, sharing and storing notes and records. In particular is the expectation that notes are kept and protected, and that a client record can take many forms, including the traditional handwritten record, or computerised, audio, visual or other forms that support specific needs. Notes should be made contemporaneously, as soon after the session as possible, and they should be legible and coherent. The contrasting views about process notes, that had occupied my team for many months, now embrace a more pragmatic simplicity. If the notes identify the client, or if the client is in any way identifiable from the notes, they are considered to form part of the client's file; if the client is not identifiable and the notes are used solely for the therapist's personal reflection and supervision, they may not be included in the client's official file and may be destroyed after they have served their purpose.

Destroying process notes that do not identify the client in any way remains counter-intuitive to many practitioners and they may be useful as a valuable area for general reflection with peers or in supervision. We need to achieve a balance in terms of serving our clients well and compliance with data protection principles, particularly for a service offering brief intervention therapy to employees, some of whom may re-present to the service more than others. Holding a 'thread of memory' about them and their life situations seems meaningful to them and us, and process notes can usefully contribute to this.

A more recent development is the inclusion in a client's file of artifacts made by them during and as part of the therapy, including artwork, creative writing and homework undertaken between sessions. In our service we might also include questionnaires and other forms used by CBT and eye movement desensitisation and reprocessing (EMDR) practitioners if they are particularly relevant to the therapeutic work.

For client records to be considered 'adequate', all information given to us about a client should be recorded and included in the client's file, and therefore may be accessible by the client under the DPA. This was the guidance we had received from the data protection officer, which we found challenging at the time but which is now considered both compliant with data protection principles and good professional practice. In a service that accepts clients by referral only, there can be a long-held tradition of 'informal' conversations with a referrer, where information about a client is received by the service but not always recorded. Although less likely to occur in a self-referral service, there can be occasions when managers, human resources staff and others wish to pass on information they believe is important for us to know. Recording these verbal and written correspondences in a client's file remains good practice; it reflects something about the client's situation that may be useful to the therapy, and it demonstrates a standard of transparency with all parties. In my current role, our service is much more responsive to the organisation, equally our client. If we are contacted by a manager who is concerned about an employee, we are more likely to supportively focus on the manager's anxieties and pressures and to explore with them how best we can maintain our respective boundaries, using the information they have given us whilst remaining honest with our client.

10.4 The influence of technology

The use of computers, tablets and mobile devices is an integral part of our daily life now, and increasingly a part of client–therapist interactions. Greater expectations on services to provide anonymised activity and outcome data have led to increased use of databases for reporting purposes. Individual practitioners and counselling and psychotherapy services enjoy much wider scope for using one or more forms of therapeutic interface with clients.

Due to the speed at which technology is developing, practitioners and services are best served by updates from BACP, other professional bodies, and data protection experts. Despite the device or method, the principles of the *Ethical Framework* (BACP, 2013) and the DPA bring us back to our fundamental obligations to our clients and profession, and encourage us to thoroughly consider what information we are collecting, holding, sharing and storing, and in whose interests we are doing so. Sending text messages and emails has become second nature to many, and easy to do almost without thinking.

Useful guidance on data sharing, in particular the *Data Sharing Checklists* (ICO, 2011a), and collecting and holding anonymised data can be obtained from the Information Commissioner's Office (ICO). The guidance is clear, accessible and supplemented by a variety of examples, and it is well worth becoming acquainted with it.

Another advent of our increased use of the Internet is the introduction of privacy notices. The ICO has published a *Privacy Notices: Code of Practice* and states that 'As a minimum, a privacy notice should tell people who you are, what you are going to do with their information and who it will be shared with' (ICO, 2010a). Two aspects of this code are relevant to services: informing clients that information about them will be held, and gaining their consent to do so. Many services and individual therapists will already comply with this code, usually through leaflets or websites. Gaining consent is more likely to be implied, as clients enter into a contract with a service or practitioner. Reflecting on the experience in my earlier post of using a contracting procedure that comprehensively informed clients of how data would be collected, stored and destroyed, what their rights were regarding this, and finally asking them to sign a confidentiality and data protection agreement, I now find this continues to meet the privacy notices code of practice, but it was far too onerous a process to implement. Now managing a service that has no waiting list, we find we are seeing people in much greater distress because we are seeing them nearly at point of contact, when their distress is great, and often we must choose between completing forms and being with the person in need who is in front of us. Here again we are seeking to find a balance, to equip our clients with information about the legal and therapeutic frame, giving them autonomy to make choices within it, and meeting them in their need. It is a good exercise to revisit this from time to time, and to seek feedback from clients, to determine whether enough is being done to inform clients and how they perceive it.

10.5 Is what we are doing enough?

How do we know if we have done enough, or made the 'right' decisions? Going back to my earlier experience in the original case study, we remained concerned about retaining some flexibility in order to be able to use our judgement and expertise; about how to enter into an ethical decision making process openly and with integrity; and how to present the need for some flexibility as necessary to therapeutic excellence. Accountability for decisions made (or not made) always rests much more heavily upon managers' shoulders than practitioners', and I was acutely aware of the enormous expectations of all stakeholders, and that managers – myself included – would be held to account in the event of something going wrong. As a manager and at the interface between the therapeutic work of our service and other external professionals, I became increasingly convinced that therapists cannot assume that other professionals will understand or comply with the principles, values, mechanisms and language of therapy. Indeed, despite a greater social acceptance and fluency in therapy, it remains a field set apart from others and it is our responsibility as therapists to value, articulate and protect both the known (theoretical and ethical frameworks) and the unknown (within the therapeutic encounter) in our work. This requires the use of our judgement and decision-making processes.

Consequently, our procedure was prefaced with the underpinning framework of: the Caldicott Principles; the relevant points of the Data Protection Act 1998; the early version of the BACP *Ethical Framework for Good Practice in Counselling and Psychotherapy* (2007) in force at that time; a statement about the complex and controversial nature of client confidentiality and note keeping; the potential for the therapist (with the collective agreement of their supervisor, manager and professional body) to use their judgement and to work outside of this procedure if necessary; and the aims and intentions of the service to provide safety to clients alongside an awareness of the needs of all parties. Such a preface may no longer be deemed useful or necessary, and perhaps best serves its purpose as a reminder of the rightful place for our expertise, judgement and professional decision-making processes.

10.6 The influence and impact of this procedure on our professional development and our practice

The procedure influenced the way in which we contracted with our clients, more clearly and comprehensively describing what they may expect from their counselling, and we had more fruitful discussions about what confidentiality meant to them within this setting.

At times, difficult questions arose amongst us, concerning what we were holding on to and why, whose interests were being served, and if or when there might be occasions when extensive notes should be retained. The session notes which formed part of the official client file were more consistent throughout the team, and counsellors made their own decisions regarding whether their process notes were either general (non-specific to any particular client) or intended for temporary use to aid their reflection on their work or to use in supervision and then shredded.

An interesting concept occurred to me through this process, and remains as true today, which I termed 'the life of the file'. It came from a realisation of just how much the paper file reflected the life of the therapy – perhaps not in terms of therapeutic dynamics and interventions, though in some cases, such as child protection or other areas of risk, it did involve noting decisions and interventions, but related more to the 'activities' (e.g. correspondence, attendance and cancellations) and the 'frame' within which it all takes place. By 'frame' I mean the agreements, intentions and understandings we are working to at this point in time, recognising that the framework may change over time, and if a client returns at a later date, that the agreements to which we work may be different, and those agreements or parameters would then become part of the file. This promotes a higher standard of duty of care for clients, should another counsellor need to see them in the future, enabling our service to 'hold a thread of memory' about them. My belief now is that a client's file deserves the quality of attention and level of responsibility that is invested in the therapeutic process. From a manager's perspective, attempting to create systems that stand in their own right, when staff come and go over the years, my challenge is to develop and embed this awareness within counsellors, who often view the administrative aspect of counselling as unnecessary, uninteresting and irrelevant, and who are unaccustomed to creating files and records as if their clients or other parties will see them.

Of great value to our team during this process have been the discussions and debates, all of which have rewarded us with glimpses of each other's beliefs and practices, previously assumed, and have led us to a better understanding of where we work in similar ways and where we diverge. At times this felt risky and mirrored a shared fear of external eyes interpreting and judging one's practice. We further embedded a systemic view of our role within a large organisation, and the needs of each party involved. Alongside this came new collaborations and understandings with our data protection officer, solicitors and principal insurance officer, which we hope to build upon as we regularly review and update this procedure.

It was hoped, at the outset, that counsellors would feel more confident and less fearful of being called to account for their work, with a written procedure in place. Although understanding of the legal and ethical responsibilities has increased, and our systems and practice are more efficient and professional, the hoped-for confidence has increased little. It was made very clear to us that we must make our own decisions about our procedure, based upon the varying opinions available to us. We remain acutely aware that in a field where our judgement is crucial in our daily encounters with clients, the judgement of others involved in processes with which we are unfamiliar, who have agendas of their own, and do not understand the values and mechanisms of therapy may hold much greater power than our own. However, it occurs to me that we are able to support ourselves by having a written procedure in place that states our intentions and our limitations in accordance with clear legal guidance, legitimising the need to use judgement and ethical decision-making processes and representing the therapeutic work in a legal, ethical and fair way through our documentation and contemporaneous notes held in our clients' files.

10.7 Reflections and conclusions

To have a written procedure for client confidentiality and record keeping in place, and one that is meaningful to us, feels a great achievement and a relief. The process has been lengthy: nearly ten months from the outset of our discussions to the implementation of the new procedure.

These reflections by some of the counsellors represent some of our struggles and achievements:

> The process made me realise what a minefield it is to develop a client file procedure within an organisation as large and complex as a local authority. It seemed an impossible task to come up with something that would satisfy the legal, insurance and ethical requirements and yet still not stifle us as counsellors in our creative practice with clients. Even though I was anxious about how the changes would work in practice, it feels as though we have adapted to the new way of working very well. I also feel more secure now in the knowledge that how we record has been scrutinised and considered at great length.

> Awareness of recording has influenced what I write, why, and to whom, during the counselling process, consciously observing a new discipline of self. To work towards accuracy, answerability and responsibility, which is influencing the systems we, the client and I, work in. It also impacts on the recording mechanisms of other departments in our organisation. I have started to experience a new freedom that has enabled me to feel that the client, the counsellor and the organisation are working in unity.

> I didn't initially feel comfortable with the additional contracting paperwork as part of the first session, and I feared it would inhibit clients who want to talk as soon as they come through the door. But what I find is that by going through the confidentiality agreement more thoroughly, a dialogue is opened up, we are engaged in a shared activity and it all feels much clearer for both of us.

> Originally I was unconvinced that it was important to have a set order of the file as long as it was complete. However, I feel the new client file format has had a much deeper effect on the way I feel about how this material is held and recorded. Somehow, with the extra clarity and a comprehensive system, it does feel that more respect is being expressed for the material and the work between the clients and ourselves. It is more pragmatic, but also impacts on a psychical level.

One of the most enlightening aspects of this process has been the presence of strong emotions that have arisen as therapists' ways of working have been called into question by the Data Protection Act and the increase in litigation. I have frequently noticed a tension and movement between confidence and anxiety: as beliefs and assumptions about confidentiality and note keeping were made explicit; as therapists began to write their notes 'as if' their client – or a court – were reading them; or as we realised that, despite all our expertise and our efforts to produce this procedure, there remains no guarantee that our notes will be seen by others as we intended when we wrote them.

Throughout the process I have noticed what seems to be the personal nature of note keeping to each practitioner, and how much meaning this has to them, a testament to a firmly protected relationship between therapist, client and notes. Our decision to make process notes and shred them after one month was a way of honouring the importance and life of that relationship, and this is something a court of law may never understand about our work.

It was probably not surprising, then, to sense the ripples of shock as the reality of the changes required were absorbed: 'How can my training and practice over all these years be wrong?' 'How can I make these changes and still feel I'm practising as well?' The anxiety raised here needed to be heard and enough time allowed for discussion, support and reassurance. This may have been one of the most fruitful steps towards understanding and accepting what have been, for some therapists, fundamental changes in their practice.

Our paperwork relating to the procedure continues to evolve, frustratingly at times, as I search for the best way of representing the integrity of the therapy in the file and also meet therapists' needs for straightforward administrative processes. However frustrating, this does ensure that our discussions continue. Each time I read again the key documents underpinning our procedure, I gain more insight into other possible interpretations and applications for our work with clients and this generates further refinements in the procedure. There is more clarity to be gained for us in the way that confidentiality and note keeping apply to counselling files that are considered health files, and we may implement changes as we begin to understand these issues.

Old habits die hard, and we still catch ourselves as we slip into well-worn ways of working or forget to document a phone call. For the most part, practitioners are now more at ease with the changes they have made, and as a result our contracting with clients is clearer, and our files are more consistent and cogent.

The process of developing a procedure for client confidentiality and record keeping has brought many achievements: we have found some degree of balance that we hope meets the needs and rights of all parties, at least at this point in time; we have sharpened our awareness of our responsibilities and accountabilities; we have found consistency in this core aspect of therapy while retaining our theoretical differences; we better understand each other and the work we do; we are more rigorous practitioners; what we previously held as assumed knowledge about these issues is more explicit, and we are more respectful. Surely our clients deserve and will benefit from this.

From a manager's perspective, it has been a rewarding opportunity to work with such an open and skilled team of counsellors and managers, to build new relationships within the organisation, to further the understanding of counselling with other professionals and gain their support, to improve the clinical governance of our service, and to begin to meet the legal and professional challenges of our time. We are far more aware of the changing interface between the therapeutic encounter, confidentiality, record keeping and the law, and the increasing challenges to practitioners to integrate the concept of accountability into their practice.

Our current procedure is far from exhaustive and definitive, and will continue to evolve as we become more familiar with the principles, laws and interpretations that inform it. My sense is that our procedure is heavily weighted towards fulfilling our data protection responsibilities, and that this may be at the cost of the therapy. With increasing complexity in our casework, we may choose to retain more case notes, either process or file notes, to keep the consistency and integrity of the therapy intact. Perhaps our greatest achievement is that we have begun to engage with these issues and principles, and we are more open to meeting future changes in the law and our profession.

As therapists working in organisations, we must actively address these cultural and organisational challenges. We are skilled at holding our confidence in the midst of the unknowns of the therapy; and we may also need to learn how to find such confidence in the face of unknown legal and organisational processes.

11 Mental Capacity, Vulnerable Adults and Consent

She was seeing pixies running around behind the coal scuttle last time she came to see me ... surely there is no way she could be able to give valid consent to counselling?

She was anorexic. She went into hospital because of her weight loss, and they wanted to detain her for treatment. She was furious.

She was the victim of sexual assault and the police tried to deter her from having therapy before the trial ... she said she needed it because she felt so vulnerable.

The researcher took evidence from all of the group, but some of them did not understand the questions they were asked.

He has dementia. He can understand and discuss things better at some times than others. He does not remember things for very long, these days. Can he make his own decision about whether to have therapy?

Working in accordance with a client's consent in confidentiality or record keeping will help to resolve most problems about records and information sharing. For those adults who are capable of understanding the issues in discussion and conveying their wishes, giving explicit consent for therapy and negotiating other terms of the therapeutic contract is a relatively unproblematic area of law and practice. The law will generally protect an adult's right to make autonomous decisions for themselves. However, therapists are often working with people who may be distressed or experiencing some impairment to their normal functioning. In this chapter we consider the ways in which mental impairment or other legal limitations might prevent a client from giving a valid consent to receiving therapy, and who might give valid consent on the client's behalf when this is required.

A client's ability to give legally valid consent to any medical, psychiatric or therapeutic assessment or treatment, or to enter into either a valid therapeutic contract or a legally binding contract for services, will depend upon their mental capacity to make an informed decision.

11.1 Mental capacity

Mental capacity is a legal concept, in which a person's ability to make rational, informed decisions is based, see 11.4. for the assessment of mental capacity and ability to give consent. It is presumed in law that adults and children over the age of 16 have the legal power to give or withhold consent in medical and health care matters, provided that they have mental capacity. This presumption is rebuttable, for example in the case of mental illness. For discussion of capacity and consent in decision making by and for children, please see Chapter 12.

Currently, the legislation regarding the mental capacity of adults has made a transition from the Mental Health Act 1983 and is now mainly embodied in the comprehensive Mental Capacity Act 2005, the Mental Health Act 2007 and subsidiary legislation. Relevant publications and websites are listed at the end of this book. For the relevant provisions applicable to Scotland, see the Adults with Incapacity (Scotland) Act 2000 and the Mental Health (Care and Treatment) (Scotland) Act 2003.

11.2 Mental disorder

The Mental Health Act 2007 makes a number of amendments to the Mental Health Act 1983, and also amends s. 40 of the Mental Capacity Act 2005. In s. 1, 'mental disorder' is now construed to mean 'any disorder or disability of the mind'. This definition specifically excludes drug or alcohol addiction (MHA 2007, s. 3). Interestingly, food addictions are not specifically mentioned. Under s. 2, a person with a learning disability (defined as 'a state of arrested or incomplete development of the mind which includes significant impairment of intelligence and social functioning') is not to be considered to be suffering from a mental disorder, or requiring treatment in hospital for mental disorder unless there is abnormally aggressive or seriously irresponsible conduct on his part.

11.3 Mental Health Code of Practice

The Mental Health Act 2007 in s. 8 adds to s. 118(2) of the *Mental Health Act: Code of Practice* (DH, 2003b) the requirement that a statement of principles shall be included to inform the decisions made by relevant mental health professionals under the Mental Health Act 2007. These principles should address issues including:

- respect for patients' past and present wishes and feelings;
- respect for diversity generally including, in particular, diversity of religion, culture and sexual orientation (within the meaning of s. 35 of the Equality Act 2006);
- minimising restrictions on liberty;
- involvement of patients in planning, developing and delivering care and treatment appropriate to them;
- avoidance of unlawful discrimination;
- effectiveness of treatment;
- views of carers and other interested parties;
- patient wellbeing and safety; and
- public safety.

This section also requires resources to be used efficiently and distributed equitably. We would suggest that the issues included in the *Code of Practice* should be considered when working with those with mental disorder.

11.4 Mental capacity and consent

There is no single test for mental capacity to consent. Assessment of mental capacity is not on a theoretical ability to make decisions generally, but is situation specific and depends upon the ability of the person to:

- take in and understand information including the risks and benefits of the decision to be made;
- retain the information long enough to weigh up the factors to make the decision; and
- communicate their wishes.

Part 1 of the Mental Capacity Act 2005 (MCA), which came into force on 1 October 2007, defines 'persons who lack capacity' and sets out the principles underpinning actions taken under the Act, including a checklist to be used in ascertaining their best interests. In particular, it requires that a person is not to be treated as lacking capacity simply because they may be making an unwise decision.

A person may be mentally incapacitated on a temporary basis (i.e. unconscious in hospital after an accident), or on a longer-term or permanent basis (i.e. those who suffer from severe long-term mental illness or other impairments of mental functioning) and in their case, the capacity to make medical decisions is likely to be assessed by a medical doctor or psychiatrist. The assessment of a person's mental capacity for other tasks may be made by others: for example, the decision on their capacity to make a will may be made by a lawyer; or the decision on whether they can engage in therapy may be made by the therapist. If there is any doubt, advice from an appropriate registered medical practitioner, psychiatrist or psychologist should be sought. If there is a dispute about a person's mental capacity to make an important medical decision, the matter should be referred to the High Court/Court of Session, which will then assist and, if necessary, make a ruling.

Part 1 of the MCA sets out the principles underpinning actions taken under the Act, including a checklist to be used in ascertaining their best interests. In particular, it requires that a person is not to be treated as lacking capacity simply because they may be making an unwise decision. The MCA also creates the *lasting power of attorney*, in which the donor will not only be able to appoint an attorney to carry out duties relating to property and financial affairs, but in addition, the attorney can be empowered to make decisions for the health and welfare of the donor, including giving or refusing consent for medical treatment or forms of therapy in circumstances where the donor has lost the mental capacity to do so for himself. For Scotland, see ss. 15 and 16 of the Adults with Incapacity (Scotland) Act 2000.

A person's capacity is relevant in therapy when dealing with issues of consent, especially when considering whether someone can give a valid consent to receive therapy or agree the terms on which therapy is being provided – including their wishes about the management of confidentiality and privacy. Capacity to give a valid consent may depend upon a number of factors, notably:

- For what action is consent being sought?
- Have all the potential benefits, risks and consequences of taking or not taking that action been fully explained and understood?
- Has the person retained the information long enough to properly evaluate it when making their decision?
- Can the person clearly communicate their decision (with help as appropriate) once it is made?
- Is the consent sought for the individual concerned, or is it for the treatment of another person?
- If consent is sought for another person, is that person an adult or a child?
- If consent is sought for a child, does the person giving consent have parental responsibility for the child?

For discussion of consent issues concerning children, see Chapter 12.

11.5 Consent for another person to act/make decisions on behalf of a vulnerable adult

On occasions, therapists may be in doubt as to whether a client can give valid consent for the therapeutic contract or therapists may need to determine issues regarding confidentiality and disclosure of information: for example, consent from another person may be necessary before engaging in therapeutic work with vulnerable adults, or for sharing information from their client record.

Therapists may be asked to work with vulnerable adults and to assist them to consider all the relevant issues in making difficult decisions (e.g. in family relationships) or when considering treatment or long-term planning for their future care. The therapist may need to work alongside or in co-operation with health care staff and others.

Adults in residential care may also wish to take advice from specialist professionals (e.g. lawyers, financial advisers) in making decisions about making wills, appointing attorneys, or dealing with their property or financial affairs. They may involve a therapist if they need to talk about the emotional aspects of these decisions. Some adults will have intermittent mental capacity to make specific decisions, see 11.4. Adults who do not have the mental capacity to make their own decisions may need others to give consent to sharing information, medical or psychological treatment, or for the day-to-day running of their affairs. The Court of Protection protects and manages the property and financial affairs of people with impaired mental capacity. The Public Guardianship Office provides administrative support for the Court of Protection in England and Wales. In Scotland, a similar role is fulfilled by the Office of the Public Guardian in terms of the Adults With Incapacity (Scotland) Act 2000, and in Northern Ireland, the role is fulfilled by the Office of Care and Protection, (Patients Section) under Part VIII of the Mental Health Act (Northern Ireland) Order 1986. In this legislation, the person who lacks mental capacity is referred to as the 'patient' and the person who looks after their affairs is called the 'controller.' For guidance see the booklets *Dealing with the Affairs of the*

Mentally Ill and *Handbook for Controllers* both available at www.dojni.gov.uk and www.courtsni.gov.uk.

An adult with mental capacity (the Donor) can appoint another person to act as their Attorney to run their affairs. These appointments may be made either with immediate effect or contingent upon a future loss of mental capacity. Under earlier legislation, the donor could create an *enduring power of attorney*, limited to running financial and property affairs; sources of information, forms and relevant websites are listed at the end of this book.

However, in England and Wales, this is a fast developing area of law, and on 1 October 2007 the Mental Capacity Act 2005 (MCA) came into full force, replacing the previous legislation. The MCA created the new *lasting power of attorney*. The major change is that the donor will not only be able to appoint an attorney to carry out duties relating to property and financial affairs, but in addition, the attorney can be empowered to make decisions on the health and welfare of the donor, including giving or refusing consent for medical treatment or therapy in circumstances where the donor has lost the mental capacity to do so for himself. The lasting power of attorney must be registered under the Court of Protection Rules 2007 immediately it is to be implemented. Information, forms and guidance from the government are available on the websites and addresses listed at the end of the book. For Scotland, see ss. 15 and 16 of the Adults With Incapacity (Scotland) Act 2000. In Northern Ireland, the law on mental capacity is in the process of change, following the recommendations of the Bamford Committee (DoJNI, 2007).

11.5.1 'Advance directive', 'advance statement', 'living will' or 'advance decision'

Therapists may be asked to assist clients in developing plans or expressing their wishes for present or future health care arrangements. While they have mental capacity, some clients may wish to make an 'advance directive' (otherwise known as an 'advance statement' or 'living will') about the forms of medical treatment to which they may (or may not) consent if they should subsequently lose the capacity to decide for themselves. Advance directives refusing treatment are legally binding, provided that they are made without duress, while the person had mental capacity, and that the circumstances to be applied are clear. Sections 24–26 of the MCA empower those who wish to do so to make 'advance decisions' concerning their wish to refuse specified treatment.

There are conditions under the new MCA. An advance decision is not applicable to life-sustaining treatment unless: the decision is verified by a statement to the effect that it is to apply to that treatment even if life is at risk; and the decision and statement comply with these rules:

- it is in writing;
- it is signed by the person or by another in their presence and by their direction, the signature is made or acknowledged by the person in the presence of a witness; and
- the witness signs it, or acknowledges his signature, in the person's presence.

There are legal provisions in the MCA to limit the types of decision that can be made by an attorney, to safeguard against misuse of advance decisions, to appoint mental capacity advocates and visitors, and to prevent the neglect or mistreatment of people with mental incapacity. See also the Adults With Incapacity (Scotland) Act 2000 and the Mental Health (Care and Treatment) (Scotland) Act 2003. Further information, the full text of the MCA, the Court of Protection Rules 2007 and government guidance including links to the relevant law, including Northern Ireland, are available from the organisations and websites listed at the end of the book.

General (non-emergency) treatment

Consent will be required either from an adult who has mental capacity, or from a person with legal responsibility for the care of a vulnerable adult with mental incapacity. Any kind of physical or psychological examination or treatment carried out without valid consent could render the practitioner liable for assault in civil or criminal law, or both.

Emergency medical treatment

If urgent medical treatment is required and there is grave risk to the client if emergency treatment is not given, medical practitioners may rely on their own clinical judgement if the patient is unable to give consent (e.g. is unconscious) and if anyone else in a position to give consent is unavailable. In the event of a psychiatric emergency, the Mental Health Act 2007 updates the Mental Health Act 1983, providing a legal basis for urgent admission to hospital and, where necessary, detention for psychiatric treatment with the signed approval of authorised doctors.

Counsellors and psychotherapists faced with clients in situations requiring urgent psychological treatment may need to make urgent referrals and disclosures for the benefit of the client. If a practitioner considers assessment or treatment necessary in the best interests of the client's safety or that of others, and consent is not forthcoming from the client, or anyone else entitled to give it, the counsellor has a discretion to make a disclosure or referral for the benefit of the client, which, if made in good faith and on reasonable grounds, may be defensible in the public interest.

The wishes of a child (whether competent under the *Gillick* guidelines or not) under the age of 18 years may be overruled by the High Court in the best interests of the child. However, once a person reaches maturity (i.e. 18 years of age), even the High Court cannot overrule their wishes about medical examination, treatment or therapy unless for any reason they lack the mental capacity to make their own decision. Note the provisions of the Mental Capacity Act 2005, under which power may be given to a 'deputy' appointed by Power or Attorney and the Court of Protection to make health and welfare decisions for another adult who does not have the mental capacity to make their own decisions.

Vulnerable adults

In relation to *lasting powers of attorney*, the attorney can be empowered to make decisions for the health and welfare of the donor, now including (at least in principle) giving or refusing consent for medical or psychiatric treatment or forms of counselling and psychotherapy in circumstances where the donor has lost the mental capacity to do so for himself. This may raise ethical and practical issues relevant to the client's consent for therapy, for example in relation to autonomy and accountability. There may be situations arising where therapy is appropriate but the client lacks the mental capacity to consent and it might be helpful for practitioners to address the issue of consent given by others for the treatment of adult clients. This may be particularly relevant to therapists working with clients with severe mental illness, or degenerative conditions such as dementia or Alzheimer's disease.

For therapy with children and vulnerable adults who are victims and pre-trial therapy with children and vulnerable adult witnesses, see Chapter 13.

12 Children, Capacity and Consent

She left home at 16 and came for counselling. She said that I was to tell no one about the abuse by her father, but I was worried because her younger sister is 11 this year and she might be the next one now that her sister has left home.

He was 14, but very bright and spiritual and he had strong religious beliefs. He wanted to decide for himself whether to have a blood transfusion, and he was adamant that he did not want one. His mother believed that his immortal soul would be in danger if he was given the blood. His father wanted him to have the transfusion as he believed that the sickle cell anaemia would kill his son otherwise.

She was eight months pregnant. She went into hospital after a road accident, and they did a Caesarean without her consent ... when she regained consciousness she was furious.

I was working with a 13-year-old lad, and we were getting on very well in the counselling. He can't speak very well, but I understood him and felt that he was beginning to trust me, then one day his mother came in and said that I was to stop working with him.

In this chapter, when we refer to 'child' and 'children' we adopt the legal definition of 'child' from the Children Act 1989, s. 105 and the Children (Scotland) Act 1995, s. 15(1) as any person who has not yet attained the age of 18 years. When we refer to 'young person' in this chapter, we mean a child over the age of 16 years. The principles of law in this chapter apply to the UK, but there are regional differences in law and practice, and the law in Scotland is covered where specifically mentioned. For child care practice in Wales, see CAFCASS Cymru and the Welsh government guidance and references at the end of this book. For an overview of relevant legislation and child law and practice in Northern Ireland, see the recent publication by BAAF: *Child Care Law: A summary of the law in Northern Ireland* (Long, 2013).

For an explanation of what is meant by 'mental capacity' and 'consent' as legal concepts, see Chapter 11.

Working with appropriate consent is one of the best ways of solving any problems over confidentiality or record keeping. Therapists are often working with children and young people who may be distressed or experiencing some impairment to their normal functioning or who have not yet reached legal adulthood. In this chapter we will consider the situations in which a child can give valid consent to receiving therapy, and in circumstances when the child cannot give their own valid legal consent, who can give consent on the child's behalf when this is required.

A child or young person's ability to give legally valid consent to any medical, psychiatric or therapeutic assessment or treatment, or to enter into either a valid therapeutic contract or a legally binding contact for services, will depend upon their mental capacity to make an informed decision: that is, whether they can fully understand and agree the terms on which therapy is being provided, and the context in which it is offered. It is presumed in UK law that adults and children over the age of 16 have the legal power to give or withhold consent in medical and health care matters, provided that they have full mental capacity. This presumption is rebuttable, for example in the case of mental illness. A refusal of necessary medical or psychiatric treatment by young people over the age of 16 but under the age of 18 may be overruled by the High Court/Court of Session (more of this later).

On occasions, therapists may be in doubt as to whether a child client can give valid consent for the therapeutic contract. Therapists may be asked to assist children and families to consider all the relevant issues in making difficult decisions, for example in family relationships, or when considering treatment or long-term planning for a child's future care. The therapist may need to work alongside or in co-operation with schools, health care staff and others. Consent from another person may be necessary before engaging in therapeutic work with children or young people or for sharing information about the child.

12.1 Consent: children and young people under the age of 18

Therapists working with children and young people will need to have valid consent to enter into the therapeutic contract. A child is defined in law as a person under the age of 18 (the Children Act 1989, s. 105 and the Children (Scotland) Act 1995, s. 15(1)). Under the Family Law Reform Act 1969 and the Age of Legal Capacity (Scotland) Act 1991, a child aged 16 or over can give valid legal consent to medical or psychological treatment, provided that they have the necessary mental capacity.

In England, the refusal of medical treatment by a young person over the age of 16 with mental capacity may nevertheless be overruled by the High Court where necessary. All too often, professionals make the erroneous assumption that all parents can make medical and therapeutic decisions for their children. As a result, therapists and other professionals may inadvertently act without appropriate legal consent. This section seeks to clarify the law in this field.

'Parent' is usually interpreted as meaning the biological mother and father or adoptive parent of a child, but in some legislation the term may include other people who are not the biological parents but who have parental responsibility for the child. People may wrongly assume that all parents have the power to make decisions for their children. This is emphatically (and perhaps surprisingly) not so. The ability of a parent, or anyone else, to make a decision for their child depends on whether they have 'parental responsibility', which is the legal basis for making decisions about a child, including consent for psychological therapy or medical treatment.

12.2 Parental responsibility

The Children Act 1989 (CA 1989) created the concept of 'parental responsibility', defined in s. 3(1) as 'all the rights, duties, powers, responsibilities and authority which by law the parent of a child has in relation to a child and his property'. In England, Northern Ireland and Wales, parental responsibility may subsist until the child reaches eighteen years, or in some circumstances it may expire or be brought to an end earlier by a court order (see Hershman and McFarlane (2013)). For Scotland, see the Children (Scotland) Act 1995, s. 1. More than one person can have parental responsibility for a child at the same time. It cannot be transferred or surrendered, but aspects of parental responsibility can be delegated (see the CA 1989, s. 2(9) and the Children (Scotland) Act 1995, s. 3(5)). For Northern Ireland, see the Children (Parental Responsibility Agreement) Regulations, Northern Ireland 1996, and also for parental responsibility in Northern Ireland see (Long, 2013).

12.2.1 Mothers and married fathers

Every mother (married or not) of a child born to her, and every father who is married to the child's mother at the time of or subsequent to the conception of their child, automatically has parental responsibility for their child, which may be shared with others, but will be lost only by death or adoption.

12.2.2 Unmarried fathers

Unmarried fathers may acquire parental responsibility for their biological child in one of several ways, the first three of which can only be removed by order of the court:

- In England, from 1 December 2003, an unmarried father automatically acquires parental responsibility for his child if, with his consent, he is named as the child's father on the registration of the child's birth. This law does not operate retrospectively. For Scotland, see the Family Law (Scotland) Act 2006, s. 23.
- By formal Parental Responsibility Agreement signed by the mother and father, witnessed by an officer at court, then registered. Copies may be obtained for a fee, in a similar way to obtaining a birth certificate: see Parental Responsibility Agreement Regulations S.I.1991/1478 and the Children (Scotland) Act 1995, s. 4.
- A court making an order awarding parental responsibility to him, consistent with the interests of the child.

Parental responsibility can also be acquired by a child's biological father through:

- Parental responsibility awarded along with a residence order directing the child to live with the father.
- Appointment as child's guardian (operates when appointment takes effect after the death of the appointer).
- Marriage to the child's mother.
- Adoption of the child.

12.2.3 Acquisition of parental responsibility by others

Parental responsibility may be acquired by others in a variety of ways:

- Adoption. In this case, the parental responsibility held by all others prior to the adoption will be lost.
- The child's mother may enter into a parental responsibility agreement with her married or civil partner (subject to the agreement of the father if he has parental responsibility) (CA 1989, a 4A (1) as inserted by the Adoption and Children Act (ACA) 2002, s. 112 and amended by the Civil Partnership Act (CPA) 2004, s. 75 (1)). The married or civil partner of a mother may seek a parental responsibility order from the court (CA 1989, a 4A (1) as inserted by ACA 2002, s. 112 and amended by CPA 2004, s. 75 (1)). In Scotland, the married or civil partner may seek an order under s. 11 of the Children (Scotland) Act 1995.
- The child's father (if he has parental responsibility) may enter into a parental responsibility agreement with his married or civil partner (subject to the agreement of the child's mother) (CA 1989, a 4A (1) as inserted by ACA 2002, s. 112 and amended by CPA 2004, s. 75 (1)).
- The married or civil partner of a father with parental responsibility may seek a parental responsibility order from the court (CA 1989, a 4A (1) as inserted by ACA 2002, s. 112 and amended by CPA 2004, s. 75 (1)).
- Step-parent adoption by the married or civil partner of the mother of a child born through assisted reproduction (the Human Fertilisation and Embryology Act (HFEA) 1990 was not amended by CPA 2004).
- A parental order under s. 30 HFEA 1990 declaring a married couple to be the parents of a child born through surrogacy arrangements. This order operates like adoption, and the child's surrogate birth mother loses her parental responsibility.

The right of a civil partner to acquire parental responsibility in the examples in 12.2.3. above were extended to married partners as a result of new legislation allowing same sex marriage, see the Marriage (Same Sex Couples) Act 2013.

In the other situations listed below, parental responsibility may be acquired and shared with those who already have it in relation to the child, but the exercise of parental responsibility may be limited by the court in various ways.

Parental responsibility may also be acquired through:

- Residence order awarded by the court (CA 1989, s. 8 and s. 12), Children (Scotland) Act (C(S)A) 1995, s. 11.
- Guardianship (CA 1989, s. 5), C(S)A 1995, s. 7.
- Care order made under CA 1989, s. 31 (parental responsibility is acquired by the local authority), see CA 1989, s. 33 (3), s. 86 C(S)A 1995.
- Emergency Protection Order (but the duration and exercise of parental responsibility is limited).
- Special guardianship.
- There is an additional provision in s. 3 (5) of the Children Act 1989 that those without parental responsibility may 'do what is reasonable in all the circumstances to safeguard and promote the welfare' of a child in their care, for example allowing a babysitter or relative to take a child in their care for medical help in an emergency, see also C(S)A 1995, s. 5.

12.3 Medical or psychiatric examination, therapy or assessment of children

12.3.1 What constitutes valid consent in law for medical examination for diagnosis or treatment of a child or young person under the age of 18?

- Consent of a person with parental responsibility for the child.
- Consent of the young person, if aged over 16 (under the Family Law Reform Act 1969, s. 8 (1), Age of Legal Capacity (Scotland) Act 1991, s. 1).
- Consent of a child aged under 16, if they have sufficient age and understanding of the issues involved and the consequences of consent (i.e. the child has sufficient age and understanding to make his own medical decisions as defined in the case of *Gillick v West Norfolk and Wisbech Area Health Authority and Another* [1986] (the Gillick case), Age of Legal Capacity (Scotland) Act 1991, s. 2 (1) and (4).
- A direction of the High Court/Court of Session.

A distinction must be made at the outset between examinations and assessments for diagnosis and treatment including therapy, and those purely for forensic (court) purposes.

12.3.2 General (non-emergency) treatment

Consent will be required from an older child (16 or over), or the child if under 16 but has sufficient age and understanding to make his own medical decisions in the guidelines in the Gillick case. For a younger child, consent is needed from a person with parental responsibility for the child (see 12.3). Any kind of physical examination carried out without such consent could render the practitioner liable for assault in civil or criminal law, or both.

12.3.3 Emergency medical treatment

If this is medically required and there is grave risk to the child if emergency treatment is not given, practitioners may rely on their own clinical judgement if those in a position to give consent are unavailable.

12.3.4 Where treatment is necessary but there is no consent

If a practitioner considers assessment or treatment necessary and consent is not forthcoming from any of those entitled to give it, the High Court may use its powers to act in the best interests of a child under 18, authorising the requisite assessment or treatment as lawful. If a problem arises concerning consent, the legal department of the local authority or health service, and professional organisations, may provide advice and assistance, and a direction may be sought from the High Court, if necessary using the 'out of hours' court service for emergencies.

12.3.5 What if those with parental responsibility refuse, but the child consents?

If the child is over 16 or has mental competence to make decisions in the context of the Gillick case, the child's consent is valid.

If the child is not competent in the context of the Gillick case, the child's consent is not valid. If examination or treatment is advised, obtain legal advice and if necessary a court order may be sought. The High Court will make an order if it is in the best interests of the child and the parents' consent is being unreasonably withheld.

12.3.6 What if those with parental responsibility for the child disagree with each other?

If the child is over 16 or competent in the context of the Gillick case and the child consents, this is valid and can be accepted.

If the child is not competent in the context of the Gillick case, the child's consent is not valid. If examination or treatment is advised, the parties in disagreement should obtain legal advice and, if necessary, they may apply to the court to resolve their dispute with a Specific Issue Order made under s. 8 of the Children Act 1989 and s. 11(2)(e) of the Children (Scotland) Act 1995.

12.3.7 What if a child refuses a medical examination, assessment, treatment or therapy?

A young child (i.e. under the age of 16 and not competent under the guidelines in the 'Gillick case') cannot give a valid consent, and so they also cannot give a valid refusal. If there is any issue about the competence of the child to make an informed decision, this issue can, if necessary, be referred for expert opinion and/or to the High Court.

A child over the age of 16 has the right to refuse medical examination or treatment, see the Family Law Reform Act 1969, s. 8 (1), but in some situations the High Court may overrule their refusal.

A child under the age of 16 has a similar right of refusal if they are of sufficient age and understanding to comprehend their circumstances and the potential benefits and risks of the treatment proposed to make an informed decision. They must have an understanding of the issues, including the risks and benefits involved and the consequences of refusal: that is, the child is 'competent' as defined in the case of *Gillick v West Norfolk and Wisbech Area Health Authority and Another* [1986]. However, the High Court can accept parental consent or it may overrule a refusal in the best interests of the child. In the case of *Re W (A Minor: Medical Treatment)* [1992], Lord Donaldson, supported by Lord Balcombe, said unequivocally, 'No minor of whatever age has power, by refusing consent to treatment, to override a consent to treatment by someone who has parental responsibility for the minor, and a fortiori a consent by the court.' In *Re L (Medical treatment: Gillick competency)*

[1998], Lord Donaldson reiterated that position, adding that nevertheless, such a refusal is a very important consideration in making clinical judgements, and for the parents and the court in deciding whether themselves to give consent.

The High Court will make decisions in situations where doctors, children, young people, (or those with parental responsibility) face serious dilemmas. If a child over 16, or competent under the 'Gillick' guidelines, has a diagnosed clinical need for treatment but refuses to have it, despite those with parental responsibility for the child having given their consent, if the doctors feel that the proposed treatment is medically necessary, but feel that in all conscience they cannot (or should not) proceed against the child's wishes, legal advice may be sought and the matter referred to the High Court, which is empowered to make a decision in the best interests of a child under the age of 18. The High Court may then, after considering all the circumstances, declare the proposed medical treatment to be lawful.

Once a person reaches maturity (i.e. 18 years of age), even the High Court cannot overrule their wishes about medical examination, treatment or therapy unless for any reason they lack the mental capacity to make their own decision. Note the provisions of ss. 15–20 of the Mental Capacity Act 2005, under which a 'deputy' may be appointed by the Court of Protection to make health and welfare decisions for another adult who does not have the mental capacity to make their own decisions.

12.4 Control by courts of examinations of children for purely forensic (court) purposes

Therapists may be asked to carry out an assessment of a child or young person and possibly also to provide a report and attend court to give evidence. In the case of child protection or family conflict, for example care proceedings or contested contact matters, one or more of the parties may disagree with the assessment and require a second opinion. Repeated medical and psychiatric examinations for forensic purposes can cause a child unnecessary stress. The Children Act 1989 and the Children (Scotland) Act 1995 and their subsidiary rules empower the court within the context of court proceedings including emergency protection, child assessment, interim care, and care or supervision applications, to regulate such examinations and make appropriate directions, which may nominate the practitioner(s) to carry out the examination or assessment, the venue, those to be present, and those to whom the results may be given. Breaches of these rules are viewed seriously, and the court has power to disallow any evidence obtained without compliance with the rules.

12.4.1 The child's right to refuse forensic examinations and assessments

A child of sufficient age and understanding may make an informed decision to refuse a forensic examination or assessment, even if it has been authorised by the court. A child's ability to refuse will depend on factors including age, understanding and the information given. Practitioners should ensure that a child who is competent to make a decision is given an explanation appropriate for their age of what is proposed and the potential consequences of refusal. A note should be made of the information given to the child and of the substance of the questions and answers on which the practitioner's assessment of the child's capability to make decisions is based. That note may later be required in court if the child's capability is questioned.

In care, supervision, child assessment and emergency protection proceedings brought under the Children Act 1989 and child protection proceedings under the Children (Scotland) Act 1995, a Children's Guardian/Principal Reporter should be available to assist the court in ascertaining the child's views and advising the court on the best interests of the child. When a child is brought to a doctor or therapist for a forensic examination or assessment in accordance with a direction of the court, but then refuses to comply, the examination or therapy should not proceed, but the matter should be referred back to the court.

13 Victims, and Pre-trial Therapy with Vulnerable Adults and Children

He had an accident that damaged his ability to speak. He wants to give evidence. Can he do so? What help is there for him in court?

She suffers from mental illness – and I'd like to support her in court. Is she a vulnerable witness? If she is, does this entitle her to my support?

He remembers the mugging and it still upsets him, especially at night. If I give him therapeutic help for the post-traumatic stress, can he still give evidence about the mugging if they catch the criminal?

He has dementia, and they think he is not able to give any evidence, but they have not made a final decision. He says that he needs some support from his GP and the surgery counsellor for his stress. How can we help him without compromising the case?

My client is 14, and she had told me that she was 'date raped'. She wants to tell the police and knows that the man may be prosecuted. How can I help her as a therapist before the trial? Are there rules or procedures that I have to follow when working with her?

The lad is subject to an interim care order and they want me to give evidence at the full care proceedings hearing. I have not given evidence before – what should I know and how can I find the information I need?

Working in pre-trial therapy with children and vulnerable adult witnesses is complex. The police, courts and helping professions attempt to meet the needs of the victim and also that of justice, and various guidance documents have been in the process of development. There have been changes in the system of pre-trial support, part of which includes referral for counselling and psychotherapy. This chapter explores issues that extend beyond the strict limits of confidentiality and record keeping, because legal proceedings may not only pose considerable challenges to confidentiality, but also may create additional responsibilities for record keeping and therapists' accountability for their records, particularly in relation to pre-trial work with children and vulnerable adults as victims and as witnesses. The full raft of guidance available on work with witnesses is available on the Crown Prosecution Service (CPS) website (www.cps.gov.uk) and is listed in the references at the end of the book. Please note that some of the guidance documents show their issue date, but, strangely, not all of them. Some on the website are revisions of earlier documents. The current versions of all the guidance listed can be read online or downloaded as PDFs from the CPS website.

Not all successful criminal investigations lead directly to a prosecution. In some cases, issues are identified which lead the Director of Public Prosecutions (DPP) and the CPS to pursue an alternative course. The *Code for Crown Prosecutors* (CPS, 2013) available at www.cps.gov.uk, gives guidance on the principles to be applied when prosecutors are making decisions about prosecutions. A major concern is the protection of vulnerable witnesses, balanced against the need to maintain justice.

In the *Code for Crown Prosecutors*, there are particular considerations for the victim, see:

'c) What are the circumstances of and the harm caused to the victim?

The circumstances of the victim are highly relevant. The greater the vulnerability of the victim, the more likely it is that a prosecution is required. This includes where a position of trust or authority exists between the suspect and victim.

A prosecution is also more likely if the offence has been committed against a victim who was at the time a person serving the public.

Prosecutors must also have regard to whether the offence was motivated by any form of discrimination against the victim's ethnic or national origin, gender, disability, age, religion or belief, sexual orientation or gender identity; or the suspect demonstrated hostility towards the victim based on any of those characteristics. The presence of any such motivation or hostility will mean that it is more likely that prosecution is required.

In deciding whether a prosecution is required in the public interest, prosecutors should take into account the views expressed by the victim about the impact that the offence has had. In appropriate cases, this may also include the views of the victim's family.'

(CPS, 2013, section 4.12, p. 8)

The impact on the health and welfare of the victim may be a cogent consideration for the prosecutor when deciding whether to go ahead with a prosecution, but the view must be balanced with the need for justice:

'Prosecutors also need to consider if a prosecution is likely to have an adverse effect on the victim's physical or mental health, always bearing in mind the seriousness of the offence. If there is evidence that prosecution is likely to have an adverse impact on the victim's health it may make a prosecution less likely, taking into account the victim's views.

However, the CPS does not act for victims or their families in the same way as solicitors act for their clients, and prosecutors must form an overall view of the public interest.'

(CPS, 2013, section 4.12, p. 9)

It may be, therefore, that the needs of a vulnerable victim or child witness are such that they are unable to give cogent evidence; or that the trial would have such a deleterious impact on a vulnerable witness's health and welfare that CPS may decide not to prosecute. The pre-trial therapy guidance makes it absolutely clear that the welfare of the vulnerable witness is considered of primary importance.

Witnesses and victims may not always come within the definition of 'vulnerable' but still may need support. Those that are regarded as 'vulnerable' either because of their own personal circumstances, or from the nature of the crime, or both, are automatically entitled to support. In 13.1 we explore the definition of 'vulnerable' in this context. For the current arrangements for witness and victim support, see the DPP's *Code of Practice for Victims of Crime* (MoJ, 2013); and its supporting public information materials; *The Witness Charter: Standards of Care for Witnesses in the Criminal Justice System* (MoJ, 2013); and *Working with Victims and Witnesses* (MoJ, 2013), all available online at http://www.justice.gov.uk. The referral methods and levels of support offered are explored at 13.3–13.5.

13.1 Who is a vulnerable adult?

The term 'vulnerable adult' (as opposed to the more specific term 'vulnerable or intimidated witness') might include a person who has a mental illness, a mental disorder, or a person who lacks mental capacity. Some of these terms are defined below. For a definition of mental capacity, see Chapter 11, which explores mental capacity and consent in relation to therapeutic work with vulnerable adults. Briefly, for reference here, the Mental Health Act 1983 is amended by the Mental Capacity Act 2005, the Mental Health Act 2007 and the Mental Capacity Act 2005 (Appropriate Body) (England) Regulations 2006 S.I. 2006 No. 2810. For Scotland, see the Adults with Incapacity (Scotland) Act 2000 and the Mental Health (Care and Treatment) (Scotland) Act 2003.

Section 1 of the Mental Health Act 2007, in defining 'mental disorder' as 'any disorder or disability of the mind,' does not include drug or alcohol addiction. Under s. 2 of that Act, a person with a learning disability (defined as 'a state of arrested or incomplete development of the mind which includes significant impairment of intelligence and social functioning') is not to be considered to be suffering from a mental disorder, or requiring treatment in hospital for mental disorder unless there is abnormally aggressive or seriously irresponsible conduct on his part. Those working in therapy or research with clients with drug or alcohol addictions or learning disability therefore are not treated under this legislation as working with clients with mental disorder. Interestingly, food addictions are not included in the definition.

Section 8 of the Mental Health Act 2007 adds to s. 118(2) of the *Mental Health Act 1983 Code of Practice* the requirement that a statement of principles shall be included to inform the decisions made by relevant mental health professionals under the Mental Health Act 2007. These principles should address issues including:

- respect for patients' past and present wishes and feelings;
- respect for diversity generally including, in particular, diversity of religion, culture and sexual orientation (within the meaning of s. 35 of the Equality Act 2006);

- minimising restrictions on liberty;
- involvement of patients in planning, developing and delivering care and treatment appropriate to them;
- avoidance of unlawful discrimination;
- effectiveness of treatment;
- views of carers and other interested parties;
- patient wellbeing and safety; and
- public safety.

This section also requires resources to be used efficiently and distributed equitably. We would suggest that the issues included in the *Mental Health Act 1983 Code of Practice* should be considered when working with those with mental disorder, and, although not compulsory, are relevant to all work with vulnerable adults.

13.2 Young people, children and police enquiries

Research and the forensic enquiries made by police and the courts are similar, in that the quality and reliability of the evidence gathered is regarded as important. It is relevant therefore to consider the approach taken by the police and courts to vulnerable witnesses, whether children or adults, from this perspective. A 'vulnerable adult' or 'vulnerable witness' is defined by law and government guidance in various ways, according to the context in which the terms are used (see section 13.1).

Under current PACE legislation, 17-year-olds are treated as adults while held by police, which means their parents or another 'appropriate adult' are not contacted to offer support and advice if the young person is taken into custody, unless they are deemed to be 'vulnerable'. The situation has been criticised by the Prisons Inspectorate, routinely pointing to the fact that under all other UK law and international treaty obligations, 17-year-olds are treated as juveniles. The previous Labour government committed to 'bringing the legislation into line' with other policies, but the present government is currently of the view that changes to the system will not be made.

Under the UN Convention on the Rights of the Child, 17-year-olds should be treated as children by all agencies of the law including police. Practitioners working with children and young people might make carers and/or those with parental responsibility for children aware of this provision.

13.3 'Vulnerable witnesses' in the context of court proceedings (eligible for 'special measures')

Under recent guidance, the *Vulnerable and Intimidated Witnesses: A Police Service Guide* (MoJ, 2011a), certain witnesses may be regarded as 'vulnerable or intimidated', and entitled to special measures for their protection in court. For a definition of special measures, see section 13.4.

13.3.1 Young people under the age of 18

Under s. 16 of the Youth Justice and Criminal Evidence Act 1999 (as amended by the Coroners and Justice Act 2009). Children are defined as vulnerable by reason of their age (s. 16[1]). The Act makes all children under 18 years of age, appearing as defence or prosecution witnesses in criminal proceedings, eligible for special measures to assist them to give their evidence in court. See also, *Guidelines on Prosecuting Cases of Child Sexual Abuse,* an online document available on www.cps. gov.uk. This places an emphasis on the best interests of the victim or witness (see sections 32–34), and confirms that there should be provision for pre-trial therapy for child witnesses, referring to the CPS guidance *Provision of Therapy for Child Witnesses Prior to a Criminal Trial* discussed in 13.5.

13.3.2 Vulnerable adult witnesses

The document *Vulnerable and Intimidated Witnesses: A Police Service Guide* (MoJ, 2011a), contains some prompts intended to assist in recognising vulnerable adult witnesses.

In addition to the witness who is under the age of 18 at the time of the hearing, three other types of vulnerable witness are identified by s. 16(2) Youth Justice and Criminal Evidence Act 1999. Briefly, vulnerable adult witnesses are those who have a mental disorder, learning disability or physical disorder/disability that is likely to have an impact on the quality of their evidence, including:

- witnesses who have a mental disorder or any disability of the mind as defined by the Mental Health Act 1983 (as amended by the Mental Health Act 2007);
- witnesses significantly impaired in relation to intelligence and social functioning (witnesses who have a learning disability); and
- witnesses who have a physical disability – witnesses in this category are only eligible if quality of evidence that is given by them is likely to be diminished by reason of the disorder or disability (Youth Justice and Criminal Evidence Act 1999: s. 16[1][b]).

Wherever a reference is made in the legislation to the 'quality of a witness's evidence' for the purposes of defining a witness as vulnerable or intimidated, and in terms of access to special measures, it refers to the 'completeness, coherence and accuracy' of the evidence, and 'coherence' refers to a witness's ability in giving evidence to give answers which address the questions put to the witness and can be understood both individually and collectively (s. 16[5]).

The court must take account of the views of the witness in determining whether a witness may be regarded as vulnerable by virtue of a disorder or disability (s. 16[4]).

Achieving Best Evidence in Criminal Proceedings: Guidance on Interviewing Victims and Witnesses, and Using Special Measures (MoJ, 2011b) (Achieving Best Evidence) was produced by the Ministry of Justice, the CPS, the Department for Education, the Department of Health and the Welsh Assembly government, and describes good practice in interviewing witnesses, including victims, to enable them to give their best evidence in criminal proceedings. It recognises mental disorder, but states that this may be the most difficult category to identify for support through special measures because of the fluctuating nature of many mental disorders. The provisions from the Mental Health Act 2007 (which we explored earlier in section 13.1) may be relevant for consideration. A person with mental disorder may need special assistance only at times of crisis.

Note that a brief interview may not reveal mental disorder, but if clear evidence and/or a clear diagnosis becomes available which suggests the need for special measures, then these should take account of any emotional difficulties so as to enable the witness to give evidence with the least possible distress. Currently there is no accepted and consistent approach to the assessment of witness competence. It is likely that varying criteria may be used by experts called to make assessments. In addition, mental instability might be aggravated by alcohol, drugs and withdrawal from drugs. The effect may be temporary, and the time elapsed before a witness is able to give clear evidence will vary according to the type and severity of the intoxication from a few hours to a few days.

Achieving Best Evidence (MoJ, 2011b) also defines specific terms, including:

Significant Impairment of Intelligence and Social Functioning (Learning Disability)

2.67 Learning disability is not a description of one disability, but a collection of many different factors that might affect a person's ability in relation to learning and social functioning to greatly varying degrees. While some 200 causes of learning disability have been identified, most diagnoses are still 'unspecified learning disabilities'. People with high support needs may be easily identified but people with mild or moderate learning disabilities may be more difficult to identify.

2.68 It is impossible to give a single description of competence in relation to any particular disability, because there is such a wide range of abilities within each in terms of degree of intellectual and social impairment. However, there are some indicators that may help identify a witness with a learning disability.

2.69 Though generalisations cannot be made, some characteristics may exist in relation to some syndromes. For example, witnesses with autistic spectrum disorder, which includes Kanner's syndrome and Asperger's syndrome, have a huge range of abilities/disabilities, but:

They often have difficulty in making sense of the world and in understanding relationships;

They are likely to have little understanding of the emotional pain or problems of others; and

They may display great knowledge of certain topics and have an excellent vocabulary, but could be pedantic and literal and may have obsessional interests.

Some people with learning disabilities are reluctant to reveal that they have a disability, and may be quite articulate, so that it is not always immediately obvious that they do not understand the proceedings in whole or in part.

Physical Disability

2.71 Recognition of this type of disability is less likely to be a problem, although some disabilities may be hidden, but it is important to be aware of whether or how a physical disability may affect the person's ability to give a clear statement. Most witnesses will be able to give evidence with support.

2.72 Some physical disabilities may require support. Hearing or speech difficulties may require the attendance of a skilled interpreter and/or intermediary.

Witnesses with a Mental Disorder

2.73 A mental disorder does not preclude the giving of reliable evidence. However, for many disorders there is a need to protect the witness from additional stress and provide support to enable them to give reliable evidence. The recall of traumatic events can cause significant distress, and recognition of the mental state of the witness and its effect on their behaviour is crucial. There is also the need to ensure that the type of behaviour is identified, as far as possible.

2.74 Witnesses with a mental disorder, such as schizophrenia or other delusional disorders, may give unreliable evidence through delusional memories or by reporting hallucinatory experiences, which are accurate as far as the witness is concerned but bear no relationship to reality (e.g. they might describe a non-existent crime). Challenges to these abnormal ideas may cause extreme reactions and/or distress. Interviewers should probe these accounts carefully, sensitively and in a non-judgemental way with a view to identifying which elements of the account may be delusional and which elements might have a firmer foundation in reality.

2.75 Witnesses may suffer from various forms of anxiety through fear of authority, exposure or retribution. Extreme fear may result in phobias, panic attacks or unjustified fears of persecution. Anxious witnesses may wish to please, they may tell the interviewer what they believe they wish to hear or fabricate imaginary experiences to compensate for loss of memory. The evidence given by depressed witnesses may be influenced by feelings of guilt, helplessness or hopelessness. Witnesses with antisocial or borderline traits may present with a range of behaviours such as deliberately giving false evidence. These disorders cause the most difficulties and contention in diagnosis, and require very careful assessment.

2.76 Witnesses, particularly some older witnesses, may also have dementia, which can cause cognitive impairment. A psychiatrist or clinical psychologist with experience of working with older people should be asked to assess their ability to give reliable evidence and the effect such a procedure might have on their health and mental welfare.

2.77 Witnesses with a mental disorder may show some of the behaviour seen in witnesses with a learning disability, such as confusion, memory loss and impaired reasoning. For this reason, many of the interview practices that are likely to help witnesses with a learning disability may also benefit witnesses with a mental disorder. Properly preparing the witness for the interview may help to identify and reduce confusion, emotional distress and anxiety. Cognition may not be an immediate difficulty, but attention to the way a statement is given and how questions are posed must always be considered.

2.78 The witness may wish to please the person in authority. They may be suspicious of the person, aggressive, or wish to impress the interviewer. Interviewing teams should be aware of such possibilities. Consultation with people who know the witness well should give some indication of their likely behaviour and some suggestions as to how interviewers can best interact with the witness.

2.79 Confusion may be exacerbated by the use of drugs or alcohol or withdrawal from drugs. An assessment should include information as to how this is likely to affect the interview, and how long this effect is likely to last.

2.80 Preparation of the witness for the interview and a rapport stage prior to formal questioning during the interview is essential. This will allow the witness to have some familiarity with the personnel who will be involved in the interview, including the interviewer, interview monitor and intermediary (where used).

Witnesses with a Significant Impairment of Intelligence and Social Functioning (Learning Disability)

2.81 Some witnesses with a learning disability may wish to please people in authority. Some may be suspicious of people, or aggressive, or may wish to impress the interviewer. Interviewing teams should be aware of such possibilities. Consultation with people who know the witness well should give some indication of their likely behaviour and some suggestions as to how interviewers can best interact with the witness.

2.82 Some witnesses with a learning disability may show confusion, memory loss and impaired reasoning. Properly preparing the witness for the interview may help to identify and reduce confusion, emotional distress and anxiety.

2.83 In some instances of mild and moderate learning disability, a difficulty with cognition may not be immediately apparent. The experience that many people with learning disabilities have of discrimination towards them in society is likely to act as an incentive to conceal or minimise their disability whenever possible. Where there are concerns that a witness has a learning disability, even if the extent of the disability is considered to be relatively mild, it is essential that a great deal of care is taken in framing questions and evaluating the witness's response to them.

2.84 Some witnesses with a learning disability communicate using a mixture of words and gestures (e.g. Makaton signs/symbols when used as an augmentative communication system). While an intermediary should be considered in every case where a witness has a learning disability, the services of an intermediary are essential in circumstances where a witness communicates using a mixture of words and gestures.

2.85 Some witnesses with a learning disability do not use speech but communicate using alternative methods of communication. Such alternative methods include sign and symbol systems. Examples of sign systems include Makaton signing and Sign-a-long (these systems may be used either as an augmentative system with speech or as an alternative system without it). Examples of symbol systems include Rebus, Bliss and Makaton. The symbols may be printed on boards or cards, or contained in booklets. They vary from being iconic and concrete to being more abstract in their composition. They may be personalised and can be composed of words, pictures and symbols. While an intermediary should be considered in every case where a witness has a learning disability, the services of an intermediary are essential in circumstances where a witness uses an alternative method of communication instead of speech.

(Ministry of Justice, 2011b)

13.4 Special measures for vulnerable witnesses

For a definition, see *Special Measures* (CPS available at www.cps.gov.uk).

'Special Measures' are a series of provisions that help vulnerable and intimidated witnesses give their best evidence in court and help to relieve some of the stress associated with giving evidence. Special measures apply to prosecution and defence witnesses, but not to the defendant.

Many witnesses experience stress and fear during the investigation of a crime and subsequently when attending court and giving evidence. Stress can affect the quantity and quality of communication with, and by, witnesses of all ages. Some witnesses may have particular difficulties attending court and giving evidence due to their age, personal circumstances, fear of intimidation or because of their particular needs.

The Youth Justice and Criminal Evidence Act 1999 (YJCEA) introduced a range of measures that can be used to facilitate the gathering and giving of evidence by vulnerable and intimidated witnesses. The measures are collectively known as 'Special Measures' and are subject to the discretion of the court.

There is not room here to explore special measures in detail, for which please refer to the guidance. Useful points in brief (this list is not exhaustive):

- Eligibility for special measures are explained in the guidance, and are based on the witness' vulnerability and/or experience or fear of intimidation.
- All child witnesses under 18 are entitled to special measures.
- All witnesses with mental disorder, significant impairment of intelligence and social functioning, or physical disability or physical disorder are regarded as vulnerable in the terms of this guidance.
- Intimidated witnesses may include: those suffering from fear and distress, those who have suffered sexual abuse, domestic violence, witnessed offences with guns and knives, racially motivated crime and repeat victimisation, and witnesses who self-neglect, self-harm, or are elderly and/or frail.

Being eligible for special measures does not mean that the court will automatically grant them. The court has to satisfy itself that the special measure or combination of special measures is likely to maximise the quality of the witness's evidence before granting an application.

While the legislation distinguishes between vulnerable and intimidated witnesses in respect of the criteria for their eligibility for special measures, it is important to remember that:

- some witnesses may be vulnerable as well as intimidated;
- other witnesses may be vulnerable but not subject to intimidation;
- and others may not be vulnerable but may be subject to intimidation.

It is important not to attempt to categorise witnesses too rigidly.

13.4.1 Child witnesses

Under section 101 of the Coroners and Justice Act 2009, amending section 21 of the Youth Justice and Criminal Evidence Act, all child witnesses are in the same position and entitled to special measures.

For all child witnesses there is a presumption that they will give their evidence in chief by video-recorded interview and any further evidence by live link unless the court is satisfied that this will not improve the quality of the child's evidence.

However, a child witness may opt out of giving their evidence by either video-recorded interview or by live link or both, subject to the agreement of the court. If the child witness opts out then there is a presumption that they will give their evidence in court from behind a screen. Should the child witness not wish to use a screen they may also be allowed to opt out of using it, again subject to the agreement of the court.

In deciding whether or not to agree to the wish of the child witness the court must be satisfied that the quality of the child's evidence will not be diminished.

Where a video-recorded interview is made before a child witness's 18th birthday, the witness is eligible for video-recorded evidence in chief and live link special measures directions after his/her 18th birthday.

13.4.2 Types of special measures available

The special measures available to vulnerable and intimidated witnesses, with the agreement of the court, include:

* screens (available for vulnerable and intimidated witnesses): screens may be made available to shield the witness from the defendant;
* live link (available for vulnerable and intimidated witnesses): a live link enables the witness to give evidence during the trial from outside the court through a televised link to the courtroom. The witness may be accommodated either within the court building or in a suitable location outside the court;
* evidence given in private (available for some vulnerable and intimidated witnesses): exclusion from the court of members of the public and the press (except for one named person to represent the press) in cases involving sexual offences or intimidation by someone other than the accused;
* removal of wigs and gowns (available for vulnerable and intimidated witnesses at the Crown Court): removal of wigs and gowns by judges and barristers;
* video-recorded interview (available for vulnerable and intimidated witnesses): a video-recorded interview with a vulnerable or intimidated witness before the trial may be admitted by the court as the witness's evidence-in-chief. For adult complainants in sexual offence trials in the Crown Court a video-recorded interview will be automatically admissible upon application unless this would not be in the interests of justice or would not maximise the quality of the complainants evidence. Section 103 of the Coroners and Justice Act 2009 relaxes the restrictions on a witness giving additional evidence in chief after the witnesss video-recorded interview has been admitted.

- examination of the witness through an intermediary (available for vulnerable witnesses): an intermediary may be appointed by the court to assist the witness to give their evidence at court. They can also provide communication assistance in the investigation stage approval for admission of evidence so taken is then sought retrospectively. The intermediary is allowed to explain questions or answers so far as is necessary to enable them to be understood by the witness or the questioner but without changing the substance of the evidence;
- aids to communication (available for vulnerable witnesses): aids to communication may be permitted to enable a witness to give best evidence whether through a communicator or interpreter, or through a communication aid or technique, provided that the communication can be independently verified and understood by the court.

This is our brief précis of the guidance provisions:

Special measures will not be automatically available at trial and the prosecutor must make an application to the court with the consent of the witness (some witnesses may prefer to give evidence without special measures). The court will need to be told about any views expressed by the witness generally, and the specific views of the witness when determining who should accompany the witness if s/he gives evidence by live link.

With regard to intimidated witnesses, the court must, or should, take into account certain factors when assessing whether the witness qualifies for any of the special measures. The factors include:

- The nature and alleged circumstances of the offence;
- The age of the witness;
- The social and cultural background and ethnic origins of the witness;
- Any religious beliefs or political opinions of the witness;
- The domestic and employment circumstances of the witness; and
- Any behaviour towards the witness on the part of the accused, their family or associates, or any other witness or co-accused (this may be particularly relevant in cases of domestic violence).

Witnesses who have given video-recorded evidence can refresh their memory by viewing it again, but see the guidance for the principles on which this is allowed.

13.5 Pre-trial counselling and psychotherapy with children and vulnerable adults

Cases continue to be reported in the press where witnesses involved in the judicial process have been severely affected or re-traumatised by the police investigation and the court process. Some witnesses have been so affected by the judicial process that they have become ill, made attempts on their own life, or in some cases, have committed suicide following their provision of evidence in court. This has led to renewal of concerns about the welfare of vulnerable adult and child witnesses and a re-examination of the way in which they are treated and the support they receive during a police investigation and throughout the judicial process. There is cogent evidence to support the argument that witness support and psychological assistance for vulnerable witnesses should be able to continue when necessary, after the court case has finished.

13.5.1 Current guidance relevant to pre-trial therapy

Earlier, in the introduction to this chapter we looked at the *Code for Crown Prosecutors* (CPS, 2013) which gives guidance on the principles to be applied when prosecutors are making decisions about prosecutions. We noted that one of the concerns is the protection of vulnerable witnesses, balanced against the needs of maintaining justice.

In 2001, the CPS published two guidance documents: Provision of Therapy for Vulnerable or Intimidated Adult Witnesses Prior to a Criminal Trial: Practice Guidance and Provision of Therapy for Child Witnesses Prior to a Criminal Trial: Practice Guidance. These two documents are now available online and as PDFs, along with other current guidance relevant to the protection of children, victims and vulnerable witnesses, on the CPS website www.cps.gov.uk. The website (visited on 25 May 2014) describes several of the documents as 'updated in 2014', however, in the case of these two guidance documents, the wording currently remains unchanged from the earlier versions. We suggest that readers watch out for revisions, as the documents need some updating, for example, the pre-trial therapy for children guidance refers in section 1.9 to the child protection document Working Together to Safeguard Children (DoH, 1999) and in force now is a much newer version: Working Together to Safeguard Children (DE, 2013). It is possible that these two CPS documents may be revised in the future. They contain similar provisions regarding pre-trial therapy, and we have been involved in discussion about potential future revisions, bringing them in line with the publication of other guidance and developments in child protection, possibly reconsidering the definitions of counselling and psychotherapy, and also, given the similarity of the two documents, there might be a potential usefulness in amalgamating them into one comprehensive guidance.

It will be seen that, although the interests of the client are paramount, confidentiality is limited in that therapists working with vulnerable clients in pre-trial therapy will have to agree with the client to allow disclosure of the fact that therapy is taking place, and also to the disclosure of client records, or such information or parts of client records as the courts may direct.

Also relevant to pre-trial therapy are the *Guidelines on Prosecuting Cases of Child Sexual Abuse* (CPS, 2013). The sections on counselling and therapy clarify the policy that should be followed:

1. The CPS guidance *Provision of Therapy for Child Witnesses Prior to a Criminal Trial* is clear that the best interests of the victim or witness are the paramount consideration in decisions about therapy. There is no bar to a victim seeking pre-trial therapy or counselling

and neither the police nor the CPS should prevent therapy from taking place prior to a trial. Prosecutors should be familiar with the content of the CPS guidance on pre-trial therapy so that they can advise police and witnesses on the correct approach.

2. Providers of counselling or therapy should ensure that records are kept and that the child or young person (and if relevant, parents or guardian) is advised at the start of the process that there may be a requirement to disclose the fact that counselling has taken place, particularly if detail of the alleged offending is raised. Experience over a number of years has shown that properly conducted and recorded counselling or therapy has not caused problems with the criminal trial process. Where the therapist or counsellor is known to the investigation, they should be briefed at an early stage to inform them about the court process and their disclosure obligations.

Prosecutors have a duty to disclose the fact that a victim has undergone therapy or counselling and to disclose any other matter which is determined by the usual tests as to whether it is relevant to an issue in the case. This is part of the continuing duty on the CPS to disclose (Ministry of Justice, 2013).

13.5.2 Consents and pre-trial therapy

Practitioners working with vulnerable adults and children will need to have valid consent to enter into a therapeutic contract (see Chapters 11 and 12), and if the client is involved in a court process, as we have seen in 13.5.1, additional confidentiality issues are involved in the therapeutic process, because there will inevitably be a need to share a certain amount of information between professionals, and also to disclose information from client records to the courts when ordered to do so.

The law and guidance surrounding the provision of pre-trial support, including therapy, with children and young people includes resources for children in need under s. 17 and Schedule 2 of the Children Act 1989 as amended, and services to protect children from abuse. The CPS guidance on pre-trial therapy (*Provision of therapy for vulnerable or intimidated adult witnesses prior to a criminal trial: Practice Guidance* and *Provision of therapy for child witnesses prior to a criminal trial: Practice Guidance* (www.cps.gov.uk) were both published in 2001 as part of a raft of resources, see 13.5.1. Until further revised or withdrawn, these remain as guidance to police, CPS and therapists. The guidance in relation to pre-trial therapy for children is worded similarly to that for vulnerable adults, but attention is given to the additional issues of consent and child protection. The key issues relevant to both these guidance documents are addressed below.

Key issues for pre-trial therapy

Pre-trial discussions   A key issue in a criminal trial (and to some extent in civil trials, too) is that pre-trial discussions of any kind with a witness may have a potential effect on the reliability, actual or perceived, of the evidence of that witness and the weight which will be given to their evidence in court. Therapy is regarded as a form of pre-trial discussion. Pre-trial discussions may lead to allegations of influencing the witness by coaching and, potentially, could lead to the failure of the criminal case. It should also be borne in mind that the professionals concerned may themselves be called to court as witnesses in relation to any therapy undertaken prior to the criminal trial.

If therapy is necessary for the welfare of the witness, and the nature of the therapy may affect the evidence, the overarching concept in both sets of guidance is the primary importance of the welfare of the witness, even at the cost of the trial if necessary and the guidance regarding child witnesses is crystal clear on this:

4.1 The Crown Prosecution Service is responsible for reviewing and conducting the majority of criminal cases involving child victims and witnesses. Once a Crown Prosecutor considers that there is a realistic prospect of conviction, the public interest must be considered. A primary consideration for Crown Prosecutors when taking decisions in these circumstances is the best interests of the child.

The guidance then refers to the safeguarding of therapy:

4.2 The prosecution in these criminal cases must do what it can to:

- identify cases in which the provision of therapy before the criminal trial might be thought to have some material impact on the evidence;
- assess the likely consequences for the criminal trial in these cases;
- ensure that these cases are dealt with as quickly as possible;
- safeguard the confidentiality of therapy sessions wherever possible whilst ensuring that the defence and the court are aware of the existence of information which might undermine the prosecution case or assist the defence.

(*Provision of therapy for child witnesses prior to a criminal trial: Practice Guidance*).

A crucial point made by the guidance is that the decision whether a child should or should not have therapy is <u>not</u> that of the CPS or the police:

4.3 Whether a child should receive therapy before the criminal trial is not a decision for the police or The Crown Prosecution Service. Such decisions can only be taken by all of the professionals from the agencies responsible for the welfare of the child, in consultation with the carers of the child and the child him or herself, if the child is of sufficient age and understanding.

4.4 The best interests of the child are the paramount consideration in decisions about the provision of therapy before the criminal trial. In determining what is in the best interests of the child, due consideration should be given to ascertaining the wishes and feelings of the child, in a manner which is appropriate to the child's age and understanding. When working with the child either for assessment or therapeutic purposes, account should be taken of the child's gender, race, culture, religion, language and (if appropriate) disability.

The welfare of the child is important, even if it costs the case:

> 4.5 If there is a demonstrable need for the provision of therapy and it is possible that the therapy will prejudice the criminal proceedings, consideration may need to be given to abandoning those proceedings in the interests of the child's wellbeing. In order that such consideration can be given, it is essential that information regarding therapy is communicated to the prosecutor.

But the case need not necessarily be jeopardised:

> Therapy may be delayed until after the trial:

> 4.6 Alternatively, there may be some children for whom it will be preferable to delay therapy until after the criminal case has been heard, to avoid the benefits of the therapy being undone.

Or therapy can be carried out in such a way as not to jeopardise the trial:

> 4.7 While some forms of therapy may undermine the evidence given by the witness, this will not automatically be the case. The Crown Prosecution Service will offer advice, as requested in individual cases, on the likely impact on the evidence of the child receiving therapy.

Records and disclosures in pre-trial therapy (for both child and adult witnesses)   For therapists working in the field of pre-trial therapy, constant practice updating is a necessity. Cases often involve complex situations, and practitioners need to keep up with constantly changing law, policies and practice.

Not only do we need to be familiar with relevant child law, and the provisions of guidance such as *Working Together to Safeguard Children* (DfES, 2013) or any subsequent amended version, but in private practice we have to develop and match our own policies and procedures in line with current guidance and legislation. For therapists working in the NHS, local authority and government regulated practice, national policies will bind practitioners contractually to compliance with government guidance. Practitioners working in contexts such as NHS, education, etc., should be fully aware of the terms under which they are required to work, and ensure that clients understand and agree to abide by these terms.

The documents *Provision of Therapy for Vulnerable or Intimidated Adult Witnesses Prior to a Criminal Trial: Practice Guidance* and the *Provision of Therapy for Child Witnesses Prior to a Criminal Trial: Practice Guidance* (both online and as PDFs at CPS at www.cps.gov.uk) are almost identical in their wording of provisions regarding record keeping and information sharing and the use of therapy and so are treated together in this paragraph. This similarity of wording includes assessment, therapists' training, and therapeutic approaches. Examples are taken below from both sets of guidance.

Disclosure of information concerning the pre-trial therapy is likely to be required by the court, and it follows that practitioners should be very careful and accurate in their record keeping. In pre-trial working, therapists must pay strict attention to accuracy and the inclusion of sufficient detail for the primary therapeutic purpose, but at the same time bearing in mind that the notes potentially could be used as evidence. Clients should be made aware of the limits of confidentiality (child clients should have explanations at an age-appropriate level), and therapists should explain the need for professionals to share information for the protection of the child as well as for the interests of justice, and the possible use of client records for court purposes.

For the content of client notes, see *Provision of Therapy for Vulnerable or Intimidated Adult Witnesses Prior to a Criminal Trial: Practice Guidance*:

> 11.4 Records of therapy (which includes videos and tapes as well as notes) and other contacts with the witness must be maintained so that they can be produced if required by the court. They should include, in the case of therapy, details of those persons present and the content and length of the therapy sessions. It is not expected, for practical reasons, that verbatim written records will be kept.

> 11.5 At the outset of therapy an understanding should be reached with the witness and, where appropriate, those who are emotionally significant to the witness of the circumstances under which material obtained during therapy might be required to be disclosed. Maintaining trust will remain important and it can be confirmed that those aspects of the therapy that have no material relevance to criminal proceedings will not have to be disclosed. However, what is 'relevant' may change as the case progresses and so confidentiality cannot be guaranteed.

Therapy should not start until a statement has been taken:

> 11.6 In newly arising allegations, therapy should not usually take place before a witness has provided a statement or, if appropriate, before a video-recorded interview has taken place. However, in existing cases where therapy is already under way, a decision about how to proceed may be best made after discussion at a multi-disciplinary meeting which includes the therapist. Clearly, when therapeutic work is in progress, disruption of therapy should be avoided even if new investigations must be conducted. If it is decided that leading questions or interpretations must be used to help a witness in psychotherapy, then the evidential implications of this should be understood and made clear.

> 11.7 If the prosecutor advises that the proposed therapy may prejudice the criminal case, this should be taken into account when deciding whether to agree to the therapy. It may still be in the best interests of the witness to proceed with the therapy.

Requests for information to be obtained from third parties may be made at various stages in a criminal case by:

- the police;
- the prosecutor;

- the defence;
- the court.

The *Provision of Therapy for Child Witnesses Prior to a Criminal Trial: Practice Guidance* (CPS) makes it clear that disclosure should be used carefully, and

> 3.11 Disclosure should not be viewed as a tool to enable the prosecution or defence to satisfy their curiosity. It is a principle designed to ensure that information that is of genuine relevance to a criminal case is available to the parties and the court.

This guidance goes on to explain more about disclosure:

> 3.12 The requests should explain the issues in the case, so far as they are known, and be reasonably precise. Speculative inquiries are discouraged. The purpose should be to elicit a genuine and focused search for relevant documents or information. Careful maintenance of records of therapy will facilitate this focused approach. Where a therapist receives a request for information or documents, legal advice should be obtained before complying with the request. If, for example, the therapist is employed by a Social Services Department or NHS Hospital, the legal department of such a Department or Hospital will provide advice.
>
> 3.13 In addition to informal requests for information, if there are real grounds to believe that material which could affect the outcome of the prosecution is being withheld, an application may be made to the court for a witness summons to obtain the material. If, as will usually be the case, a therapist, having taken appropriate legal advice, believes that the material should not be disclosed, he or she may oppose the witness summons application. In that case the court may hold a hearing at which the therapist's employer may be legally represented. The court, having heard representations from the advocate representing the applicant for the witness summons and the advocate for the therapist's employer, will decide whether or not to issue a summons requiring the disclosure of the material.
>
> [Authors' Note: A self-employed therapist may attend court (e.g. a directions hearing), in his or her own right.]
>
> 3.14 Because of the recognition that maintaining trust is central to the provision of therapy, it will usually only be appropriate to breach confidentiality in compliance with a court order, as outlined in paragraph 3.13 above. Those aspects of the therapy that have no material relevance to criminal proceedings should not have to be disclosed. However, the issue of relevance may need to be reviewed at different stages of the criminal case, as more becomes known about the prosecution and defence cases.
>
> 3.15 Confidentiality cannot, therefore, be guaranteed in advance. Bearing this in mind, it is important that an understanding is reached with the vulnerable or intimidated adult witness (and, where appropriate, any other emotionally significant person) at the outset of any therapy undertaken of the circumstances under which material obtained during treatment may be required to be disclosed.

The CPS have a duty to attend to confidentiality issues, including therapy; see:

4.1 The Crown Prosecution Service is responsible for reviewing and conducting the majority of criminal cases involving adult vulnerable or intimidated witnesses. Once a crown prosecutor considers that there is a realistic prospect of conviction, the public interest must be considered.

4.2 The prosecution in these criminal cases must do what it can to:

- identify cases in which the provision of therapy before the criminal trial might be thought to have some material impact on the evidence;
- assess the likely consequences for the criminal trial in these cases;
- ensure that these cases are dealt with as quickly as possible;
- safeguard the confidentiality of therapy sessions wherever possible whilst ensuring that the defence and the court are aware of the existence of information which might undermine the prosecution case or assist the defence.

These questions are not unique to therapy which takes place before the criminal trial, but the ethical, medical, welfare and legal issues are of particular importance in these cases.

4.3 Whether a vulnerable or intimidated witness should receive therapy before the criminal trial is not a decision for the police or the Crown Prosecution Service. Such decisions can only be taken by the vulnerable or intimidated witness, in conjunction with the professionals from the agencies providing service to the witness.

4.4 The best interests of the vulnerable or intimidated witness are the paramount consideration in decisions about the provision of therapy before the criminal trial. In determining what is in the best interests of the vulnerable or intimidated witness, it will be essential to consider the wishes and feelings of the witness and, where appropriate, of those who are emotionally significant to the witness. The witness will need to be given information on the nature of the therapy proposed in a form which is accessible. Account should be taken of issues associated with gender, race, culture, religion, language, disability and any communication difficulties both in initial discussions about the proposed therapy and in the provision of the therapy itself.

4.6 If there is a demonstrable need for the provision of therapy and it is possible that the therapy will prejudice the criminal proceedings, consideration may need to be given to abandoning those proceedings in the interests of the wellbeing of the vulnerable or intimidated witness. In order that such consideration can be given, it is essential that information regarding therapy is communicated to the prosecutor.

Assessment of the need for pre-trial therapy   In addition to the guidance on pre-trial therapy, practitioners are referred to the revised *Code of Practice for Victims of Crime* (Ministry of Justice, 2013).

The *Provision of Therapy for Vulnerable or Intimidated Adult Witnesses Prior to a Criminal Trial: Practice Guidance* (CPS), provides that:

8.1 Assessment of the need for therapy during the pre-trial period (when the vulnerable or intimidated witness may become a witness in the subsequent trial) should only be undertaken following consultation with:

- the witness;
- where appropriate, those who are emotionally significant to the witness;
- the relevant professionals.

The police and the Crown Prosecution Service should be informed about any planned or ongoing therapy at the assessment stage.

The guidance goes on in s. 8.2 to provide for a meeting of 'all relevant professionals' to discuss an assessment and treatment strategy, at which the views of the witness and those emotionally significant to them would be made known and considered as part of the decision-making process if the witness is not present at the meeting. This may include decisions about support from other agencies, including therapy. Issues to be considered would include the funding of therapy, transport to appointments, family work, and inter-agency professional communication. This, of course, all has a bearing on confidentiality and sharing information in the context of pre-trial therapy, which would need appropriate consent.

Sections 8.5–8.9 deal with consideration of the type of therapy appropriate, and the impact of therapy on the case, giving priority to the best interests of the vulnerable or intimidated witness. The process of assessment requires some relevant experience and training, and need not necessarily be carried out by the person who will provide the therapy. Section 9 deals with the important pre-trial assessment issues, including special needs, interpreters, and hearing or speech difficulties.

There is guidance in Section 9 on how to conduct an assessment in a way that does not further traumatise or confuse a vulnerable witness, and the appropriate use of placements in a therapeutic environment.

What type of therapy is appropriate for pre-trial work?   We cannot go into detail here about the specific modalities and therapeutic approaches that could be risky for pre-trial working, and those that would be less likely to jeopardise evidence in court proceedings, as this would be beyond the remit of this book. Both guidance documents: *Provision of Therapy for Child Witnesses Prior to a Criminal Trial: Practice Guidance* (CPS at www.cps.gov.uk) and *Provision of Therapy for Vulnerable or Intimidated Adult Witnesses Prior to a Criminal Trial: Practice Guidance.* (CPS at www. cps.gov.uk) refer briefly to helpful and unhelpful therapy approaches, but there is a grey area in establishing specific kinds of pre-trial therapy that are considered appropriate for witnesses in order not to prejudice the case. Clearly, if a witness needs the type of therapy that necessitates talking in detail about the events material to the case (e.g. some sorts of trauma therapy may involve intensive discussion or imaginal re-exposure to the traumatic events), then this may raise the concern that the therapy may potentially influence the evidence by 'rehearsing the witness' or by affecting the witness' recall of the event. However, if such therapy is absolutely necessary in the interests of the witness' mental health and welfare, then, as we have seen, the trial may have to be abandoned if evidence vital to the case may be contaminated.

Both the guidance documents give generalised warnings about potential problem areas, including therapist interpretations and 'recovered memories' surfacing in therapy and the importance of a therapist being open-minded about the fact or fantasy of a client's material. *Provision of Therapy for Vulnerable or Intimidated Adult Witnesses Prior to a Criminal Trial: Practice Guidance* also warns that:

10.3 Interpretative psychotherapy may present evidential problems even if carefully conducted. The professional background and training of the therapist, the provision of adequate supervision arrangements, the appropriateness and robustness of the policies of the agency providing therapy will all help to obviate problems.

10.4 There are therapeutic approaches that would very definitely present problems as far as evidential reliability is concerned. These would include hypnotherapy, psychodrama, regression techniques and unstructured groups.

Part V

Practice Dilemmas: scenarios on confidentiality and disclosures for reflection and discussion

14 Responding to Dilemmas – Ethical and Legal Practice

I am not sure how to apply general legal principles to the dilemmas that I sometimes encounter in my work with clients.

My heart sinks when a client starts to raise issues where I might need to break their confidentiality. I don't imagine that I will ever feel comfortable breaking a confidence but it would help if I was surer of my grounds for doing so … Sometimes keeping confidences is a burden too. I am holding information that causes me to feel anxious but I can do nothing with it. I am left hoping that I am doing the right thing and watching how things work out.

It might be easier to feel with client confidences that it is 'not my problem', but it becomes my problem when I feel I ought to tell someone about what I know. It is so hard to know what to do.

It's the nature of a dilemma. You feel damned if you do and damned if you don't. It's a dilemma because it isn't clear what to do for the best. Legal dilemmas are particularly tricky because I have to look beyond my area of expertise.

Sometimes I don't know what to do when colleagues are concerned. I know I should do my best to protect clients and standards of our profession, but it is difficult to know what to do and where to go.

I worry about a client telling me about something illegal they have done – I don't want to cause trouble for them, especially if it is all in the past … the decision might be easier to make if the illegal thing is happening now and someone is at risk.

My colleague, a fellow therapist, confessed that he has been very emotionally labile recently, very quickly angry, and has lost his temper with family and staff. I'm worried about his contact with his young and vulnerable clients – what should I do?

In the earlier parts of the book, we have taken a wide-ranging overview of the law concerning confidentiality and privacy and the application of the law to therapists' responsibilities. As we worked on the first edition of this book we became aware that some situations arising in the course of therapy are experienced with some frequency, and in the workshops that followed on from the publication of the book we heard quite often about certain types of dilemmas, so we felt that readers might like to have specific guidance for those situations, gathered together in one place. In this chapter, we explore the legal and ethical issues that might arise from these dilemmas and we have directed attention to the relevant law.

We start by considering in 14.1 the circumstances in which the client may be at risk of inflicting harm on others, before considering in 14.2 the situations where the client may be at risk of harm. We go on in 14.3 to look at managing confidentiality around the 'guilty secrets' or 'confessions' that arise in the course of therapy. The next section 14.4 deals with whistle-blowing and managing confidentiality in the workplace. The next section 14.5 considers situations in which children and young people are vulnerable to abuse, and the chapter closes at 14.6 with a series of questions and issues to be considered when thinking through any challenging dilemma over confidentiality.

14.1 A client at risk of harming others

An acute ethical dilemma for therapists arises when clients threaten significant harm to others or clients reveal that they are actively involved in serious crime that harms others or the community. Clients who attempt to insist on confidentiality in these circumstances are asking for a degree of respect to be shown for their own rights that they are unwilling to show to others. The therapist may experience this as a question of personal and professional integrity over how far they are willing to protect the client or be morally implicated in the client's actions. The law takes a less personal approach by directing attention to where the balance of the public interest lies and the existence of any legal duties. Table 14.1 shows a variety of criminal actions and how the law approaches breaches of confidentiality.

14.2 Clients at risk of causing harm to themselves

In Table 14.2 we consider different situations that are likely to be encountered by therapists in which clients are considered to be at serious risk of harming themselves. This guidance relates to situations where there is no prior agreement that a therapist may seek assistance for a client, even if this means breaching confidentiality, or the client is refusing to permit a referral. As always, the best way of resolving difficulties over confidentiality is with the client's consent whenever possible.

14.3 Managing confidentiality around 'guilty secrets' and 'confessions'

As therapists, we are likely to hear many 'confessions' and 'secrets' in the course of our work. Clients may admit to having done something illegal in the past, or talk about an illegal act that they are planning in the future. In this situation, we have to refer back to the general principles outlined in Chapters 3 and 7. We should disclose confidential information only when the law requires us to do so, or where the law allows us to do so, or where the client consents for us to do so.

Table 14.1 *Deciding whether to breach confidentiality to prevent clients harming others*

Situation	Breaching confidentiality	Legal authorities
Preventing acts of terrorism, or bringing terrorists to justice in the UK, and the offence of 'tipping off'	There is a duty to disclose specified types of information, and it is an offence to interfere with an ongoing investigation, e.g. by 'tipping a person off': see Chapter 3.	Sections 38B and 39 of the Terrorism Act 2000.
Information about fundraising, use of money or property, or money laundering to assist acts of terrorism	There is a duty to disclose information about specified activities, if the information is acquired in the course of a trade, profession, business or employment: see Chapter 3.	Sections 15, 16, 17, 18 and 19 of the Terrorism Act 2000.
Preventing or assisting detection of drug trafficking and money laundering	Respond in the same way as for any serious crime. For the current law on requirements to report drug trafficking or money laundering which may affect therapists, see Chapter 3.	Drug Trafficking Act 1994, ss. 53–54. Proceeds of Crime Act 2002.
Prevention of 'serious crime' (see the Serious Crime Act 2007 and the Glossary on p. 185 for examples of serious crime)	A therapist, acting in good faith, may, at their discretion notify appropriate persons or authorities. A court will not impose any penalties for breach of confidence when the breach is considered to be in the public interest. Such breaches are 'defensible'. A client cannot insist on confidentiality over serious crime.	In common law, the public interest in the prevention and detection of serious crime is greater than in protecting confidences. The law of equity contains the principle that 'There is no confidence in iniquity' (i.e. no one can be legally bound to secrecy about crime). Balance of public interest (e.g. as against the client's wishes) in common law.
Prevention of *serious physical harm* likely to be inflicted by client on another adult	A breach of confidence is defensible in order to protect someone from serious physical harm inflicted by a client where the information is given in good faith, the belief in the risk is reasonably well founded, and the information is restricted to that necessary to prevent the harm, and communicated in confidence to either the authorities or to the intended victim	Common law – balance of public interest. Legal advice should be sought if circumstances permit this. In an emergency situation, it may be better to avert a serious and real risk of harm by warning the potential victim, if they are unaware of the danger, or by informing the police in order to prevent immediate injury. This type of dilemma may arise when providing couple counselling, while also working with one of them individually.

(Continued)

Table 14.1 (Continued)

Situation	Breaching confidentiality	Legal authorities
		Consider issues in the Disclosure Checklist on p. 173.
		Where a client is likely to harm another of the therapist's clients, failure to act to protect the victim may amount to professional negligence. The ethical issues are increased when seeing a client who is intending to inflict harm on another person who is also your client, without one or both clients knowing that the other is receiving therapy from you.
Prevention of *psychological harm* likely to be inflicted by client on another adult	No general grounds to breach confidentiality	In the case of children, the child protection procedures apply to protect children from *all* forms of harm (see below).
		The common law balance of public interest requires prevention of serious *physical* harm. However, the law in relation to adults is moving towards taking substantial *psychological* harm more seriously, e.g. in cases of harassment or stalking, especially if psychological harm may lead to psychiatric illness, or where it is being inflicted on a vulnerable person. The law provides specific protection against stalking, harassment and discrimination in many circumstances, but it is less clear whether these situations would justify a breach of confidence. Work with the client's consent or seek legal advice.
Knowledge of significant harm being caused or likely to be caused to a child/ young person		Child protection procedures apply to protect children from *all* forms of harm – mental physical and emotional.
		See Table 14.3 later in this chapter.

Table 14.2 *Deciding whether to breach confidentiality to protect clients at risk of harm to themselves*

In all these situations it may be helpful to consider the issues in the Disclosure Checklist (on p. 173), in supervision, and where appropriate, with advice and with the client.

Situation	Breaching confidentiality	Legal authorities
Prevention of serious physical harm being inflicted by client on self, whether life threatening or not, *in a way that may place others at risk of serious physical harm*	Respond as though for prevention of serious crime where crime might result or on the balance of public interest to prevent serious physical harm to others.	Balance of public interest.
Prevention of self-inflicted serious physical harm to an *adult* client *where the harm is restricted to that person*	May be defensible to consult a doctor, psychiatrist, or other specialist in mental health on a confidential basis to investigate the possibility of compulsory assessment or treatment *where mental illness is suspected* or where mental capacity is an issue. If the client explicitly refuses permission to seek medical assistance for the treatment of physical injuries. Check the client's mental capacity – is the client's ability to think clearly affected by the injuries? If the client explicitly refuses permission to seek medical assistance for the treatment of physical injuries, a doctor may only act without a patient's consent to save life in a situation of medical emergency or where the patient has no mental capacity to consent or refuse, e.g. is unconscious. If a patient has given prior instructions, e.g. an Advance Directive refusing resuscitation, then the doctor's provision of treatment in an emergency may be subject to this.	No case law could be discovered but disclosure and referral may be defensible on the balance of public interest – depending on the circumstances. There is no general right to breach confidentiality against the express wishes of the client. Persuasion to accept help is legally safer. Adults may refuse treatments for physical illnesses or offers of assistance even if it seems contrary to their best interests or unreasonable (*St George's Healthcare NHS Trust v S* [1999]).

(Continued)

Table 14.2 *(Continued)*

In all these situations it may be helpful to consider the issues in the Disclosure Checklist (on p. 173), in supervision, and where appropriate, with advice and with the client.

Situation	Breaching confidentiality	Legal authorities
Prevention of self-inflicted serious physical harm by someone under the age of 18	There is no general legal requirement to breach confidentiality but therapists working in public authorities or associated organisations may be obliged to do so in accordance with child protection law and guidance and in compliance with their contract of employment. All therapists should comply with child protection law and take note of current guidance (see p. 173).	The public policy relevant to child protection and the balance of public interest in common law favours ensuring that children and young persons under 18 are protected and therefore would support a therapist who, to prevent serious harm to a child, breaches confidence, in good faith and for reasonable cause, to obtain assistance or advice to protect a child, even against the young person's express wishes. Consider the issues in the Disclosure Checklist (p. 173).
Seeking treatment for minor or superficial self-inflicted harm by someone between 16 and 18 years old	The express wishes of the person concerned should normally be respected. However, mental capacity should be carefully considered along with the issues on the Disclosure Checklist (p. 173).	Family Law Reform Act 1969; Age of Legal Capacity (Scotland) Act 1991.
Seeking treatment for minor or superficial self-inflicted harm by someone under 16	The express wishes of someone who is competent to make their own decisions in the terms of the *Gillick* case, i.e. having sufficient age, intelligence and understanding to understand the consequences of declining treatment should normally be respected. However, consider the issues in the Disclosure Checklist (p. 173). Where someone lacks the mental capacity to give consent, consider seeking the involvement and consent of someone with parental responsibility (PR). The consent of one person with PR is sufficient if there is more than one person with PR. Whilst the young person's wishes and feelings should be taken into account, their welfare should be paramount and guide any further action.	*Gillick v West Norfolk and Wisbech Area Health Authority* [1985]; Age of Legal Capacity (Scotland) Act 1991. See Lord Fraser's judgement in the Gillick case.

There are certain situations where we have a statutory duty to disclose information (e.g. terrorism) and where tipping the client off that we will make the disclosure might constitute a criminal offence. In other situations, we have to answer questions from the police about who was driving, if the information is requested in road traffic cases, and give information about the whereabouts of a child if required to do so under the Children Act 1989. We also have to answer requests for information from the court or law enforcement officers made under the Serious Crime Act 2007.

We are also duty bound to obey court orders requiring information, documents such as client records, or requiring our attendance as a witness in court. If we have recorded in the client notes the client's words making a confession or other statements, or we have paraphrased the clients words in the client notes, then those notes will be produced as part of the client record.

The law allows us to make disclosures of confidential information, without penalty for breach of the therapy contract or an action in negligence, if we can show that the public interest outweighs the client's individual interests and/or the client's wishes. Therefore, if a client tells us that they are planning a criminal act, or planning suicide, and the impact of that action might cause serious harm to others, then we would be protected if we feel it necessary to make a disclosure in the public interest to keep those at risk safe. Where the client alone is at risk from suicide, see section 14.2 and Table 14.2 where we have discussed confidentiality for clients with suicidal feelings or intent.

If the client consents to disclosure of their information, then we do not have a problem. However, wherever possible, check with the client that they fully understand the effects of disclosure before doing so. All too often, clients sign a disclosure form (e.g. police or a solicitor might obtain a client's signed consent to disclose counselling records in a court case) without the client having understood the full implications of the disclosure. If in doubt, a therapist can ask that the court make a direction for disclosure of the notes, and ask to be present when the direction is given, to make any necessary representations to the court about which parts of the notes are relevant, or where necessary, to ask the court to restrict who will see them. See *Therapists in Court* (Bond and Sandhu, 2005) for full discussion of all aspects of evidence and court hearings.

14.4 Dilemmas in managing confidences in the workplace

14.4.1 Illness or overwork and fitness to practise

Where therapists are overworked and/or stressed by work or life events, they may become physically ill, or they may suffer from psychological distress or an illness which affects their ability to be fully present and alert in the moment with their clients (e.g. see section 14.4.2 on vicarious trauma, compassion fatigue and 'burn out'). In these situations, a therapist may feel that they have become temporarily or permanently 'unfit to practise'. Part of the role of supervision is to help therapists to take a subjective and objective look at their current situation and to recognise those times when they may need to take a break. The break may be for the benefit of clients or to meet the needs of the therapist. 'Unfit to practice' is a term which may be perceived by some therapists as implying a judgement about their professionalism, but in fact most of us have times in our lives when we recognise that we need to take a break, and the process of reflection on ourselves and our practice, with a clear recognition of our own periods of unfitness to practise, is a highly appropriate and professional activity.

As therapists, we have a legal duty of care to our clients which must be fulfilled. There may sometimes be difficult situations when a therapist colleague or supervisee does not see their situation objectively, and despite advice from their supervisor or colleagues or management, may not want to accept that they should take a break from practice. A supervisor has a duty of care to the therapist in contract and tort, but importantly, also owes a duty of care to the therapist's clients. If a therapist is not heeding professional advice, then it may be the role of colleagues, management or supervisors to advise the therapist's professional body of the situation if there are reasonable grounds to consider that the therapist's clients are at risk.

We have been asked whether a GP can certify that a therapist is 'fit for work', and this is a difficult point. Many GPs have no formal training in counselling and psychology, and they may not be fully aware of the requirements of therapy practice. A person may be certified generally by their GP as 'fit for work', but the certification of fitness may depend on the patient's own reports of their symptoms, and fitness may also vary according to the type of work to be undertaken. A therapist, for example, may be physically fit for some forms of work, but not psychologically fit to provide the level of concentration, empathy, skill and sustained care necessary to meet the demanding client needs of therapy practice, and the greater the complexity or demanding nature of the therapy practice may necessitate higher consistent levels of therapist competence and fitness.

14.4.2 Vicarious trauma, compassion fatigue and 'burn-out'

The symptoms of post-traumatic stress include hypervigilance, anxiety, avoidance and emotional numbing, and they often overlap with symptoms of other disorders including substance abuse, anxiety, panic attacks and depression. Post-traumatic stress reaction is not confined to those who directly experience trauma. The syndromes of 'compassion fatigue', 'burn-out' and 'vicarious trauma' are encountered by professionals and helpers who may themselves experience the symptoms of post-traumatic stress. In professional and volunteer helpers, the phenomenon of 'compassion fatigue' may arise from a combination of the nature of the work and from post-traumatic stress. Professionals and helpers working in physically demanding or stressful work situations (e.g. in refugee camps etc.) may find themselves working long hours, possibly in difficult conditions and perhaps feeling that they have inadequate training and experience to deal with the specific problems they are facing. Therapists working with traumatised clients in different environments, with appropriate training and good support may nevertheless be constantly faced with their clients' experiencing of highly traumatic events, and this is particularly true of therapists working with client groups who have experienced situations of abuse, violence and addiction.

From a psychoanalytic perspective, transference and counter-transference may operate to affect the therapist's perceptions and reactions to their clients, and this may cause difficulties in sustaining the therapeutic relationship and in offering appropriate empathy with clients who have experienced trauma. For example, a client affected by horrific experiences may unconsciously try to shock the therapist with the horror of their story:

> Patients' experiences may be so horrific that in telling their story they unconsciously try to shock the therapist or to elicit feelings of horror or guilt in such a way that the patient has assumed the perpetrator role and the therapist is now the victim. (Klain and Paviæ, 1999: 467)

As a result of all these factors, therapists may at some time in their careers experience a level of post-traumatic stress, compassion fatigue or 'burn-out'. Compassion fatigue is characterised by a defensive withdrawal from the close supportive relationships with clients or others required in the course of daily professional duties. The therapist may feel (or be) unwilling or unable to engage or cope with the stress of empathic communication and rapport. Therapists may find that they are bodily and emotionally exhausted, depressed, lacking in energy, anxious, lacking in self-confidence and feeling helpless, perhaps combined with fatigue, loss of appetite or sleep disturbances – all symptoms of 'burn-out'.

Preparation for exposure to trauma reduces the likelihood of adverse psychological effects occurring. The process of preparation for forthcoming stress is sometimes referred to as 'stress inoculation'. The way forward, therefore, for therapists facing stressful situations is preparation first, good support and supervision during the work, and rest and self-care afterwards.

We should also mention the benefits of 'post-traumatic growth', a phenomenon where people triumph over adversity despite, or perhaps because of their suffering. The phenomenon of positive psychological growth following suffering was noted and considered by psychologists in different circumstances some fifty years ago and the term 'post-traumatic growth' was first used by Tedeschi and Calhoun in 1995 to describe their perceptions of a new phenomenon. They identified this in clients who had experienced trauma, in which they identified three broad areas of change: self-perception; relationships with others; and philosophy of life (Tedeschi, 1999; Tedeschi and Calhoun, 1995). Tedeschi and Calhoun (1996) subsequently devised the 'Post-traumatic Growth Inventory', a measurement scale addressing these three areas of growth.

14.4.3 'Whistle-blowing' on colleagues' bad practice

This is one of the areas where morality, ethics and law meet, and sometimes the boundaries between them seem unclear. No professional is likely to feel entirely happy about reporting the bad practice or professional misconduct of another person, especially a colleague with whom they work. However, in some situations, 'whistle-blowing' may be necessary to maintain good professional practice, and it may be permitted or even required within an agency policy (contractually agreed by all the agency's employees) or required by law (e.g. reporting terrorist activities under the Terrorism Act 2000 or by an order of a court).

There are other situations where whistle-blowing is not specifically required by law or agency policy, but is left to the therapist's discretion. Therapists may encounter situations where they discover the criminal acts of colleagues (e.g. a therapist sexually assaulting clients, or mistreating vulnerable adults), or they may witness bad practice leading to a risk of potential harm to a child or vulnerable adult, where therapists might feel that whistle-blowing is morally justified. The issue then for the therapist is whether whistle-blowing is *legally* defensible, for example in the public interest (i.e. that the protection of the general public may justifiably outweigh personal or private rights, such as confidentiality).

Where a colleague has been clearly warned about their conduct and has failed to make changes, or where the colleague conceals their conduct from management or their professional organisation, practitioners may feel that whistle-blowing may be the only way left to stop the bad practice continuing.

Bear in mind that the law prohibits attacks on the reputation of another and court cases can be brought for slander (untrue verbal allegations damaging the reputation of another) and libel (similar untrue and damaging allegations made in writing), but a defence to both of these would be that the allegations made were true and that disclosure was made in the public interest. See section 15.6 for further exploration of thinking through disclosures.

14.4.4 Disclosures in institutional settings

The dilemmas that arise for therapists working in institutional settings (e.g. prisons, residential care, hospital care etc.) arise mainly from observation or knowledge of bad professional practice, and consideration about what to do. Often in such a situation there is a close knit community which is working in the context of specific policies and procedures, and also possibly a hierarchical management structure. The principles of 'whistle-blowing' discussed in section 14.4.3 and all the decision-making process in section 14.6. apply here. In addition, there is often a concern about how others might feel about any disclosure of poor practice; therapists may fear peer pressure, and/or fear the reactions of management or reprisals from anyone who resents actions which may cause difficulties for others or upset the structure of the organisation.

We cannot tell you what to do in such a situation because circumstances will vary so much. However, there are ways set out earlier in this chapter to help therapists think through the dilemma systematically, with the help of supervision or mentoring. It is important to check the context and source of the information, for example whether the information or concern is soundly based (i.e. based on fact, sound evidence or a rational and reasonable concern), and also whether disclosure would be made in the public interest, or help to prevent harm, and/or operate for the protection of the therapist or others.

14.5 Abuse of children

The legal framework and guidance concerning the protection of children and young people has undergone many substantial changes in recent years. There is now greater emphasis on hearing 'the voice of the child', and in the context of child care legislation, children and young people are able to participate more fully in court proceedings about them and in decisions made about their care.

At the same time, as a result of significant failures in the child care and protection system, further measures are being developed to encourage and facilitate better inter-agency co-operation and information sharing in child protection work; this is discussed in Chapters 7 and 12.

As children's circumstances differ, each decision has to be case specific, and therapists working in this field need a sound basic knowledge of the current child protection law and government guidance to provide a safe framework in which these difficult decisions can be made. Table 14.2 covers some of the issues which practitioners have found helpful to consider in their decision making. Further information, guidance and resources can be found below in this chapter, in Chapter 12, and in the References at the end of the book.

Failure to comply with child protection law and procedures (when under an obligation to do so) that results in further harm to a child client could lead to that child potentially having future legal claims against the therapist. The grounds for legal action may surface many years later, when the harm suffered by the child is discovered and quantified. Legal liability might arise against the therapist in negligence or breach of contract but is not restricted to these. These grounds for claims are less likely to apply where the young person concerned was at the time over 16, or had sufficient mental capacity to be considered competent in accordance with the *Gillick* case, and had explicitly refused their consent to disclosure.

Therapists working in local authorities, health services and any other agencies or organisations regulated by child protection legislation have a duty to comply with the child protection procedures set out in Part 1 of *Working Together to Safeguard Children: A Guide to Inter-Agency Working to Safeguard and Promote the Welfare of Children* (DfES, 2013). Therapists in private practice should be aware of these provisions, and also refer to *What to Do if You are Worried that a Child is Being Abused* (DfES, 2006a).

Table 14.2 *(Continued)*

In all these situations it may be helpful to consider the issues in the Disclosure Checklist (on p. 173), in supervision, and where appropriate, with advice and with the client.

Situation	Breaching confidentiality	Legal authorities
Prevention of self-inflicted serious physical harm by someone over the age of 16 but under the age of 18	Young people over 16 are treated as adults regarding consent, but are still subject to child protection legislation and to the authority of the High Court/Court of Session. There is no general legal requirement to breach confidentiality but therapists working in public authorities or associated organisations may be obliged to do so under child protection law and government guidance, and in compliance with their contract of employment. See Chapter 12, and if necessary seek legal advice.	The public policy and the balance of public interest in common law favours child protection. In situations of sufficient seriousness, the balance of public interest would protect a breach of confidence to obtain professional assistance or advice in confidence, even against the young person's express wishes. The therapist should have a reasonably held belief that the risk to a child is real, serious and immediate, and that disclosure is necessary to prevent serious harm to a child. The High Court/Court of Session may sanction life-saving treatment against a young person's express wishes. Family Law Reform Act 1969.
Seeking treatment for minor or superficial self-inflicted harm by someone between 16 and 18 years old	The express wishes of the person concerned should normally be respected, but consider the person's mental capacity and the Disclosure Checklist, see p. 173.	
Seeking treatment for minor or superficial self-inflicted harm by someone under 16	The express wishes of someone who is competent to make their own decisions in the terms of the *Gillick* case, i.e. having sufficient age, intelligence and understanding to understand the consequences of declining treatment, should normally be respected. However, consider the issues in the Disclosure Checklist (p. 173). Where someone lacks the mental capacity to give consent, consider seeking the involvement and consent of someone with parental responsibility (PR). The consent of one person with PR is sufficient if there is more than one person with PR. Whilst the young person's wishes and feelings should be taken into account, their welfare should be paramount and guide any further action.	*Gillick v West Norfolk and Wisbech Area Health Authority* [1985]. Lord Fraser's judgement in the above case.

14.6 Prevention of significant harm to children and young people under 18 years

All therapists, whether employed or self-employed, must abide by the general law applicable in their jurisdiction. See Chapters 7 and 12 for more on information sharing between professionals in the context of child protection law and guidance.

Everyone employed by government organisations (e.g. schools, health services, and social care services) must comply with the child protection procedures laid down by government. Therapists employed by non-government agencies or organisations (e.g. those with funding from health and social services) may also have a duty to comply with government guidance. They will therefore have an obligation to report the risk of serious harm from child abuse under their contract of employment.

The legal obligations of a therapist working outside organisations covered by child protection legislation are less clear, but therapists in private practice working with children and families are well advised to develop and implement a child protection policy which complies with current child protection procedures.

Current law has moved in the direction of enabling professionals to share information about vulnerable children and adults so that they can be better protected. It has also strengthened the requirements for many professionals to actively share information on a confidential basis. This follows thirty years of inquiries into the deaths of children caused by neglect and abuse in which it emerged that several professionals were concerned about the child but only knew about a small part of the total circumstances. It seemed that each professional held one or two pieces of the jigsaw sufficient to cause concern but no one held sufficient pieces to make the entire picture from which the full danger to the person concerned was apparent: see *Beyond Blame* (Reder et al., 1994).

Table 14.3 highlights some issues that should be considered when someone discloses abuse of a child or young person.

The tipping point which led to the Children Act 2004 and the development of new policy and practice in Every Child Matters (2004a) was the tragic death of Victoria Climbié in February 2000:

> Victoria spent much of her last days, in the winter of 1999–2000, living and sleeping in a bath in an unheated bathroom, bound hand and foot inside a bin bag, lying in her own urine and faeces. It is not surprising then that towards the end of her short life, Victoria was stooped like an old lady and could walk only with great difficulty. (Lord Laming, 2003)

Lord Laming's report revealed both the ways in which determined abusers can seek to hide from the authorities and a catalogue of poor practice by those responsible for child protection and the care of vulnerable children. It also reveals how inadequate protection systems compound the difficulties for any vulnerable person asking for help to escape abuse. Gradually, since the Children Act 1989, which provides that the child's wishes and feelings should be taken into account, more attention has been paid to listening to children and taking what they say seriously.

Table 14.3 *Issues to be considered when someone discloses abuse of children and young people under 18 years*

In all cases where there is any child protection concern, discuss the issues in supervision, and seek additional advice, e.g. from lawyers or social services where necessary. See Chapters 7 and 12, and *Guidance: Working Together to Safeguard Children: A Guide to Inter-Agency Working to Safeguard and Promote the Welfare of Children* (DfES, 2013), see www.education.gov.uk, and *What to Do if You are Worried a Child is Being Abused* (DfES, 2006a); *Information Sharing: A Practitioner's Guide* (DfES, 2006b); *Confidentiality: Protecting and Providing Information* (GMC, 2004a); and *Confidentiality* (GMC, 2009). These and many other useful guidance documents are listed in the References at the end of the book.

Type of disclosure	Issues to be considered
An adult who discloses that they have abused children in the past	<ul><li>Are they likely to do this again?</li><li>Are there children at imminent risk from them now?</li><li>Are the authorities aware of this past abuse already?</li><li>This is a serious crime (see above).</li></ul>
An adult who admits to causing any present harm or is likely to cause any future harm to a child, e.g. sexual, physical, emotional or through neglect	<ul><li>What is the harm that this person admits to causing?</li><li>Are the authorities aware of this situation already?</li><li>If the person is an active paedophile, then children may be actually suffering significant harm now and may be at risk in the future.</li><li>Child sexual abuse constitutes grounds for an inquiry by social services and is potentially a serious crime (see above).</li><li>Causing any harm (e.g. physical, emotional or through neglect) to a child is also potentially criminal and in any event may constitute grounds for an investigation by social services.</li></ul>
Young person over 16 with mental capacity or competent in the guidelines of the *Gillick* case tells you of abuse they suffered in the past or are suffering now	If they refuse their explicit consent to disclose, their decision should be respected, but …<ul><li>Ask yourself, why are they telling you this, now, as a trusted adult?</li><li>Bear in mind that other children in the family/neighbourhood may be at risk.</li><li>Wherever possible, especially if other children are at risk, persuade the child to allow you to refer with their consent, and support the child through the subsequent process.</li><li>If the child refuses consent for disclosure, then you have to weigh up client's wishes versus public interest – and whether to breach without client consent and to be able to justify that decision.</li></ul>

Type of disclosure	Issues to be considered
Child under 16 and who is *not* competent in the guidelines of the *Gillick* case, tells you of abuse they suffered in the past or are suffering now	• Ask yourself, why are they telling you this, now, as a trusted adult? • They do not have legal capacity to refuse consent to disclose/refer. • The child victim may have suffered significant harm and also be at risk of future harm. • Government agencies and health authorities have a duty to protect the child and act in the public interest. • Local authorities have a duty to investigate and to provide help and protection for children under the age of 18 in need or at risk of significant harm (Children Act 1989, Children Act 2004, Children (Scotland) Act 1995). Act in accordance with current child protection law and procedures, see *What to Do if You are Worried a Child is Being Abused* (DfES, 2006a) and *Working Together to Safeguard Children* (DfES, 2013). • Bear in mind that other children in the family/neighbourhood may be at risk. • Not only child protection issues here but also potentially serious crime. • No duty to tell those with parental responsibility if to tell them might put this child or other children at risk of further abuse or if they are the alleged abusers. Under child protection procedures, social services would conduct an investigation (in certain cases jointly with the police) and they will handle any necessary communication with those with parental responsibility.
Young person under the age of 18 or a younger child admits to causing significant harm to another child	• Ask yourself, why are they telling you this, now, as a trusted adult? • The child causing the harm may themselves be in need of help as well as the child victim. • The child victim may have suffered significant harm and also be at risk of future harm. • Local authorities are under a duty to provide help and protection for children under the age of 18 (Children Act 1989 s. 17, Children (Scotland) Act 1995). • Local authorities are under a duty to investigate where there is a risk of significant harm to a child. • Act in accordance with current child protection law and procedures. See *What to Do if You are Worried a Child is Being Abused* (DfES, 2006a) and *Working Together to Safeguard Children* (DfES, 2013). • Bear in mind that other children in the family/neighbourhood may be at risk.

Despite this, some children still remain unheard and further deaths have resulted since the Children Act 2004, including baby Peter C, a 17-month-old boy who died in London on 3 August 2007, suffering from appalling injuries inflicted over a period of around eight months, despite the fact that he had been seen repeatedly by Haringey social care staff. Peter's death triggered further enquiries into the efficacy of social care, and Lord Laming was requested to review the impact of his own earlier report on the death of Victoria Climbié. This may have to be reviewed again since it seems that the child protection system failed again to protect another young child from an appalling death in 2013 following prolonged and systematic sadistic torture in his home. Sadly, there are still more of these cases of which the public may be unaware. Children seeking help should have opportunities readily available to speak with professionals and trusted adults, and young children who are thought to be possible victims of abuse should be regularly seen by professionals and/or medically examined as appropriate and necessary. Teachers, doctors and other professionals, including counsellors, may be the first recipients of a child's disclosure of abuse or neglect. Victoria Climbié never got as far as seeing a counsellor. Baby Peter was too young, and the suffering of the latest boy to die in 2013 went unnoticed by school, social services or other professionals.

It is salutary to ask ourselves how we as therapists would respond in a similar situation in judging the balance between respecting privacy and confidentiality and the dangers to the child concerned or the balance between the rights of a child and the rights of the adult 'carers' responsible for them. Children's services are regularly being revised and restructured, and therapists may become involved in working for or alongside child protection services.

We are only too aware, from our personal practice and from what other therapists have told us, that many who consider making a referral of a child or a vulnerable adult to social services or other helping agencies hesitate to do so. They feel they are stopped from acting, partially because of concern to protect their client's privacy and from respect for what has been disclosed in confidence but also because they have had experience of, or have heard from others about, situations where the child protection system appears to have failed. In the worst cases, a failure of the child protection system may have left a young person more vulnerable to further abuse and perhaps also destroyed the therapeutic relationship in the process of disclosure, so that even their therapeutic support may have been lost. What we have to consider is whether this fear really constitutes a valid reason not to refer. We must ask ourselves why the child is telling us, now, about the abuse they are suffering or have suffered. It is likely that they are telling us as a trusted adult now because they actually want and need help (or perhaps they want to have help for a younger sibling), but are afraid of possible consequences or don't know how to get the help they need. We can help our child clients by being as well informed as we can, and by empowering the child as much as we can in the context of the child protection process, and by staying alongside the child to support them throughout the child protection process, and afterwards to help their recovery.

As therapists, we must remember that we have only our client's perspective of the situation and therefore we often do not know the wider picture. In addition, we may not have specialist training and experience in child protection and so there may be many factors of which we are unaware. If we refer a client on, for example within the child protection framework, we are placing that child within the care of a team of professionals, who together have a much wider body of shared experience and expertise and access to resources than we have, and who have the ability to investigate the bigger picture and act appropriately to protect the client's welfare. Recent developments in services may mean that we as therapists may become part of that team, continuing to support clients through the protective process, and if so, we can do our best to make sure that it works for them. It may be that as a profession we need to develop collective strategies through our professional bodies to monitor our experiences of the new services and to participate at a collective level to remedy any deficiencies. It may not be the legal framework that is failing vulnerable children, but the inadequacy of systems and practice. This is another theme to emerge from the Laming Reports.

All therapists should become familiar with the current government guidance, *What to Do if You are Worried a Child is Being Abused* (DfES, 2006a). Those working within the NHS should also refer to *Confidentiality: NHS Code of Practice* (DH, 2003a). Note that these may be updated, so keep an eye on the websites www. education.gov.uk and www.gov.uk. Therapists working in England can find statutory and non-statutory guidance on inter-agency collaboration at those websites, and in *Working Together to Safeguard Children: A Guide to Inter-Agency Working to Safeguard and Promote the Welfare of Children* (DfES, 2013) and *Information Sharing: A Practitioner's Guide* (DfES, 2006b). The general principles of this guidance apply across England, although names of agencies and roles may vary across the different local authorities.

Further resources providing information on child protection, the Children Act 1989, the Children Act 2004 and child protection in Scotland, Northern Ireland and Wales are included at the end of this book.

Issues to be considered during dilemmas over confidentiality are presented in Box 14.1.

Box 14.1   Issues to be considered during dilemmas over confidentiality

With all clients, including those who have refused consent, discuss with the client if appropriate, consider and ideally also discuss in supervision these issues:

- What is the likelihood of serious harm in this case?
- Is this serious harm imminent?
- If I refer, what is likely to happen?
- If I do not refer, what is likely to happen?

(Continued)

(Continued)

- Do the likely consequences of non-referral include any serious harm to the client or others?
- If so, are the likely consequences of non-referral preventable?
- What would have to happen to prevent serious harm to client or others?
- Is there anything I (or anyone else) can do to assist in preventing this harm to my client or others?
- What steps would need to be taken to implement such assistance?
- How could the client be helped to accept assistance/the proposed action?
- Does my client have the mental capacity to give explicit informed consent (or refusal of consent) at this moment in time?
- If the client does not have mental capacity, then what are my professional responsibilities to the client and in the public interest?
- If the client has mental capacity, but does not consent to my proposed action (e.g. my proposed referral to a GP), what would be my legal and professional situation if I went ahead and did it anyway?

Further guidance on issues of consent and mental capacity can be found in Chapters 11 and 12.

14.7 Thinking through dilemmas in confidentiality

14.7.1 Making decisions about disclosures

These reflection questions may assist, considered perhaps with the help of an independent supervisor or mentor:

How has this information become known – is it hearsay or is there objective or corroborative evidence for it?

If there is no clear factual objective evidence for the concern, is the report based on a reliable source on which it is reasonable to rely?

Is anyone at risk of harm? Who is at risk of harm?

What is the nature of any risk?

How serious and how imminent is the risk?

Would disclosure mean that the risk to the client or others may be significantly reduced or come to an end?

Does law, guidance or agency policy and procedure require disclosure of these circumstances? If so, it is easier to follow the procedures laid down. If not, is it in the public interest to make a disclosure?

To whom should disclosure be made?

What is the best way to make a disclosure? (Are there any set procedures for this?)

Box 14.2 presents a useful disclosure checklist.

Box 14.2   Disclosure Checklist

When making decisions about disclosure and information sharing, it may help to consider these points:

- Is this information regulated by the Data Protection Act 1998 (DPA) and/or the Freedom of Information Act 2000 (e.g. do the records comprise client-identifiable sensitive personal data held on computer or in a relevant filing system)?
- Were the notes made by a professional working for a public body in health, education or social care? If so, the Freedom of Information Act 2000 applies.
- What are the relevant rights of the person concerned under the Human Rights Act 1998?
- If working in the health community, is disclosure compliant with the *Caldicott Principles and Guidance* (DH, 2010a)? See also *Confidentiality: NHS Code of Practice, and the Confidentiality: NHS Code of Practice Supplementary Guidance: Public Interest Disclosures* (DH, 2003a; 2010b).
- Is there a legal requirement to share this information (e.g. a statutory duty or a court order)?
- What is the purpose of sharing the information?
- If the information concerns a child or young person under 18, see *Working Together to Safeguard Children* (DfES, 2013). If it concerns a vulnerable adult, is sharing the information in their best interests?
- Is the information confidential? If so, do you have consent to share it?
- If consent is refused, or there are good reasons not to seek consent, does the public interest outweigh the client's wishes, and/or justify or necessitate sharing the information?
- What is the most appropriate way to share this information?
- Is the decision, date, method and rationale for sharing the information recorded?

Best practice also requires that we record a note of our actions so that there is openness, transparency and clarity for future reference in the client record.

Make a record of:

- the date the information is disclosed;
- the information that has been shared;
- who the information has been shared with;
- how the information was shared (e.g. letter, phone call etc.);
- whether client consent was obtained, and if so, the details and date; and
- if no client consent, the reason for disclosure without consent.

Useful Organisations and Contacts

Please note that websites tend to change quite often, and so we recommend that if you cannot find any of these organisations on the web address given, try entering the organisation's name in a general Google or other search.

Organisations

Action on Elder Abuse, Astral House, 1268 London Road, London SW16 4ER. Freephone helpline: 0880 8808 8042, Website: www.elderabuse.org.uk

Adoption UK, 46 The Green, South Bar Street, Banbury OX16 9AB. Tel: 01295 752240, Fax: 01295 752241, Helpline: 0844 848 7900 (10 a.m. to 4 p.m.), Website: www.adoptionuk.org

Age Concern, Astral House, 1268 London Road, London SW16 4ER. Tel: 020 8765 7200, Website: www.ageconcern.org.uk

Alert, 27 Walpole Street, London SW3 4QS. Tel: 020 7730 2800, Website: www.donoharm.org.uk

Alzheimer's Society, Gordon House, 10 Green Coat Place, London SW1P 1PH. Helpline: 0845 300 0336, Website: www.alzheimers.org.uk

Aware: A voluntary organisation in Ireland that aims to provide support group meetings for people with depression and their families. Website: www.aware.ie

BAAF (British Association for Adoption and Fostering), Saffron House, 6–10 Kirby Street, London EC1N 8TS. Tel: 020 7421 2600, Fax: 020 7421 2601, Email: mail@baaf.org.uk, Website: www.baaf.org.uk

Barnardo's Fostering and Adoption Agency, Tanners Lane, Barkingside, llford, Essex, IG6 1QG. Tel: 0208 550 8822, Website: www.barnardos.org.uk

Breathing Space: A free and confidential phone line service for any individual, particularly young men, experiencing low mood or depression, or who are unusually worried and in need of someone to talk to. Website: www.breathingspacescotland.co.uk

British Association for Counselling and Psychotherapy, BACP House, 15 St John's Business Park, Lutterworth, Leicestershire LE17 4HB. Tel: 01455 883300, Fax: 01455 550243, Email bacp@bacp.co.uk, Website: www.bacp.co.uk

British Medical Association, Tavistock Square, London WC1 9JP. Tel: 020 7383 6286. Website: www.bma.org.uk

British Psychological Society, St Andrews House, 48 Princess Road East, Leicester LE1 7DR. Tel: +44 (0)116 254 9568, Fax: +44 (0)116 227 1314, Email: enquiry@bps.org.uk, Website: www.bps.org.uk

Bullying Online: A UK charity helping parents and pupils deal with school bullying. Website: www.bullying.co.uk

Cam's Den: An emotional wellbeing website for children aged 7–10 years. Website: www.camsden.co.uk

Care Quality Commission (CQC), Website: www.cqc.org

Carers UK, Ruth Pitter House, 20–25 Glasshouse Yard, London EC1A 4JT. Carers line Tel: 0808 808 7777; 020 7490 8824, Website: www.carersuk.org

ChildLine: The UK's free, national helpline for children and young people in trouble or danger. Website: www.childline.org.uk

Children and Families Advisory Service Wales (CAFCASS Cymru), Website: wales.gov.uk/cafcasscymru/home/?lang=en

Childrens' Trust, Website: www.thechildrenstrust.org.uk

Commission for Health Care Audit and Inspection, Website: www.health-carecommission.org.uk and also see www.opsi.gov.uk

Commission for Social Care Inspection (CSCI), Website: www.csci.org.uk

Connexions, Website: www.connexions-direct.com

Contact the Elderly, 15 Henrietta Street, Covent Garden, London WC2E 8QG. Freephone: 0800 716543, Website: www.contact-the-elderly.org

Court of Protection, see Public Guardianship Office below.

Crown Prosecution Service (England and Wales), has headquarters in London and York, and operates under a structure of 42 areas in England and Wales. London Office: 7th Floor, 50 Ludgate Hill, London EC4M 7EX. Tel: 020 7796 8000, Fax: 020 7710 3447, Website: www.cps.gov.uk

CyberMentors, about young people helping and supporting each other online. If you want to talk to someone about bullying or just want to chat about something that is bothering you, just drop a CyberMentor a message or ask to chat to them online. The site is safe and secure; you can keep all your chats and messages private. There are also counsellors available for anything really serious. Website: cybermentors.org.uk

Dementia Care Trust, Kingsley House, Greenbank Road, Bristol BS5 6HE. Tel: 0870 443 5325, 0117 952 5325, Website: www.dct.org.uk

Dignity in Dying (formerly the Voluntary Euthanasia Society), 181 Oxford Street, London W1D 2JT. Tel: 0870 777 7868, Email: exit@euthanasia.cc, Website: www.dignityindying.org.uk

Down's Syndrome Association, 155 Mitcham Road, London SW17 9PG. Tel: 020 8682 4001, Website: www.downs-syndrome.org.uk

Foundation for People with Learning Disabilities, 7th Floor, 83 Victoria Street, London SW1H 0HW. Tel: 020 7802 0300, Website: www.learningdisabilities.org.uk

General Medical Council, 178 Great Portland Street, London W1W 5JE. General Enquiries Desk: 020 7580 7642, Website: www.gmc-uk.org

Get Connected: Supports young people's emotional wellbeing by ensuring that they find access to the most appropriate help on any issue wherever they are in the UK. Website: www.getconnected.org.uk

Hands On Scotland: A new NHS website resource for anybody working with children and young people. Website: www.handsonscotland.co.uk

Headway (brain injury association), 4 King Edward Court, King Edward Street, Nottingham NG1 1EW. Helpline: 0808 800 2244, 0115 924 0800 (Nottingham), 020 7841 0240 (London), Website: www.headway.org.uk

Help the Aged, St James' Walk, Clerkenwell Green, London EC1R 0BE. Free welfare rights advice line, Tel: 0808 800 6565, Website: www.helptheaged.org.uk

Help the Hospices, Hospice House, 34–44 Britannia Street, London WC1X 9JG. Helpline: 0879 903 3903, Website: www.hospiceinformation.info

HM Chief Inspector of Education, Children's Services and Skills, Website: www.ofsted.gov.uk

HM Revenue and Customs, Website: www.hmrc.gov.uk

Information Commissioner's Office, Wycliffe House, Water Lane, Wilmslow, Cheshire SK9 5. Tel: 0303 123 1113, Website: www.ico.gov.uk

Learning and Skills Council, Website: www.lsc.gov.uk

Linacre Centre for Healthcare Ethics, 60 Grove End Road, London NW8 9NH. Tel: 020 7806 4088, Website: www.linacre.org

Manic Depression Fellowship, Castle Works, 21 St George's Road, London SE1 6ES. Tel: 020 7793 2600, Website: www.mdf.org.uk

MedicAlert Foundation, 1 Bridge Wharf, 156 Caledonian Road, London N1 9UU. Tel: 0800 581 420, Website: www.medicalert.org.uk

Mencap, 123 Golden Lane, London EC1Y 0RT. Helpline: 0808 808 1111, Tel: 020 7454 0454, Website: www.mencap.org.uk

Mind (National Association for Mental Health), 15–19 Broadway, Stratford, London E15 4BQ. Tel: 020 8519 2122, Mind infoline: 08457 660 163, Website: www.mind.org.uk

Motor Neurone Disease Association, PO Box 246, Northampton NN1 2P2. Tel: 01604 250505, Helpline: 08457 626262, Website: www.mndassociation.org.uk

National Assembly for Wales, Information on guidance in Wales. Website: www.wales.gov.uk

National Autistic Society, 393 City Road, London EC1V 1NG. Tel: 020 7833 2299 Helpline: 0870 600 8585, Website: www.nas.org.uk

Northern Ireland Courts Service, Website: www.courtsni.gov.uk

NSPCC, Website: www.nspcc.org.uk

Official Solicitor, 81 Chancery Lane, London WC2A 1DD. Tel: 020 7911 7127, Website: www.officialsolicitor.gov.uk

Ofsted, Piccadilly Gate, Store Street, Manchester, M1 2 WD. Tel: 0300 123 1231, Textphone: 0161 618 8524, Email: enquiries@ofsted.gov.uk, Website: www.ofsted.gov.uk

Patient's Association, PO Box 935, Harrow, Middlesex HA1 3YJ. Tel: 020 8423 9119, Helpline: 0845 608 4455, Website: www.patients-association.com

Patient Concern, PO Box 23732, London SW5 9FY. Tel: 020 7373 0794, Website: www.patientconcern.org.uk

Patient Information Advisory Group (PIAG): Provides the minutes of PIAG meetings and guidance on the use of powers provided under s. 60 of the Health & Social Care Act 2001 which allow confidentiality requirements to be set aside in limited circumstances for purposes such as research and public health work. PIAG also provides guidance on issues of major significance that are brought to its attention. Website: www.hpa.org.uk

Prevention of Professional Abuse Network (POPAN), 1 Wyvil Court, Wyvil Road, London SW8 2TG. Tel: 020 7622 6334, Support line: 0845 4 500 300, Website: www.popan.org.uk

Public Guardianship Office, Archway Tower, 2 Junction Road, London N19 5SZ. Customer service helpline: 0845 330 2900, Enquiry line: 0845 330 2900, Website: www.guardianship.gov.uk

Reach Out: Aims to improve young people's mental health and wellbeing by building skills and providing information, support and referrals in ways we know work for young people. Website: www.reachout.com

Rescare (The National Society for mentally disabled people in residential care), Third Floor, 24–32 Stephenson Way, London NW1 2HD. Helpline: 0808 808 0700, Website: www.rescare.org.uk

Respond, Third Floor, 24–32 Stephenson Way, London NW1 2HD. Helpline: 0808 808 0700, Website: www.respond.org.uk

Rethink (formerly National Schizophrenia Fellowship), 17 Oxford Street, Southampton SO14 3DJ. General enquiries: 0845 456 0455, Advice line: 020 8974 6814, Website: www.rethink.org

Samaritans, Freepost RSRB-KKBY-CYJK, Chris, PO Box 90 90, Stirling FK8 2SA, Tel: 08457 90 90 90, Email: jo@samaritans.org, Website: www.samaritans.org

SANE, 1st Floor, Cityside House, 40 Alder Street , London E1 1EE. Helpline: 0845 767 8000, Website: www.sane.org.uk

Scope (Major disability charity with a focus on cerebral palsy), 6 Market Road, London N7 9PW. Tel: 020 7619 7257, Cerebral palsy helpline: 0808 800 3333, Website: www.scope.org.uk

Scottish Voluntary Euthanasia Society, Website: www.euthanasia.cc/vess.html

Solicitors for the Elderly, PO Box 9, Peterborough PE4 7NN. Tel: 01733 326769, Website: www.solicitorsfortheelderly.com

Speakability, 1 Royal Street, London SE1 7LL. Tel: 020 7261 9572, Helpline: 080 8808 9572, Website: www.speakability.org.uk

Stroke Association, Stroke House, 240 City Road, London EC1V 2PR. Tel: 020 7566 0300, Helpline: 0845 30 33 100, Website: www.stroke.org.uk

Teens First For Health – by Great Ormond Street Hospital: Website providing mental health advice for teenagers. Featuring an A–Z of mental health topics, people's real stories, information on drugs, lifestyle, therapies and more. Website: www.childrenfirst.nhs.uk/teens/health/mental_health/index.htm

TheSite: A website providing factsheets and articles on key issues facing 16–24-year-olds, as well as hosting a community area for peer-to-peer support. Website: www.thesite.org

Values into Action, Oxford House, Derbyshire Street, London E2 6HG. Tel: 020 7729 5436, Website: www.viauk.org

VOICE UK, Wyvern House, Railway Terrace, Derby DE1 2RU. Tel: 01332 345346, Fax: 01332 295670, Email: voice@voiceuk.org.uk, Website: www.voiceuk.org.uk

Youthspace: A website aimed at people aged 14–25 experiencing mental health problems which offers information, films made by young people and clinical advice. Website: www.youthspace.me

Useful internet sites

Courts and legal information relevant to capacity and consent

Enduring Power of Attorney (EPA) see www.guardianship.gov.uk

High Court of Justice, see www.justice.gov.uk. Address for correspondence: The Court Manager, Room E08, Royal Courts of Justice, The Strand, London WC2A 2LL. Telephone: 020 7947 7309 (Customer Service Manager), Fax: 020 7947 7339 (Customer Service Manager). In case of difficulty out of hours, contact the Royal Courts of Justice on Tel: 020 7947 6260.

Lasting Power of Attorney, see www.guardianship.gov.uk. From 1 October 2007, the EPA was replaced by the *Lasting Power of Attorney* made under the Mental Capacity Act 2005. Detailed information and all the relevant forms and guidance are available on the website.

Scottish Courts www.scotcourts.gov.uk

*Addresses and contact numbers for **other courts** are to be found at www.hmcourtsservice. gov.uk/HMCSCourtFinder*

Websites providing information on consent, capacity and ethics:

Adoption UK, 46 The Green, South Bar Street, Banbury OX16 9AB. Tel: 01295 752240, Fax: 01295 752241, Helpline: 0844 848 7900 (10 a.m. to 4 p.m.), Website: www.adoptionuk.org

British Association for Adoption and Fostering (BAAF), Saffron House, 6–10 Kirby Street, London EC1N 8TS. Tel: 020 7421 2600, Fax: 020 7421 2601, Email: mail@baaf.org.uk, Website: www.baaf.org.uk

British Medical Association, www.bma.org.uk, and specifically:

Ethics: www.bma.org.uk/ap.nsf/Content/Hubethicshandbook

Children: www.bma.org.uk/ap.nsf/Content/Hubethicschildren

Confidentiality: www.bma.org.uk/ap.nsf/Content/Hubethicsconfidentiality

Consent and capacity: www.bma.org.uk/ap.nsf/Content/Hubethicsconsentandcapacity

Health Records: www.bma.org.uk/ap.nsf/Content/Hubethicshealthrecords

Human Rights: www.bma.org.uk/ap.nsf/Content/HubethicshumanrightsReproduction Issues, www.bma.org.uk/ap.nsf/ Content/Hubethicsreproduction issues

General Medical Council, www.gmc-uk.org, and specifically:

Good medical practice: www.gmc-uk.org/guidance/current/library/confidentiality.asp www.gmc-uk.org/guidance/good_medical_practice/index.asp

Confidentiality: protecting and providing information: www.gmc-uk.org/guidance/current/library/confidentiality.asp

Confidentiality: frequently asked questions: www.gmc-uk.org/guidance/current/library/confidentiality_faq.asp

The General Medical Council (Fitness to Practise) Rules Order of Council 2004

Seeking patients' consent: the ethical considerations: www.gmc-uk.org/guidance/current/library/consent.asp

Accountability in multi-disciplinary and multi-agency mental health teams: www.gmc-k.org/guidance/current/library/accountability_ in_multi_teams.asp

Government guidance on consent, capacity and ethics

Caldicott Guardian Manual, 2010, report on the Review of Patient-identifiable Information by the Caldicott Committee, chaired by Dame Fiona Caldicott in 1997. Report and principles available from www.dh.gov.uk/en/index.htm or www.dh.gov/publications

National Assembly for Wales, information on guidance in Wales: www.wales.gov.uk

NHS The Information Governance Toolkit (IGT), provides guidance on how organisations should satisfy confidentiality, data protection, information security, freedom of information, records management and information quality requirements. Extensive knowledgebase of exemplar documents, guidance materials and useful links. An e-mail helpline for assistance with the IGT (content, technical advice and administration issues) is: helpdesk@cfh.nhs.uk, and general website is: www.igt.connectingforhealth.nhs.uk (accessed 27 January 2013).

Patient Information Advisory Group (PIAG), provides the minutes of PIAG meetings and guidance on the use of powers provided under s. 60 of the Health & Social Care Act 2001 which allow confidentiality requirements to be set aside in limited circumstances for purposes such as research and public health work. PIAG also provides guidance on issues of major significance that are brought to its attention and its guidance is published at www.advisorybodies.doh.gov.uk/piag

Scottish Courts, www.scotcourts.gov.uk

Scottish Executive (2002) *'It's Everyone's Job to Make Sure I'm Alright': Report of the Child Protection Audit and Review*. Edinburgh: Scottish Executive. Available at www.scotland.gov.uk/Resource/Doc/47007/0023992.pdf (accessed 24/4/14).

Scottish Executive (2004) *Protecting Children and Young People: The Charter*. Edinburgh: Scottish Executive. Available at www.scotland.gov.uk/Resource/Doc/1181/0008817.pdf (accessed 24/4/14).

Scottish Executive (2004) *Protecting Children and Young People: The Framework for Standards*. Edinburgh: Scottish Executive. Available at www.scotland.gov.uk/Resource/Doc/1181/0008818.pdf (accessed 24/4/14).

The Scottish Office (1998) *Protecting Children – A Shared Responsibility. Guidance on Inter-Agency Co-operation*. London: The Scottish Office. Available at www.scotland.gov.uk/Topics/People/Young-People/children-families/17834/14723 (accessed 24/4/14).

The Scottish Office (1998) *Protecting Children – A shared responsibility. Guidance for Health Professionals in Scotland*. London: The Scottish Office. Available at www.scotland.gov.uk/Topics/People/Young-People/ children-families/17834/14723 (accessed 24/4/14).

Useful resources for research guidance

Code of Human Research Ethics (2010), The British Psychological Society. Available at www.bps.org.uk/sites/default/files/documents/code_of_human_research_ethics.pdf (accessed 27/4/14).

The Research Ethics Guidebook, Economic & Social Research Council Available at www.ethicsguidebook.ac.uk/EthicsPrinciples (accessed 27/4/14).

ESRC Framework for Research Ethics (2nd edn 2010, updated September 2012). Available at www.esrc.ac.uk/_images/framework-for-research-ethics-09-12_tcm8-4586.pdf (accessed 27/4/14).

Governance Arrangements for Research Ethics Committees: A Harmonised Edition (May 2011), Department of Health. Available at www.gov.uk/government/uploads/system/uploads/attachment_data/file/213753/dh_133993.pdf (accessed 27/4/14).

Good Research Practice: Principles and Guidelines (July 2012), Medical Research Council. Available at www.fdanews.com/ext/resources/files/Clinical_Trials_Advisor/CTA_Docs/Medical-Research-Council-Good-Research-Practice.pdf (accessed 27/4/14).

Glossary

These are brief explanations of some of the most important terms used in this book. For further details please refer to the relevant chapter.

Anonymised data Data from which the client cannot be identified by the recipient of the information. The name, address and full post code must be removed together with any other information which, in conjunction with other data held by or disclosed to the recipient, could identify them. Unique numbers may be included only if recipients of the data do not have access to the 'key' to trace the identity of the client.

Caldicott Guardians are appointed to protect patient information in health and social care. They should be existing members of the management board or senior management team, senior professionals, or hold responsibility for promoting clinical governance or equivalent functions within organisations providing health or social care. In 2006, the DH produced the *Caldicott Guardian Manual* for their guidance. See also *Confidentiality: NHS Code of Practice* (DH, 2010b).

Caldicott Principles Six principles for testing whether to disclose patient-identifiable information as part of recommendations on information sharing within the NHS and between NHS and non-NHS organisations: see the *Report on the Review of Patient-Identifiable Information* (DH, 2006) by a committee chaired by Dame Fiona Caldicott in 1997 (the Caldicott Committee).

Circle of confidentiality A group of people sharing confidential information with the client's consent, for example a health care team, or a counselling organisation with group supervision.

Client records Generic term which includes all notes, records, memoranda, correspondence, photographs, artifacts and video or audio recordings relating to an identifiable client, whether factual or process related, and in whatever form they are kept.

Clinical audit Evaluation of clinical performance against standards or through comparative analysis, to inform the management of services. Studies that aim to derive, scientifically confirm and publish generalisable knowledge that constitute research and are not encompassed by the definition of clinical audit in this document.

Competent adult A person aged over 18 and mentally capable of giving valid consent.

Confidentiality A wide ranging duty of managing information in ways that keep it secure and control its disclosure. It is concerned with protecting information that is identifiable with a specific person, typically because the person is named, but the law will also protect the confidences of people whose identity can be deduced from the available information, perhaps because the listener knows some of the circumstances of the person being referred to. Thoroughly anonymised information in which the identity of specific people cannot be discerned is not protected by the law of confidentiality.

Data Defined in s. 1 (1) of the Data Protection Act 1998 to mean information held about a person which is processed automatically, is part of a relevant filing system, or is part of an accessible record. Data may therefore include: computer-based records and certain manual records, tape, video and audio recordings, laboratory results, notes, memoranda and so on. The term 'data' otherwise denotes a collection of statistical or other information gathered in the course of research. (Also see **personal data** and **sensitive personal data** below.)

Data controller Defined in s. 1 (1) of the Data Protection Act 1998 to mean a person who (either alone or jointly or in common with other persons) determines the purposes for which and the manner in which any personal data are, or are to be, processed.

Data processor Defined in s. 1 (1) of the Data Protection Act 1998 to mean any person (other than an employee of the data controller) who processes the data on behalf of the data controller.

Data subject Defined in s. 1 (1) of the Data Protection Act 1998 to mean an individual who is the subject of personal data.

Duty of confidence A duty of confidence will arise whenever the party subject to the duty is in a situation where he either knows or ought to know that the other person (about whom he holds information) can reasonably expect his privacy to be protected.

Explicit consent Term used in the Data Protection Act 1998 to mean consent which is absolutely clear and specific about what it covers, that is, not implied by surrounding circumstances. Explicit consent may be given orally, but for the avoidance of doubt it is always best to have it confirmed in writing wherever possible. The clearest form is signed consent with no ambiguity and a full statement of the purposes for which it was given. Wherever the DPA refers to explicit consent in a record, then it must be in writing. See the Data Protection Act 1998 – Legal Guidance at www.ico.gov.uk.

Express consent This involves active affirmation, which is usually expressed orally or in writing. If clients cannot write or speak, other forms of unequivocal communication of consent may be sufficient.

Forensic In general terms, forensic simply means court-related, that is, a forensic report is one ordered by the court or prepared for use in court; forensic evidence is evidence used in court cases and so on.

Health care team The health care team comprises the people providing clinical services for each patient and the administrative staff who directly support those services.

Implied consent Agreement which is inferred from circumstances. For example, implied consent to disclosure may be inferred where clients have been informed about the information to be disclosed and the purpose of the disclosure, and that they have a right to object to the disclosure, but have not objected.

Incompetent adult A person aged 18 or over and who lacks the mental capacity to give valid consent.

Mental capacity See Chapter 11 for details of mental capacity in adults. Mental capacity is a legal concept, according to which a person's ability to make rational, informed decisions is assessed. It is assumed in law that adults and children of 16 or over have the mental capacity and therefore the legal power to give or withhold consent in medical and health care matters. In England and Wales, see the Mental Capacity Act 2005. In Northern Ireland see the Bamford Committee Report *A Strategic Framework for Adult Mental Health Services (AMH) Report* (2005), available at www. dhsspsni.gov.uk. In Scotland, s. 1 (1)(b) of the Age of Legal Capacity (Scotland) Act 1991 provides that a person of 16 years of age or over has legal capacity to enter into any transaction, which includes medical and health care matters. Section 2 (1) provides that a person under the age of 16 can consent to a transaction of a kind commonly entered into by persons of his age and circumstances and on terms which are not unreasonable, and s. 2 (4) specifically provides that a person under the age of 16 years shall have the legal capacity to consent to any surgical, medical or dental procedure where, in the opinion of a qualified medical practitioner attending him, he is capable of understanding the nature and possible consequences of the procedure or treatment. These presumptions and rules are rebuttable, for example in the case of mental illness. A refusal of necessary medical treatment by young people over the age of 16 but under 18 may be overruled by the High Court (or Court of Session in Scotland). There is no one test for mental capacity to consent. Assessment of mental capacity is situation specific, and will depend upon the ability of the person to take in, understand and weigh up information including the risks and benefits of the decision to be made, and to communicate their wishes.

Parental responsibility The legal basis for decision making in respect of children under the age of 18, created by the Children Act 1989 and defined in s. 3 (1) as 'all the rights, duties, powers, responsibilities and authority which by law the parent of a child has in relation to a child and his property'. It is possible that the definition of parental responsibility may be further clarified in new legislation currently under consideration. More than one person can have parental responsibility for a child at the same time. It cannot be transferred or surrendered, but aspects of parental responsibility can be delegated (Children Act 1989 s. 2 (9)). See Chapter 11 for further details. (For the equivalent provisions in Scotland, see ss. 1–3 of the Children (Scotland) Act 1995.)

Patient-identifiable information Facts or professional opinions about a client or patient learned in a professional capacity and from which the identity of the individuals concerned can be identified.

Personal data Information relating to a specific individual.

Processing Defined in s. 1 (1) of the Data Protection Act 1998 to mean, in relation to information or data, obtaining, recording or holding the information or data or carrying out any operation or set of operations on the information or data, including: (a) organisation, adaptation or alteration of the information or data; (b) retrieval, consultation or use of the information or data; (c) disclosure of the information or data by transmission, dissemination or otherwise making available; or (d) alignment, combination, blocking, erasure or destruction of the information or data.

Public interest The interests of the community as a whole, or a group within the community or individuals.

Relevant filing system Defined in s. 1 (1) of the Data Protection Act 1998 as any set of information that is structured either by reference to individuals or to criteria relating to individuals in such a way that specific information relating to an individual is readily accessible. In a relevant filing system, data about specific individuals can be located by a straightforward search.

Sensitive personal data Defined in s. 2 of the Data Protection Act 1998 as information about a specific individual which relates to: racial or ethnic origin, political opinions, religious beliefs or other beliefs of a similar nature, trade union membership, physical or mental health condition, sexual life, criminality (alleged or proven), and criminal proceedings, their disposal and sentencing.

Serious crime Although the definition of serious crime is not entirely clear in law, the Department of Health has offered the following guidance:

> Murder, manslaughter, rape, treason, kidnapping, child abuse or other cases where individuals have suffered serious harm may all warrant breaching confidentiality. Serious harm to the security of the state or to public order and crimes that involve substantial financial gain and loss will generally fall within this category. In contrast, theft, fraud or damage to property where loss or damage is less substantial would generally not warrant breach of confidence. (DH, 2003a: 35)

Soft law A term used to describe guidance, departmental circulars, codes of practice, charters, memoranda of understanding and recommendations in departmental and inter-departmental reports.

Supervision In the psychoanalytic tradition and in most therapeutic approaches in the USA, supervision is seen as supporting trainees who, on completion of their training, may work unsupervised. In Britain there is a tradition of independent supervision which continues throughout the training and the working life of the therapist, in which the supervisor is regarded as an independent facilitator with a specific role to support and mentor professional practice.

References

Please note that websites and web links tend to change quite often, and so we recommend that if you cannot find any of these organisations on the web address given, try entering the document title, author, or organisation's name in a search engine.

BACP (2013) *Ethical Framework for Good Practice in Counselling and Psychotherapy*. Lutterworth: British Association for Counselling and Psychotherapy. Available at www.itsgoodtotalk.org.uk (accessed 28/4/14).

Bamford Committee Report (2005) *A Strategic Framework for Adult Mental Health Services (AMH) Report*. Available online and as pdf at www.dhsspsni.gov.uk

Bond, T. (2010) *Standards and Ethics for Counselling in Action*. London: SAGE.

Bond, T. and Mitchels, B. (2008) *Confidentiality and Record Keeping in Counselling and Psychotherapy*. London: SAGE.

Bond, T. and Sandhu, A. (2005) *Therapists in Court: Providing Evidence and Supporting Witnesses*. London: SAGE.

Bond, T. and Mitchels, B. (2014) *G2 Breaches in Confidentiality*; BACP Information Sheets. Lutterworth: British Association for Counselling and Psychotherapy.

BPS (2005) *Professional Practice Guidelines for Counselling Psychologists*. Leicester: British Psychological Society.

BPS (2006) *Code of Ethics and Conduct*. Leicester: British Psychological Society.

Brazier, M. (2003) *Medicine, Patients and the Law*. London: Penguin.

Clarkson, P. (1995) *The Therapeutic Relationship*. London: Whurr.

Cooper, M. (2008) *Essential Research Findings in Counselling and Psychotherapy*. London: SAGE.

Crown Prosecution Service (CPS) Guidance, all available on www.cps.gov.uk

CPS (2001) *Provision of Therapy for Child Witnesses Prior to a Criminal Trial: Practice Guidance*. London: Crown Prosecution Service (England and Wales). Available at www.cps.gov.uk (accessed 28/4/14).

CPS (2001) *The CPS: Provision of Therapy for Vulnerable or Intimidated Adult Witnesses Prior to a Criminal Trial: Practice Guidance*. London: Crown Prosecution Service (England and Wales). Available at www.cps.gov.uk (accessed 28/4/14).

CPS (2013) *Code for Crown Prosecutors*.

CPS (2011) *Achieving best evidence in criminal proceedings: Guidance on interviewing victims and witnesses, and using special measures*.

DfES (2004a) *Every Child Matters: Change for Children Programme*. Ref: DfES/1081/2004. London: Department for Education and Skills. Available at www.everychildmatters.co.uk (accessed 28/4/14).

DfES (2006a) *What to Do if You are Worried a Child is Being Abused – Summary*. Nottingham: DfES Publications. Available at www.gov.uk (accessed 28/4/14).

DfES (2006b) *Information Sharing: Practitioner's Guide: Integrated Working to Improve Outcomes for Children and Young People*. Norwich: The Stationery Office. Available at www.everychildmatters.gov.uk (accessed 24/4/14).

DfES (2013) *Working Together to Safeguard Children: A Guide to Inter-Agency Working to Safeguard and Promote the Welfare of Children*. Norwich: The Stationery Office. Available at www.education.gov.uk (accessed 24/4/14).

DH (2000) *No Secrets: Guidance on Developing and Implementing Multi-Agency Policies and Procedures to Protect Vulnerable Adults From Abuse*. London: Department of Health. Available at www.gov.uk (accessed 24/4/14).

DH (2003a) *Confidentiality: NHS Code of Practice*. London: Department of Health. Available at www.gov.uk (accessed 24/4/14).

DH (2003b). *Research Governance Framework for Health and Social Care*, 2nd edn in draft. London: Department of Health.

DH (2006) *Report on the Review of Patient-Identifiable Information*. London: Department of Health. Available at www.wales.nhs.uk (accessed 24/4/14).

DH (2010a) *The Caldicott Guardian Manual 2010*. Norwich: The Stationery Office. Available at http://systems.hscic.gov.uk (accessed 24/4/14).

DH (2010b) *Confidentiality: NHS Code of Practice: Supplementary Guidance: Public Interest Disclosures*. Norwich: The Stationery Office. Available at www.gov.uk (accessed 29/4/14).

DH (2013) *Mental Health Act 2007: Response to Health Select Committee* Department of Health. Available at www. gov.uk DH (2014) *Review of the operation of Sections 135 and 136 of the Mental Health Act (Consultation Paper)* Department of Health. Available at www. gov.uk

Director of Public Prosecution Guidance available online at http://www.justice.gov.uk

CPS (2013) *Guidelines on Prosecuting Cases of Child Sexual Abuse*.

MoJ (2013) *Code of Practice for Victims of Crime*.

MoJ (2013) *The Witness Charter: Standards of Care for Witnesses in the Criminal Justice System*.

MoJ (2013) *Working with Victims and Witnesses*.

MoJ (2011a) *Vulnerable and Intimidated Witnesses: A Police Service Guide*.

DLA Piper (2014) *Data Protection Laws of the World*. Available at www.dlapiperdata protection.com (accessed 29/4/14).

Feltham, C. (ed.) (1999) *Understanding the counselling relationship*. London: Sage.

GMC (2000a) *Seeking Patients' Consent: The Ethical Considerations*. London: General Medical Council.

GMC (2004a) *Confidentiality: Protecting and Providing Information*. London: General Medical Council. Available at www.gmc-uk.org (accessed 24/4/14).

GMC (2004b) *General Medical Council (Fitness to Practise) Rules Order of Council 2004*. London: General Medical Council.

GMC (2006) *Good Medical Practice*. London: General Medical Council.

GMC (2009) *Confidentiality*. London: General Medical Council. Available at www.gmc-uk.org (accessed 24/4/14).

GMC (2012) *Good Medical Practice*. London: General Medical Council.

Hackney, H. and Goodyear, R. (1984) *Carl Rogers' Client-Centred Approach to Supervision. Client Centered Therapy and the Person Centered Approach*. R. Levant, J. Shlien (eds), New York: Praeger.

Hawkins, P. and Shoet, R. (1996) *Supervision in the Helping Professions*. Milton Keynes., Philadelphia: Open University Press.

Hershman, A. and McFarlane, D. (2014) *Children Law and Practice*. Bristol: Family Law. (Encyclopaedia which is regularly updated throughout the year).

HCPC (2012) *Standards of Conduct, Performance and Ethics*. London: Health & Care Professions Council. Available at www.hpc-uk.org (accessed 29/4/14).

Home Office (2007) *Achieving Best Evidence in Criminal Proceedings: Guidance on Interviewing Victims and Child Witnesses and Using Special Measures*.

IACP (2005) *Code of Ethics and Practice* (Information Sheet 7). Wicklow: Irish Association for Counselling and Psychotherapy.

ICO (2001) *Data Protection Act 1998 Legal Guidance*. Wilmslow: Information Commissioner's Office.

ICO (2010a) *Privacy Notices: Code of Practice*. Wilmslow: Information Commissioner's Office. Available at https://ico.org.uk (accessed 24/4/14).

ICO (2010b) *A Complete Guide to Notification*. Wilmslow: Information Commissioner's Office.

ICO (2011a) *Data Sharing Checklists*. Wilmslow: Information Commissioner's Office.

ICO (2011b) *Data Sharing Code of Practice*. Wilmslow: Information Commissioner's Office. Available at http://ico.org.uk (accessed 24/4/14).

ICO (2011c) *Advice on How to Safeguard Your Personal Information*. Wilmslow: Information Commissioner's Office.

ICO (2012a) *Anonymisation: Managing Data Protection Risk – Code of Practice*. Wilmslow: Information Commissioner's Office. Available at http://ico.org. (accessed 24/4/14).

ICO (2012b) *A Practical Guide to IT Security*. Wilmslow: Information Commissioner's Office.

ICO (2013) *How do I Handle Subject Access Requests?* Wilmslow: Information Commissioner's Office.

Jacobs, M. (ed.) (1996) *In Search of Supervision*. Buckingham, Philadelphia: Open University Press.

Jacobs, M. (2007). *G3 Dual Roles – Blurring the boundaries in professional relationships. BACP Information Sheets*. Lutterworth: British Association for Counselling and Psychotherapy.

Jackson, E. (2006) *Medical Law, Texts and Materials*. Oxford: Oxford University Press.

Klain, E. and Paviae, L. (1999). 'Countertransference and empathic problems in therapists/helpers working with psychotraumatized persons.' *Croatian Medical Journal*, 40(4): 466–472.

Law Commission (1981) *Breach of Confidence* (Cmnd 8388). London: HMSO.

Long, M. (2013) *Child Care Law in Northern Ireland: A summary*. London: BAAF.

Lord Laming (2003) *The Victoria Climbié Inquiry: Report of an Inquiry by Lord Laming*. Norwich: The Stationery Office.

McLeod, J. (2014) *Doing Research in Counselling and Psychotherapy*. London: SAGE.

Mearns, D. (2008) *G4 Counselling and Psychotherapy Workloads. BACP Information Sheets*. Lutterworth: British Association for Counselling and Psychotherapy.

Ministry of Justice (2008) *The Public Law Outline: Guide to Case Management in Public Law Proceedings*. London: Ministry of Justice. Available at www.familylaw.co.uk (accessed 28/4/14).

Ministry of Justice (2011a) *Vulnerable and Intimidated Witnesses: A Police Service Guide*. London: Ministry of Justice. Available at www.justice.gov.uk (accessed 28/4/14).

Ministry of Justice (2011b) *Achieving Best Evidence in Criminal Proceedings: Guidance on Interviewing Victims and Witnesses, and Guidance on Using Special Measures*. London: Ministry of Justice. Available at www.justice.gov.uk (accessed 28/4/14).

Ministry of Justice (2013) *Code of Practice for Victims of Crime VICTIMS' CODE*. London: The Stationery Office. Available at www.cps.gov.uk (accessed 28/4/14).

Mitchels, B. and Bond, T. (2008) *Essential Law in Counselling and Psychotherapy*. London: BACP and Sage.

Mitchels, B. and Bond, T. (2010) *Essential Law for Counsellors and Psychotherapists*. London: BACP and Sage.

Mitchels, B. and Bond, T. (2011) *Legal Issues Across Counselling and Psychotherapy Settings: A Guide for Practice*. London. BACP and Sage.

Page, S. and Wosket, V. (1998) *Supervising the Counsellor*. London: Routledge.

Pattenden, R. (2003) *The Law of Professional–Client Confidentiality: Regulating the Disclosure of Confidential Personal Information*. Oxford: Oxford University Press.

Pattinson, S. D. (2006) *Medical Law and Ethics*. London: Sweet & Maxwell.

Proctor, B. (1986) 'Supervision: a co-operative exercise in accountability', in M. Marken and M. Payne (eds), *Enabling and Ensuring: Supervision in Practice*. Leicester: National Youth Bureau.

Reder, P., Duncan, S. and Gray, M. (1994) *Beyond Blame: Child Abuse Tragedies Revisited*. London and New York: Routledge.

Scottish Executive (2002b) *'It's Everyone's Job to Make Sure I'm Alright': Report of the Child Protection Audit and Review*. Edinburgh: Scottish Executive. Available at www.scotland.gov.uk (accessed 24/4/14).

Scottish Executive (2004a) *Protecting Children and Young People: The Charter*. Edinburgh: Scottish Executive. Available at www.scotland.gov.uk (accessed 24/4/14).

Scottish Executive (2004b) *Protecting Children and Young People: The Framework for Standards*. Edinburgh: Scottish Executive. Available at www.scotland.gov.uk (accessed 24/4/14).

Scottish Executive (2008a) *Interviewing Child Witnesses in Scotland*. Available at www.scotland.gov.uk

Scottish Executive (2008b) *Code of Practice to Facilitate the Provision of Therapeutic Support to Child Witnesses in Court Proceedings*. Edinburgh: Scottish Executive.

Scottish Office (1998a) *Protecting Children – A Shared Responsibility. Guidance on Inter-Agency Co-operation*. London: The Scottish Office. Available at www.scotland.gov.uk

Scottish Office (1998b) *Protecting Children – A Shared Responsibility. Guidance for Health Professionals in Scotland*. London: The Scottish Office. Available at www.scotland.gov.uk

Syme, G. (2003) *Dual Relationships in Counselling and Psychotherapy*. London: Sage.

Tedeschi, R. G. and Calhoun, L. G. (1995) *Trauma and Transformation: Growing in the Aftermath of Suffering*. Thousand Oaks, CA: Sage.

Tedeschi, R. G. and Calhoun, L. G. (1996) 'The post-traumatic growth inventory: Measuring the positive legacy of trauma.' *Journal of Traumatic Stress*, 9: 455–471.

Tedeschi, R. G. (1999) 'Violence transformed: post-traumatic growth in survivors and their societies'. *Aggression and Violent Behaviour*, 4: 319–341.

Trumble, W. R. and Stevenson, A. (eds) (2002) *The Shorter Oxford English Dictionary on Historical Principles*. Oxford: Oxford University Press.

Tudor, K. and Worrall, M. (2004) *Freedom to Practice*. Ross on Wye: PCCS Books.

Further Reading

Please note that websites and web links tend to change quite often, and so we recommend that if you cannot find any of these organisations on the web address given, try entering the document title, author, or organisation's name in a search engine.

BMA (2000) *Consent, Rights and Choices in Health Care for Children and Young People*. London: BMA.

BMA (no date) *Mental Capacity Tool Kit*. London: BMA. Available at bma.org.uk (accessed 24/4/14).

Bond, T. (1990) 'Counselling supervision–ethical issues', *Counselling, Journal of the British Association for Counselling*, 1(2): 43–46.

Bond, T. (2004) *Ethical Guidelines for Researching Counselling and Psychotherapy*. Rugby: British Association for Counselling and Psychotherapy.

Bond, T., Mitchels, B. (2014) *G2 Breaches in Confidentiality*. BACP Information Sheets. Lutterworth: British Association for Counselling and Psychotherapy.

Bond, T. and Jenkins, P. (2014) *G1 Access to Records of Counselling and Psychotherapy*. BACP Information Sheets. Lutterworth: British Association for Counselling and Psychotherapy.

Cohen, K. (1992) 'Some legal issues in counselling and psychotherapy', *British Journal of Guidance and Counselling*, 20(1): 10–26.

Crown Prosecution Service Guidance, all available on www.cps.gov.uk

Code for Crown Prosecutors (CPS, 2013)

Achieving best evidence in criminal proceedings: Guidance on interviewing victims and witnesses, and using special measures (2011) PDF

The Prosecutors' Pledge (online) PDF

CPS policy on prosecuting criminal cases involving children and young people as victims and witnesses (online) PDF

Supporting victims and witnesses with a learning disability (in English, Welsh and Easy Read) PDF

Supporting victims and witnesses with mental health issues (in English, Welsh and Easy Read) PDF

Shaping Our Lives – Consultation on cases involving people with mental health problems (2009) Consultation report (online)

Crimes against older people – prosecution policy PDF

Crimes against older people – prosecution guidance PDF

Leaflets

Witnesses and best evidence – About meeting with the Crown Prosecution Service prosecutor

Your Meeting with The Crown Prosecution Service

Pre-trial witness interviews by prosecutors

> DfES (2004a) *Every Child Matters: Change for Children Programme.* Ref: DfES/1081/2004. London: Department for Education and Skills. Available at www.everychildmatters.co.uk (accessed 28/4/14).
>
> DfES (2013) *Working Together to Safeguard Children: A Guide to Inter-Agency Working to Safeguard and Promote the Welfare of Children.* Norwich: The Stationery Office. Available at www.education.gov.uk (accessed 24/4/14).
>
> Note that this new version of *Working Together* replaces earlier guidance on particular safeguarding issues, and in it, Appendix C lists the following helpful and fully downloadable supplementary guidance documents available:

Department for Education guidance

> Safeguarding children who may have been trafficked
>
> Safeguarding children and young people who may have been affected by gang activity
>
> Safeguarding children from female genital mutilation
>
> Forced marriage
>
> Safeguarding children from abuse linked to faith or belief
>
> Use of reasonable force
>
> Safeguarding children and young people from sexual exploitation
>
> Safeguarding children in whom illness is fabricated or induced
>
> Preventing and tackling bullying
>
> Safeguarding children and safer recruitment in education
>
> Information sharing
>
> Recruiting safely: Safer recruitment guidance helping to keep children and young people safe
>
> Safeguarding Disabled Children: Practice guidance

Guidance issued by other government departments and agencies

> Child Protection and the Dental Team: an Introduction to Safeguarding Children in Dental Practice
>
> Department of Health: Responding to domestic abuse: A handbook for health professionals
>
> Department of Health: Violence Against Women and Children
>
> Department of Health: The Framework for the Assessment of Children in Need and their Families 2000: Practice guidance
>
> Department of Health: Good Practice in Working with Parents with a Learning Difficulty
>
> Department of Health: Recognised, Valued and Supported: Next Steps for the Carers Strategy
>
> Department of Health: Mental Health Act 1983 Code of Practice: Guidance on the Visiting of Psychiatric Patients by Children
>
> Foreign and Commonwealth Office/ Home Office: Forced marriage
>
> Home Office: Guidance on Teenage Relationship Abuse
>
> Home Office Circular: 16/2005 Guidance on Offences Against Children

Home Office: Disclosure and Barring Services

Home Office: What is Domestic Violence?

Ministry of Justice: Guidance on forced marriage

Ministry of Justice: Multi-Agency Public Protection Arrangements Guidance

Ministry of Justice: HM Prison Service Public Protection Manual

Ministry of Justice: Probation Service Guidance on Conducting Serious Further Offence Reviews Framework

Missing Children and Adults – a Cross Government Strategy

NHS National Treatment Agency: Guidance on development of Local Protocols between Drug and Alcohol Treatment Services and Local Safeguarding and Family Services

UK Border Agency: Arrangements to Safeguard and Promote Children's Welfare in UKBA

Youth Justice Board: Guidance on People who Present a Risk to Children

DH (2014) *Review of the operation of Sections 135 and 136 of the Mental Health Act (Consultation Paper)* Department of Health. Available at www. gov.uk

Feldman, D. (2002) *Civil Liberties and Human Rights in England and Wales*. Oxford: Oxford University Press.

Hodson, D. (2012) *The International Family Law Practice*. Bristol: Family Law.

Long, M. (2013) *Child Care Law in Northern Ireland*. London: BAAF.

Long, M. (2004) *The Law of Children in Northern Ireland: The Annotated Legislation*. Belfast: SLS Legal Publications (NI).

Long, M. and Loughran, G. (2002) *The Law of Adoption in Northern Ireland: The Annotated Legislation*. Belfast: SLS Legal Publications (NI).

McDonald, A. (2011) *The Rights of the Child, Law and Practice*. Bristol: Family Law.

Mason, J. K. and Laurie, G. T. (2006) *Mason and McCall Smith's Law and Medical Ethics* (7th edn). Oxford: Oxford University Press.

Mearns, D. (2008) *G4 Counselling and Psychotherapy Workloads*. BACP Information Sheets. Lutterworth, British Association for Counselling and Psychotherapy.

Mitchels, B. (ed.) (2012) *Child Care and Protection: Law and Practice* (5th edn). London: Wildy, Simmonds and Hill.

North, J. (2014) *Mindful Therapeutic Care for Children*. London: Jessica Kingsley.

Reeves, A. (2010) *Working with Suicidal Clients*. London: SAGE.

Scottish Executive (2003a) *Sharing Information about Children at Risk*. Edinburgh: Scottish Executive.

Scottish Executive (2003b) *Framework for Standards and Children's Charter*. Edinburgh: Scottish Executive.

Scottish Executive (2006) *Getting it Right for Every Child*. Edinburgh: Scottish Executive.

The Scottish Executive (2008a) *Interviewing Child Witnesses in Scotland*. Available at www.scotland.gov.uk

The Scottish Executive (2008b) *Code of Practice to Facilitate the Provision of Therapeutic Support to Child Witnesses in Court Proceedings*. Edinburgh: Scottish Executive.

List of Legal Cases

A Health Authority v X [2001] EWCA Civ 2014; [2002] 2 All ER 780 (CA); affirming [2001] Lloyds Rep Med 349

A v B plc and C ('Flitcroft') [2002] EWCA Civ 337; 3 WLR 542, reversing [2001] 1 WLR 2341

A v Hoare and Others [2008] UKHL 6

Allen v British Rail Engineering CA 2001 EWCA Civ 242, [2001] ICR 942

Attorney General v Guardian Newspapers (No 2) [1988] 3 All ER 545

Boyd v US [1885] 116 US 616, 630

Campbell v Mirror Group Newspapers Ltd [2004] UKHL 22, [2004] 2 AC 457

Commissioner of Police v Ombudsman [1998] 1 NZLR 385

Douglas v Hello! [2007] UKHL 21

Durant v Financial Services Authority [2003] EWCA Civ 1746 (CA)

Gillick v West Norfolk and Wisbech Area Health Authority and Another [1986] 1 AC 1212; [1985] 3 All ER 402 (HL) [1986] 1 FLR 224; [1985] 1 All ER 533 (CA); [1985] 3 WLR 830

JD v Ross [1998] NZFLR 951

Kapadia v. London Borough of Lambeth [2000] (CA) 1 IRLR 699; 57 BMLR 170; The Times, 4 July 2000.

London Borough of Southwark v Afolabi [2003] ICR 800 CA

Malcom v Dundee City Council [2007] CSOH 38

Mr X v Hospital Z [1998] 8 SCC 296, 307

MS v Sweden [1999] 28 EHRR 313

R v Cannings [2004] EWCA Crim 1 [2004] 1 WLR 2607

Re L (Medical Treatment: Gillick Competency) [1998] 2 FLR 810, [1998] Fam Law 591

Re TG (A Child) [2013] EWCA Civ 5(at *http://www.bailii.org/ew/cases/EWCA/Civ/2013/5.html)*

Re W (A Minor: Medical Treatment) [1992] 4 All ER 627

St George's Healthcare NHS Trust v S [1999] Fam 26

Tarasoff v The Regents of the University of California [1976] 551 P 2d 334 and [1974] 529 P 2d 553–554

W v Edgell and others [1990] 1 All ER 835; Ch 359 (CA) affirming [1989] 1 All ER 801

Z v Finland [1998] 25 EHRR 371

List of Acts and Rules

Access to Health Records Act 1990
Adoption and Children Act 2002
Adults with Incapacity (Scotland) Act 2000
Age of Legal Capacity (Scotland) Act 1991
Children (Scotland) Act 1995
Children Act 1989
Children Act 2004
Children Act 2004 Information Data Base [England] Regulations 2007, S.I. 2007/2182
Children and Adoption Act 2006
Children's Hearings (Scotland) Act 2011
Children (Parental Responsibility Agreement) Regulations, Northern Ireland 1996
Civil Partnership Act 2004
Commissioner for Children and Young People (Scotland) Act 2003
Coroners (Inquests) Rules 2013
Coroners (Investigations) Regulations 2013
Coroners Allowances, Fees and Expenses Regulations 2013
Coroners and Justice Act 2009 (in force from 23 July 2013)
Court of Protection Rules 2007. SI 2007 No. 1744
Data Protection (Processing of Sensitive Personal Data) Order 2000
Data Protection (Subjects Access Modification) (Health) Order 2000
Data Protection Act 1998
Defamation Act 1996
Drug Trafficking Act 1994
Drug Trafficking Offences Act 1986
Education Act 2002
Equality Act 2006
Family Law (Scotland) Act 2006
Family Law Reform Act 1969
Family Proceedings Rules 1991, S.I. 1991/1247
Freedom of Information Act 2000
Human Fertilisation and Embryology Act 1990
Human Rights Act 1998
Latent Damage Act 1986
Limitation (Scotland) Act 1973
Limitation (Scotland) Act 1984
Limitation Act 1980

Local Government in Scotland Act 2003

Marriage (Same Sex Couples) Act 2013

Mental Capacity Act 2005

Mental Capacity Act 2005 (Appropriate Body) (England) Regulations 2006 S.I. 2006 No. 2810

Mental Health (Care and Treatment) (Scotland) Act 2003

Mental Health Act 1983

Mental Health Act 2007

Money Laundering Regulations 2007

National Care Standards (Scotland) 2010

National Guidance for Child Protection in Scotland 2010

Parental Responsibility Agreement Regulations 1991, S.I. 1991/1478

Police and Criminal Evidence Act 1984

Prescription and Limitation (Scotland) Act 1973

Prescription and Limitation (Scotland) Act 1984

Proceeds of Crime Act 2002

Protection from Harassment Act 1997

Protection of Children (Scotland) Act 2003

Protection of Children and Prevention of Sexual Offences (Scotland) Act 2005

Serious Crime Act 2007

Social Work (Scotland) Act 1968

Terrorism Act 2000

Vulnerable Witnesses (Scotland) Act 2004

Youth Justice and Criminal Evidence Act 1999

Index